Together Alone

Together Alone

PERSONAL RELATIONSHIPS IN PUBLIC PLACES

Edited by
Calvin Morrill, David A. Snow,
and Cindy H. White

UNIVERSITY OF CALIFORNIA PRESS

BERKELEY   LOS ANGELES   LONDON

University of California Press
Berkeley and Los Angeles, California

University of California Press, Ltd.
London, England

© 2005 by The Regents of the University of California

Library of Congress Cataloging-in-Publication Data

Together alone: personal relationships in public places /
edited by Calvin Morrill, David A. Snow, and Cindy
H. White

    p.   cm.
  Includes bibliographical references and index.
  ISBN 0-520-24522-9 (cloth : alk. paper)—
  ISBN 0-520-24523-7 (pbk. : alk. paper)
  1. Interpersonal relations. 2. Public spaces. I. Morrill,
Calvin. II. Snow, David A. III. White, Cindy H., 1965–
  HM1106.T64 2005
  302—dc22   2004018526

Manufactured in the United States of America
14 13 12 11 10 09 08 07 06 05
10 9 8 7 6 5 4 3 2 1

The paper used in this publication meets the minimum
requirements of ANSI/NISO Z39.48–1992 (R 1997)
(*Permanence of Paper*).

CONTENTS

FIGURES AND TABLES

FIGURES

TABLES

PREFACE

THIS BOOK IS BASED ON nine ethnographic studies on a topic that has received scant scholarly attention: personal relationships in public places. Scholars of personal relationships have traditionally explored them in the contexts of family, school, and work but rarely in public places, which traditionally have been thought of as the realm of passing strangers. To be sure, a handful of scholars have explored aspects of public sociality—namely, Paul Cressey, Fred Davis, Robert Edgerton, Erving Goffman, Jane Jacobs, Lyn Lofland, and Gregory Stone—and this volume is indebted to their contributions. But it goes beyond them by pushing the conceptual boundaries of what are usually considered personal relationships and by examining the social conditions associated with public places that both facilitate and constrain the negotiation of public personal relationships. In so doing, this volume illuminates the ironies of face-to-face social ties that paradoxically blend aspects of durability and brevity, of emotional closeness and distance, of being together *and* alone. It also suggests, metaphorically, that people are not so much "bowling alone," as Robert Putnam has argued, as they are together in disconnected niches of public sociality.[1]

This volume also spans a number of disciplines and fields of inquiry. The interactionist tradition in sociology, relationship research by communication scholars and social psychologists, and urban ethnography undergird the collection as a whole. Multiple conceptual frameworks inform each chapter, including sociological theories of gender, sexuality, and exchange; treatises on community by political scientists and historians; and cultural work on identity, place, and youth that cuts across the humanities and social sciences. The settings—ranging from city streets, bus stops, and parking lots to bars, retail establishments, and urban university recreation centers—represent places that contemporary urban dwellers not only frequent but also develop personal relationships in.[2]

Aside from its substantive focus, this book illustrates an ethnographic research strategy for examining personal relationships as people go about their daily routines in public contexts. This ethnographic approach meant that the research projects in this book unfolded over months, sometimes years, as the authors collected data and got to know the people they studied firsthand.[3] Other distinctive features also mark the authors' overall ethnographic strategy.

Most prominent among these features is a systematic approach to qualitative fieldwork and theory dubbed "analytic ethnography" by John Lofland.[4] Analytic ethnographers attempt to weave together rich interpretations of those under study while explicitly investigating how those interpretations can contribute to "the elaboration of generic understandings and propositions" about social life.[5] Thus analytic ethnographers attempt to link ethnography with theoretical development by modifying and refining existing frameworks or by developing novel conceptual leads.[6] The interpretive stance of analytic ethnography is akin to Martin Hammersly's concept of "subtle realism," in which the ethnographer "retains from naive realism the idea that research investigates independent, knowable phenomena,"[7] yet also recognizes that representations of that reality issue from multiple, valid "point[s] of view that [make] some features of the phenomenon represented relevant and others irrelevant."[8] Along these lines, our contributors illuminate the daily routines of conducting personal relationships in public places while, at the same time, drawing out the theoretical relevance of their findings.

A second prominent feature of the fieldwork in this volume is the use of team ethnography.[9] Ethnographic teams have a number of advantages underscored in many of the chapters. First, working in teams enabled greater flexibility among the authors with regard to field relations. On several teams, for example, team members adopted different roles that varied in terms of their participation in a setting and relationships with informants.[10] Such strategies thus overcame many of the difficulties that lone researchers can face with respect to avenues and barriers to multiple actors and information in the field. The availability of multiple roles also meant that the teams could capitalize on the interpersonal strengths and biographies of their members with respect to developing and managing field relations. Second, team members often adopted different interviewing techniques with the same informants. Some team members, for example, opted for techniques that employed standard question formats, while other team members adopted techniques that used "interviewing by comment" through which the researcher elicited responses from informants by declarative statements (e.g., hypotheses and humorous remarks).[11] Third, teamwork enabled team members to cross-check their data or to engage in quasi–field experiments to check the information yield from different techniques and role perspectives. These multiple data sources, in turn, enabled the triangulation of data sources gathered by multiple researchers and the incorporation of multiple perspectives and voices into the writing in each chapter.

Despite these advantages, team members also faced several challenges. First and foremost among these were the potential tensions and misinterpretations that could occur as a result of members' differential exposure to the field. The teams solved this problem by developing systematic sampling, field visit protocols, and consistent team meetings such that all members became conscious of how their fieldwork experiences informed their understandings of dynamics in the field. Moreover, some measure of differential exposure could be used as a mechanism through which interpretations and assumptions could be explicitly elaborated and revisited as team members discussed aspects of their field data.

The analysis and interpretation of field data offered another challenge for each team as members negotiated their own analytic and political commitments. Indeed, all of the authors came to their field settings with political and ideological perspectives, sometimes fully articulated and sometimes nascent. Through the course of their fieldwork and data analysis, these perspectives would sometimes emerge and at other times remain submerged within scholarly perspectives drawn from sociology, social psychology, interpersonal communication research, or cultural studies. All of these framings created the conditions for intragroup disagreements (or even conflict), which in many cases proved highly beneficial for raising questions and issues that a solo researcher might miss. All the teams were ultimately able to negotiate their own agreements in these instances. These agreements certainly influenced the arrangement of materials in each chapter, and our authors reflect on some of these issues as they discuss their field procedures at the end of each chapter.[12]

Perhaps the biggest challenge faced by our contributors involved the ethics of field research on personal relationships. One could argue that, at worst, doing ethnography of personal relationships is a way to poke one's nose into the private affairs of others for no good reason other than for the aims of "scientific understanding" or "theoretical development." Personal relationships, the argument might continue, are *personal* and should be left alone lest the relationships studied be affected in adverse ways. We have two responses to this critique. First, all the relationships studied by our contributors occurred in more or less public places. This meant, with some exceptions, that a wide range of persons enjoyed access to the places and social relationships that were observed. A good bit of eavesdropping, casual conversation, and other forms of observation ("people watching") in such places occurs naturally and for a variety of purposes, including research. As a result, many of the authors' activities during fieldwork blended into local routines and did not compromise either the individuals or the places they studied. Some authors, however, did alter the social interaction they studied, first by merely inhabiting the setting and second by creating meaningful personal relationships with their informants. Yet, as Howard Becker has argued, people in their natural settings are not easily jarred for very long from their daily routines by the mere presence of ethnographers (unless, of course, a whole herd of ethnographers appears and begins to dominate the setting).[13]

Another troubling issue, therefore, is how ethnographers use personal relationships in the service of research. For some of the authors in this collection, this issue motivated them to adopt overt roles in their research by explicitly talking with their informants while in the field about the nature of the research. This strategy put the relationships between informants and researchers on a more authentic footing while creating opportunities for data collection. In other situations, the authors revealed (or concealed) their purposes in strategic ways, which in turn sometimes created anxieties for the researcher and ambiguities for informants.

This raises yet another problem in field research: the potential impact of published accounts of fieldwork on those being studied. Traditionally, ethnographers have managed this issue by adopting standards of confidentiality with respect to the privacy of informants.[14] More recently, some ethnographers[15] have abandoned confidentiality in their published works in the spirit of explicit collaboration with and "ethical commitment"[16] to their informants. All of the authors in this volume opt for confidentiality with respect to those they studied. For some, this approach resulted from explicit concerns raised by informants about how the research would affect their interpersonal relations and reputations. For other authors, confidentiality was simply the default. All of these issues remind us that the ethical dilemmas faced by ethnographers cannot easily be managed or resolved via a priori, rigid codes of ethics and procedures that are now commonly imposed on fieldworkers by university-based institutional review boards (IRBs). The twists and turns of fieldwork mean that there is typically no one "right" answer to such dilemmas.[17] But this does not mean that "anything goes" with respect to researcher conduct in the field. Rather, it suggests that ethnographers of all stripes must remain vigilant about negotiating multiple sets of concerns: their research goals; the potential harm their work may pose for their informants and themselves; and the research guidelines of their professional associations and institutions. As Patricia and Peter Adler write:

> No matter how much ethnographic research is regulated, no matter how tight the stipulations, unanticipated situations will always arise that are not covered in a research plan or proposal. Researchers will always have to make situational decisions and interpretations about the ethical and safe thing to do. We argue that not alienating researchers and their subjects increases the chances for a proper decision. We advocate a joint, reciprocally respectful relationship, more attuned to legal nuances, that looks ahead to anticipate potential problems while still respecting the fundamental bond of obligation and trust between researchers and those whom they study.[18]

This volume experienced a long gestation, beginning with a collaboration during the early 1990s, when Calvin Morrill and David Snow offered their first co-taught graduate seminar in qualitative field methods in the Department of Sociology at the University of Arizona. After teaching the course a few times, Morrill and Snow noticed that some of its students had undertaken ethnographies of social relationships that occurred in public places. The idea for this volume began to take shape as Morrill and Snow urged students who had already taken the course, and who had done studies of relationships in public, to go back to the field and collect more data. By 2000, as Morrill and Snow both prepared to leave Arizona and join the Department of Sociology at the University of California, Irvine, nearly all the teams had completed additional fieldwork. With that, the volume began to take on its final form.

Throughout the development of the book, the editors in pairs and alone met in person and by phone several times with each other and with the contributors. Taken together, our editorial comments ran to well over 125 single-spaced pages (bolstered by hundreds of short e-mail clarifications, reminders, and updates traveling between the authors and editors). Each chapter went through a minimum of three drafts (and some, as many as five drafts). Once the final drafts from the authors had been received, a final, intensive period of editing the chapters began in 2002. In some cases, the final editing brought to the fore additional analytic insights and new applications of field data that were incorporated into each chapter. In other instances, chapter revisions led to the modification or introduction of broad themes that were integrated into the entire volume. Cindy White, who had taken the field methods seminar at Arizona (and coauthored an empirical chapter), joined the editorial team in the late 1990s. Her expertise in communication studies and the social psychology of personal relationships facilitated the development of each chapter and the entire volume.

Along the way, we drew on the support and insights of numerous people. First, we thank the countless informants who participated in the research. Without their time and patience, this project would have been impossible. We also thank the dozens of graduate students in the qualitative field methods seminar taught by Morrill and Snow at the University of Arizona and now at the University of California, Irvine, who, over the years, have offered useful ideas, examples, and critiques relevant to this volume. Carolyn J. Aman Karlin, in particular, gathered and abstracted materials on the personal relationship field. More recently, students in the seminars have read and provided useful responses to the chapter drafts. We received useful comments from those who attended a 1998 National Communication Association panel on personal relationships in public places organized by Cindy White. We also received important feedback on the project from participants at a qualitative methods workshop for graduate students in the Department of Sociology, School of Business, and School of Education at the University of Michigan that Morrill led in 2000.

Several individuals deserve special mention for their feedback on this volume. Bob Emerson generously read through a penultimate draft of the entire manuscript, offering insightful commentary on every chapter. In 2003, Jack Katz invited Morrill and Snow to present an overview of this volume at his and Emerson's "LA at Play" summer Undergraduate Ethnography Institute at the University of California, Los Angeles, funded by the National Science Foundation. The responses by students and Katz (both orally and in subsequent written comments) were quite supportive and proved valuable for completing the project. Jason Owen-Smith read early drafts of some of the chapters and made helpful comments on them and the entire volume. Christina Nippert-Eng, in a review of the entire manuscript for the University of California Press, cogently presented several useful ideas for shaping the final manuscript to make it more accessible to a wide range of audiences, as did an anonymous reviewer for the press. Two early reviews for the press of the introductory and three empirical chapters helped shape the volume in important ways. Finally, we thank Naomi Schneider of the press for her unwavering support and patience in shepherding this project on a long and winding road. And to our families and colleagues, as well as the countless persons with whom we have developed personal relationships in public places, we extend our thanks for their support of this project and particularly for their experiential testimony to the significance and importance of personal relationships in public places.

Irvine, California
October 2004

ONE

The Study of Personal Relationships in Public Places

CALVIN MORRILL AND DAVID A. SNOW

EVIDENCE OF PERSONAL RELATIONSHIPS CAN be found in almost any urban public place: a dozen teenagers hang out with each other on the sidewalk outside a market; a mother and daughter laugh playfully as they inspect decorations in a retail store; two women chat amiably with each other on a bench at a park as they watch their husbands play softball in a city league; young men and women greet each other with salutations and hugs at a local bar. Despite these commonplace observations, multiple traditions in the social sciences concerned with cities and social relationships have neglected the study of personal relationships in public places. Decades ago, the sociologists Georg Simmel and Louis Wirth claimed that urban dwellers coped with the intense sights and sounds of cities by shutting down meaningful social contact while in public.[1] Their perspectives influenced an entire generation of urban sociologists whose research rarely acknowledged personal relationships in public places. Social psychologists and communication scholars further contributed to this neglect by confining their research on relationships to long-term ties grounded in private contexts, such as households and workplaces.[2] And more recently, the political scientist Robert Putnam portrayed American public places as increasingly bereft of meaningful social relationships in his version of the age-old critique of community decline.[3]

During the latter half of the last century, urban ethnographers began to venture out in public to study, up close, the sights and sounds of everyday urban life. What they found challenged the received wisdom: public places that fostered a wide range of meaningful personal connections instead of asocial settings.[4] In this volume, the contributors take important cues from this line of inquiry to examine how people in public create, negotiate, and make sense of personal relationships. Some of the studies deal with intimate relationships that spill over from private to public places. Most focus on relationships—whether short-lived or more durable—that unfold entirely in public, yet embody some of the interactional dynamics and feel of intimate relations. The authors thus provide a unique window on personal relationships that have received little attention from social scientists but can be significant for individuals and contemporary society as a whole.[5] In so doing, the volume underscores how public sociality often creates islands where meaningful social ties are formed and maintained, even though these islands tend to be isolated from each other.

At a theoretical level, the authors focus less on individuals than on the patterned social interactions that constitute personal relationships. Thus they attempt to understand people's everyday relational practices or, put more concretely, their ways of operating as they conduct personal relationships in parks, bars, exercise facilities, public discussion groups, and retail establishments and on sidewalks and city streets.[6] To get close to those they studied, the authors used qualitative field methods, including participant observation and semistructured interviewing, that yielded data not easily generated by other methods, such as surveys or experiments. Throughout these processes, they created personal relationships with their informants that, by facilitating access and broadening their perspective, proved crucial for their research.[7] Moreover, the contributors often worked in teams, adopting different roles in the field and perspectives during data analysis, in order to approximate a range of perspectives within and across diverse settings and relationships. This strategy, in turn, maximized what the fieldworkers could inquire about and learn.[8]

In this chapter, we provide a broad conceptual orientation to the nine studies in this volume. We begin by locating the overall thrust of the volume with respect to the dominant research traditions on personal relationships. We then outline some key elements of an interactionist perspective on personal relationships in public, drawing especially from Erving Goffman and interactionist approaches to emotional expression. In the next sections, we offer some ways to think about public places and contexts, particular kinds of personal relationships that occur in public, and how people suppress, repair, and strategically manage threats to relationships in public.

THE STUDY OF PERSONAL RELATIONSHIPS IN TIME AND PLACE

Steve Duck argues that "people's lives are fabricated in and by their relationships with other people. Our greatest moments of joy and sorrow are founded in relationships."[9] As his statement suggests, personal relationships are at the core of human existence. Daily routines as well as extraordinary events are made sense of within and organized through personal relationships. Personal relationships often mediate the influences of larger economic and political institutions on individuals and can, under certain conditions, act back on those institutions.[10] Given the elemental character and scale of the subject, it is not surprising that a wide range of the social sciences, including sociology, psychology, communication studies, and anthropology, have undertaken research on personal relationships.

Figure I.I represents the dominant research traditions on personal relationships along two relevant continua: the time frame of a relationship

FIGURE I.I

Dominant Tendencies in Research on Personal Relationships by Time and Place

PLACE

PUBLIC

TIME		
Ethnographic studies on the complexities of encounters and *short-term* relationships among urban dwellers in places with broad social access and visibility (e.g., sidewalks, parks, bars, retail stores)	Ethnographic and historical studies on *long-term* relationships among urban dwellers in places that have broad social access and visibility (e.g., sidewalks, parks, bars, retail stores), but with an eye toward how such relationships contribute to community integration
TRANSITORY ——————————————————— DURABLE	
Ethnographic and biographical studies on *short-term* relationships involving subordinated persons in mainstream and normatively marginal places with restricted access (e.g., domiciles, sex workplaces, mental institutions)	Experimental and survey studies on *long-term* intimate relationships involving Anglo, middle-class persons that are explicitly or implicitly contextualized in mainstream places with restricted access (e.g., domiciles, dorms, workplaces, Internet chat rooms)

PRIVATE

(transitory to durable) and the places where a relationship is primarily grounded (public to private).[11] The bulk of previous research on personal relationships is found in mainstream "relationship research," represented in the lower right quadrant.[12] Relationship researchers devote considerable attention to long-term intimate relationships, such as marriages, close friendships, and family ties. A number of substantive issues have dominated such work, including satisfaction among relational partners, interpersonal power and dynamics, conflict, and how relationships develop from initial encounters to more intimate footings. To study these topics, relationship researchers most often plumb the experiences of Anglo-American, middle-class, heterosexual, eighteen- to twenty-five-year-old college students. As a result, a great deal is known about romance and friendship on college campuses, but little about less durable relationships or about relationships among people who do not fit that profile, such as the poor, ethnic minorities, people who are not college educated, gays and lesbians, and those who are younger or older than traditional college students.[13]

Aside from focusing on durable ties, the relationship research tradition typically contextualizes relationships in private places with little social access or visibility. *Context* generally refers to the surrounding social, cultural, and institutional environments that help define, channel, and enable social interaction.[14] Regardless of how context is defined, many relationship researchers practice what we call "context stripping" and "context glossing" in their work. In context stripping, researchers set context aside altogether to treat social interaction as though it occurred in a vacuum.[15] This is typically done in the name of isolating a set of factors hypothesized to influence an aspect of social interaction. In context glossing, researchers import thin approximations of context (typically situated in private places) into studies of social relationships through vignettes, role playing, or having participants remember aspects of relevant places or situations as they recount or enact some aspect of their personal relationships in a controlled setting. Although researchers claim certain methodological advantages to context stripping and glossing, removing personal relationships from natural social contexts constrains researchers from taking into account how enveloping material, institutional, cultural, and social conditions affect the way people interact in personal relationships. Recently, some relationship research has moved away from this trend to explore how institutionalized expectations and "relational logics" provide organizing principles for different types of relationships: for example, by influencing the definitions that people hold about personal relationships.[16] Relationship researchers have also investigated how proximate social structures, such as interpersonal networks, influence the relational choices available to people, as well as the different forms of social support needed to maintain personal relationships.[17]

Whatever the conceptual orientation, experimental and self-report methods dominate the relationship research tradition.[18] Despite the scientific advantages of experiments for isolating predictive and/or causal relationships between particular sets of variables, such methods can limit the kinds of relationships that can be approximated in or imported to controlled settings (typically, but not always, laboratories). Moreover, ongoing relationships may be unintentionally altered because of contextual conditions in the laboratory itself,[19] and studies in controlled settings may gloss over aspects of personal relationships that are continually renegotiated and redefined by individuals in natural settings.[20]

Survey methods, especially "relational inventories" and "relational diaries," continue to enjoy currency in some research programs. Relational inventories are typically organized so that respondents can check off items that elicit information about the attributes of their personal relationships (e.g., when and how did a person meet his or her relational partner).[21] Relational diaries rely on respondents' memories but require multiple entries over structured time periods, thus providing opportunities for qualitative and quantitative responses.[22] Despite the growing sophistication of these techniques, they still encounter a host of difficulties, including informant accuracy problems that raise questions about what respondents remember about their relationships and under what conditions.[23] At a more general level, self-report methods touch a classic social science problem of the complex interplay between talk, attitudes, and behavior.[24] Clearly, people do not always do what they report they do or would do. Under some conditions, talk, attitudes, and other actions are closely aligned. At other times, avowed attitudes provide after-the-fact accounts for actions that may bear little direct relationship to subsequent behavior.[25]

Beyond the lower right quadrant of Figure 1.1, we find work that is disconnected from many of the concerns associated with traditional relationship research but nonetheless provides insights into the dynamics of personal relationships as they are lived in natural contexts. Perhaps the least explored terrain in this regard is research on temporary relationships in private places (represented in the lower left quadrant of Figure 1.1). Here we encounter social connections that are nearly invisible to mainstream audiences and often involve socially subordinated persons (especially women and ethnic minorities) in both mainstream and normatively marginal places. Such research is nearly always qualitative, involving ethnography, interviews, or biographical studies that chronicle how individuals manage these circumstances. Robert Edgerton's ethnography of transient personal relationships among mental patients trying to construct "normal" private lives after being released from mental institutions offers a poignant example of this type of research.[26] More recently, Pierette Hondagneu-Sotelo's research on domestic service workers in middle-class Los Angeles and Barbara Ehrenreich and Arlie Hochschild's collection of ethnographic and biographic essays on sex workers, maids, and nannies underscore the often short-lived "serial" relationships among subordinated women and between them and their employers in the context of the global economy.[27]

Still other research, especially in urban ethnography, attempts to understand everyday life in urban public places. Scholars working along these lines are particularly attuned to how people can invest emotion and meaning in personal relationships amidst the intensity of the urban experience. The upper left quadrant of Figure 1.1 shows work that focuses on relationships occurring over brief periods in public places. From the vantage point of a mainstream relationship researcher, many of the social connections studied by scholars in this tradition would not be considered relationships at all because of their lack of durability. Nonetheless, the research traditions in this quadrant demonstrate the importance of such ties for participants and the wider social context in which they occur. Fred Davis's ethnographic study of the transitory ties between cabbies and their fares and Erving Goffman's myriad observations on the ironies of seemingly trivial but highly complex interpersonal interactions between strangers and acquaintances in public frame much of the research in this tradition.[28] Among those influenced by Goffman and Davis is Lyn Lofland, whose work on encounters and short-lived relationships in urban public settings underscores their social character and sets the tone for much of the research in this volume.[29]

The upper right quadrant of Figure 1.1 contains the vast majority of studies on personal relationships in public places. Unlike work on public, short-term relationships, much of the work in this area attempts to understand how durable ties in public undergird communities and other social institutions. William Foote Whyte's classic observations in *Street Corner Society* of the durable and very public personal relationships among "corner boys" is perhaps the most famous exemplar of this research tradition.[30]

Far from contributing to the social "disorganization" of a "slum," the ties among the youth and young adults that Whyte studied provided a foundation for social organization in Boston's North End. Observational studies of long-standing relationships among pub patrons by Mass Observation and Gregory Stone's ethnography of "personalizing" ties among retail clerks and their customers also demonstrated how regular pub going and personalizing of retail relations contribute to the integration of local communities.[31] Other well-known works in this tradition include Jane Jacobs's observational and historical work on "public characters"—individuals whose extensive ties with local community members enhance both the solidarity and security of urban neighborhoods.[32] Along these same lines, Elijah Anderson demonstrated how "Jelly's" (a Chicago bar and liquor store that working and nonworking African American men used as a regular hangout) functioned as a key focal point for its neighborhood, while Mitch Duneier ethnographically documented how Greenwich Village street vendors operated as contemporary public characters.[33]

Our brief foray through the history of research on personal relationships is not intended to be exhaustive; rather, it is meant to set the stage for presenting a theoretical approach to the naturalistic study of personal relationships in public places. That approach—like this volume—grows out of and contributes to the interactionist perspectives undergirding the research traditions in the upper quadrants of Figure 1.1.

PERSONAL RELATIONSHIPS IN PUBLIC
FROM AN INTERACTIONIST PERSPECTIVE

Up till now we have used the term *personal relationship* in unspecified ways. In this section, we provide a working definition of personal relationships from an interactionist perspective with particular attention paid to how social ties play out in public. This perspective, which has evolved from the philosophical tradition of American pragmatism, gives primacy to the interactional nexus of social relationships. Attention is specifically focused on how individuals and groups negotiate, construct, assess, and engage in social interaction within a broader cultural milieu.[34] Goffman, whose work represents a variant of the interactionist perspective, argued that the proper analytic focus for studying social relationships is the "interaction order"—a class of behaviors that involves face-to-face interaction or mediated interpersonal communication that approximates such interaction.[35] From this perspective, personal relationships are not attributes or traits of individuals; rather, they are constituted by ongoing social interaction, at the core of which are coordinated behaviors and a "working consensus" about the character of face-to-face communication, which in turn result in "situated" interdependencies.[36]

Situated Interdependence

From an interactionist perspective, social relationships can be defined according to how their interdependencies (i.e., mutual influence) are situated in social interaction.[37] To one degree or another, all social interaction involves coordination. Many social interactions, however, can be termed "encounters" because actors exhibit very little mutual influence over one another beyond what is necessary to sustain a momentary transaction.[38] Encounters can carry the seeds of social relationships if they evolve into multiple, coordinated episodes such that actors' behaviors and expectations affect one another in meaningful ways.[39] Social relationships move toward the personal to the degree that individuals become emotionally interdependent with some combination of the following dimensions: a normative dimension (e.g., the kinds of behaviors that are considered appropriate and inappropriate within the relationship), a symbolic dimension (e.g., the way one defines oneself relative to one's relational partner), and a material dimension (e.g., the relative financial resources controlled by relational partners).[40] The most socially intimate relationships thus involve the commingling of people's moralities, interpretations, hopes, aspirations, identities, financial resources, and emotional expressions.

To argue that two people are interdependent, however, does not imply they are completely or equally dependent on one another. Interdependencies can be asymmetrical, thus forming the basis for social power within relationships.[41] Personal relationships also vary by their stage of development. Although the natural development of a personal relationship is not necessarily linear and the boundaries between its stages are often difficult to discern, one could argue that interdependencies typically increase between relational partners as a relationship moves from its beginnings to a more durable footing.[42] Relational interdependencies also vary in their "scope" (i.e., how many relational dimensions form the basis for relational interdependence) and their "depth" (i.e., how strong or weak the interdependence is on any single dimension). One could imagine, for example, friends who are deeply interdependent materially (they own a business together) and moderately interdependent emotionally (they like each other and are sensitive to one another's feelings but are not terribly close) but who share little else with each other in terms of their personal tastes and preferences.

Personal relationships do not exist in a social vacuum independent of the social networks or the broad institutional and cultural contexts in which they are embedded. Social networks can provide resources that both help sustain relationships and introduce opposing interests that can weaken or rupture close social ties. In long-standing personal relationships, moreover, relational partners' personal networks can become intertwined in both depth and scope. As a result, relational dissolution among individuals involved in a long-standing personal relationship (particularly in marriage) often involves the disentangling of highly interdependent personal networks.[43] As individuals draw from their proximate social networks to constitute their personal ties, they are also oriented, in various ways, to taken-for-granted societal, ethnic, religious, and gendered premises about the definitions and dynamics of close relationships. Such premises offer "constitutive rules" that individuals draw from to define personal relationships, feed into routine practices for conducting personal relationships, and facilitate behavioral accounts for relational partners and other actors.[44]

As fundamental as interdependence is for understanding personal relationships, the term leaves a relatively abstract sense of them. Left unanswered are questions such as: How is relational interdependence constituted by interaction processes in public? How do relational partners express their feelings toward one another via social interaction in public? How do people communicate their relational ties to broader social audiences? These questions point toward social approaches to personal relationships that focus on their everyday "achievement," but with an eye toward the special challenges that public settings pose for the conduct of relationships.[45] To begin to unpack some of these issues, we turn to Erving Goffman's work on public social interaction.

Balancing "Normal Appearances" with Relational Interaction in Public

Although Goffman did not concentrate on personal relationships in public per se, his work provides a useful point of departure for their study. He argued that much of urban public life rests on people upholding the tacit working consensus surrounding ordinary social interaction and "normal appearances"—outward behavior that facilitates movement through public places, minimizes physical contact and fear, and protects valued social and moral identities.[46] On a day-to-day basis, a great deal of the subtleties and social complexities of public social interaction involves strangers who brush by one another with ritualized precision. Through these rituals, individuals enter into and navigate through public places without giving much attention to their surroundings. Conducting a personal relationship in public, however, means that actions that might be expected to be more commonly found in private are now out in the open for all to see. Such visibility can cut multiple ways. On the one hand, being out in public can create tensions as people attend to multiple sets of ground rules. At the very least, people must simultaneously present an appearance appropriate for a public place and coordinate their actions appropriately with those to whom they are personally tied. What can result is something of a balancing act between the normative demands of public sociality and personal interaction during which individuals camouflage their actions for broader audiences. At the same time, being in public can liberate relational partners from the intense scrutiny and regulation of private places (because, for example, they are youths or unmarried young adults who are intensely supervised by adults). Thus public places can free people to conduct relationships with whom and where they choose.

As Goffman noted, people conducting personal relationships in public also convey their relational status via a variety of signals that help to recalibrate, so to speak, the immediate interactional norms surrounding them. "Tie signs," for example, consist of actions that signal the characteristics of a relationship to both the principals and wider audiences. Tie signs are found in any public place as people embrace, hold hands, or move close to one another to engage in conversation. From a distance, such signs carry "obvious" meanings that the persons enacting them are "together" in some fashion and can be expected to interact with one another in more socially intimate ways than would be typically expected between two strangers in a public place.[47] Yet the meanings of an embrace can vary dramatically according to the vantage point from which it is observed or who (e.g., men, women, children) is involved. What is viewed as an innocuous embrace by some may be viewed by others as "beyond the pale" or greeted with jeers of "Get a room!" Some public contexts (e.g., bars) may display more leeway than others with regard to the physical intimacy with which tie signs are enacted.

Closely related to tie signs are "territories of the self," which are physical, stylistic, emotional, and conversational spaces claimed by participants as they interact with one another. In public, strangers typically maintain individual territories of the self (personal spaces) even in the face of intense crowding (such as in a bus or subway car at rush hour). People involved in personal relationships, by contrast, typically commingle their territories of the self and signal such mergers through tie signs. Here again, we encounter the balancing act alluded to above as relational partners whose personal spaces are joined typically navigate public places as a collective unit. Consider, for example, how two people chatting for an extended period on a sidewalk or in a retail store continuously reposition themselves so that their collective space is not encroached upon by other pedestrians.

"Civil inattention," a term coined by Goffman in *Behavior in Public Places,* offers a third example of the embodiment of tacit, normative assumptions in public that differ dramatically from the norms of social interaction undergirding personal relationships in private. The principle of civil inattention requires that strangers in public places give "enough visual notice to demonstrate that one appreciates that the other is present, while at the next moment withdrawing one's attention from him so as to express that he does not constitute a target of special curiosity or design."[48] As Lyn Lofland notes, civil inattention enables "co-presence without co-mingling."[49] Such interaction, then, limits the amount of social interaction that occurs and prevents violations of the norms of politeness and distance characteristic of much of public life. In so doing, it is diametrically opposed to the bulk of social interaction that occurs within personal relationships where the object is co-presence *with* commingling. Another example can be found in the tacit assumptions of "restrained helpfulness" in which strangers ask one another for small favors (e.g., "Could you tell me the time?" or "If you're not using this chair, would you mind if we used it at our table?"). The important qualifier here is *restrained,* which also limits the interdependencies and relational interaction that occurs between interactants. This kind of interaction stands in sharp contrast to that which characterizes a personal relationship, in which the underlying interdependencies require behaviors that go well beyond the boundaries of restrained helpfulness.

As is clear from the above examples, people must navigate multiple sets of tacit rules to enact personal relationships and public sociality, but they may not constantly and deeply reflect on those norms, what they mean, or whether they should be followed to the letter.[50] How, then, can one produce reliable evidence of such ground rules? Goffman points toward what he calls normative "transgressions"—"deviant" behaviors that can be observed in public and that reveal underlying normative strata in social interaction.[51] Such behaviors involve "situational improprieties" during the course of interaction but can also include more "serious" transgressions such as interpersonal conflict and violence and the ending of a relationship. It is in these social interactions, when people marshal "enforcement systems" against deviants, that we learn most definitively about the normative boundaries of relationships and their intersections with wider social and cultural contexts.

What emerges from this brief discussion is an image of skill at maneuvering through the tacit conventions of social interaction. For those engaged in personal relationships in public, such maneuvering is complicated by the multiple sets of rules and demands that must be managed. Further complicating these dynamics are the emotional expressions that accompany personal relationships and that are socially shaped by one's immediate surroundings (especially the public places in which people find themselves) and broader cultural frameworks for interpreting and enacting emotion.

The Social Shaping of Emotion in Public

Interactionist approaches to emotion stress its occurrence, as Jack Katz argues, via one's "readings and responses" to other persons and relevant contexts regarding what a line of action means.[52] Some emotional expressions, such as shame, can involve explicit self-searching as an individual "thinks through" what has happened, including how others will define the situation, impute social identities, and behaviorally respond. Anger, laughing, or crying, by contrast, can occur so rapidly that the "artfulness" of emotion occurs in largely intuitive and sensual ways, much as a painter adds a flurry of brush strokes while painting a canvas.[53] During these processes, individuals attend to a backdrop of "feeling rules" that help them define and enact appropriate emotions and access whatever resources (e.g., bodily, material, cultural) are available to them to constitute particular emotional displays.[54]

In public, such displays are often muted. As Spencer Cahill and Robin Eggleston argue, "[P]ublic etiquette would seem to proscribe the public expression of emotion."[55] This means, among other things, that emotions, like other aspects of relational interaction, may be camouflaged behind what appears to be conventional, distanced public social interaction. Under such conditions, individuals can "surface act," to borrow from Arlie Hochschild, to prevent intense emotional displays from reaching the surface.[56] Thus normal appearances in public can appear to be somewhat devoid of emotion, but they are not. At the very least, they require emotional management as individuals suppress emotional displays. In the context of tie signs and territories of the self that are commingled, emotional displays may be more intense; indeed, they may be expected to be more intense as the public etiquette that defines ostensibly "emotionless" public sociality is suspended. The sociological insight in all of this is that people socially shape each other's emotions.[57] Such shaping also involves multiple sets of ground rules and orientations that act in indeterminate, yet influential ways as people constitute their personal relationships.

Taken together, these observations about the rule-based character of public sociality and the social shaping of emotion provide useful points of departure for examining personal relationships conducted in public, but they provide us less leverage for analyzing the range of public places in which personal and social relationships are found. How, then, can we conceptualize the public geography and social settings where personal relationships develop?

LOCATING PUBLIC SOCIALITY IN PLACES AND REALMS

To conceptualize the public settings where personal relations are found, we must confront private-public distinctions, briefly alluded to at the outset of this chapter. These constitute one of the "grand dichotomies of Western thought" and inform a wide range of analyses in the social sciences.[58] As implied by the plural use of the term, these distinctions compose a set of differences that appear clear in the abstract but are somewhat complex as experienced. Although public-private distinctions are invoked to analyze a range of phenomena from economics to politics, we use these distinctions to better understand personal relationships in public. The first distinction we draw concerns the *places* in which personal relationships develop; the second focuses on the social nature of *realms*. By *places,* we mean geographical locales in the built environment that become imbued with particular meanings and practices regarding their access and social visibility.[59] Virtually all locales in urban settings have some set of meanings associated with them and can be located on a continuum that stretches from public places that are highly accessible and visible to all members of a community to private places that have highly restricted access (gatekeeping) and visibility. In between these poles, places of various sorts have different degrees and mixes of accessibility and visibility.[60]

This distinction, although not precise enough for some purposes, does fit with common sense. Many urban sidewalks are examples of public places where nearly anyone can walk and where visibility of others is generally high. Most domiciles are examples of private places that are restricted to family members and those whose presence is legitimated by family members. In between these extremes are places that vary widely in access and visibility but also display gatekeeping and are associated with more focused tasks, features that mark them as "quasi"-public places. Examples include retail establishments, bars, restaurants, cafés, spectating areas for various artistic or sporting performances, community centers, and public monuments.[61]

Features of the built environment strongly influence the public nature of places. The physical openness of city plazas, for example, facilitates greater access and visibility than walled-in, domiciled patios. Similarly, the openness of main artery streets makes them differ in their access and visibility from alleyways, which in turn affects the degree of publicness and privacy that can be achieved in them and the extent to which public interaction mixes people of different racial and class identities. Architectural features can also facilitate the kinds of sociality that occur in public places. Plazas with benches and seats, for example, physically "encourage" people to engage in social interaction, while long vistas can "invite" people to stop, look, and linger. The physical attributes of place can also facilitate gatekeeping by limiting particular ethnic or residential groups' entry into geographical areas.[62]

Social settings also contain different distributions of public and quasi-public places that can be used to ground personal relationships. These distributions vary by social class, ethnicity, and geographical organization (e.g., urban and rural settings). For example, middle-class urban settings typically contain few places that are not officially defined as "prime real estate" reserved for particular uses and people of middle-class status.[63] People attempting to use prime real estate public places to conduct personal relationships (e.g., teenagers hanging out with friends in fast-food restaurants or shopping center parking lots) typically are driven off the premises by those attempting to uphold the official definitions of place. Poorer areas often contain less prime real estate and ironically can offer ambiguously designated public places (abandoned buildings, empty lots, warehouse districts) that can be appropriated in a variety of ways for engaging in personal relationships. Urban ethnic enclaves have various distributions of public spatial resources, in part defined by the intersections of ethnicity, social class, and geographic locations within cities, as well as culture. Mexican and Central American immigrants to the United States, for example, sometimes carve out places on streets and neighborhoods that approximate the plazas and courtyards frequently built into the urban architecture of their homelands.[64]

In contrast to places, differences between private and public *realms* rest on the types of social relationships that predominate in a particular place rather than access and visibility. Lyn Lofland distinguishes three realms: public, parochial, and private.[65] Public realms are social settings in which fluid, impersonal relationships predominate: that is, settings in which people are typically, but not exclusively, unknown to one another or else know each other primarily in terms of impersonal roles or categories (e.g., the "street vendor," the "businessperson who waits at the bus stop," the "cop"). Personal relationships among, for example, acquaintances, neighbors, or workplace colleagues who belong to overlapping social networks constitute the parochial realm. This is the world of the neighborhood and the workplace. The private realm consists of socially intimate and closely bounded relationships that often have a pretense to, if not actual, durability.

In many instances, the type of place and the type of realm overlap in a one-to-one correspondence. Public places tend to contain public realms, and private places tend to contain private realms. Quasi-public and quasi-private places tend to contain a mixture of public and parochial realms. Experientially, however, distinguishing the social, cognitive, and cultural boundaries between private and public places and realms can become a good deal more complex.[66] Consider the stereotypical family picnic to a city park. City parks are quintessential public places because of their general accessibility and high visibility. A family is a quintessential private realm. The area in a park that the family inhabits becomes a quasi-private realm for the duration of their picnic. The place that the family occupies is also partially transformed. Access to the ramada or picnic table they occupy will be restricted to family members (or those they invite to their picnic), and a temporary sense of territoriality by family members can also develop. At the same time, the family's social interaction will still be largely visible to anyone else in the park. The public features of the territory occupied by the family picnic, especially its accessibility and visibility, return once the family leaves.

What the family-in-the-park example underscores, again, is that personal relationships that venture out into or develop primarily in public spaces are partly transformed such that they come to take on some of the interactional characteristics of the public realm. When the personal unfolds in public, various aspects of personal relationships are constrained while others are enabled, thereby affecting the types of relationships possible in such contexts. To examine these possibilities, we next discuss an expanded vocabulary of personal relationships that modifies the classic distinction between "primary" and "secondary" relationships.

EXPANDING THE VOCABULARY
OF PERSONAL RELATIONSHIPS

Just as public-private distinctions cast a long shadow across the social sciences, the dichotomy of primary and secondary relations shapes much of the received wisdom about interpersonal relationships. Viewed in terms of this dichotomy, the most emotionally invested and interdependent relationships are coded as primary (e.g., family ties, long-term romantic relationships, and close friendships), and all other relationships fall into the secondary category. This dichotomy makes more sense when one is studying variants of traditionally defined primary relationships (as most scholars of personal relationships do). But when one moves into the public or the parochial realms to observe personal relationships, the dichotomy becomes less useful. Earlier observational studies of public gathering places, such as bars or retail settings, underscored these limitations. In these settings, scholars found social relationships that were infused with personal interdependencies and had episodic durations (relational partners might interact with each other in intervals over extended periods of time— e.g., meeting once per week or month) and in which the interactants might not even know each other's surnames. These kinds of relationships do not fit neatly into the primary category because they do not typically have the interdependent scope and depth of primary relations. At the same time, lumping them together as secondary relations glosses over their significance and meaning. As a result, such observations require an expanded vocabulary that moves beyond the primary-secondary dichotomy to explore relationships that exist in the interstices of the primary-secondary divide and mix relational purposes from both primary and secondary categories.[67] We draw from a variety of sources to identify two types of personal relationships—"fleeting personal relationships" and "anchored personal relationships"—that are especially relevant beyond private places and realms.[68]

Fleeting Personal Relationships

The public realm, by definition, contains a large volume of social encounters that do not constitute personal relationships. When such encounters are emotionally colored and evince some level of interdependence between individuals but have a transient nature, they take on the interactional characteristics of a fleeting relationship. Thus the fleeting relationship lies beyond the "familiar stranger" phenomenon, identified by Stanley Milgram and associates, in which urban dwellers develop relationships at a distance with those they recognize and observe repeatedly but with whom they never interact.[69] Familiar strangers are found in many public places frequented by large aggregates of "regulars," including commuter trains and buses, city parks, and large urban public university campuses. Examples of fleeting relationships, by contrast, include friendly chats between dog owners as they walk their dogs, extended conversations among seatmates in buses and airplanes, conversations among patrons as they watch others or react to various televised or immediate events in a bar, and extended, helpful interactions among retail customers.[70]

The transient character of fleeting relationships, however, does not mean that relational players necessarily invest little significance in these types of ties. On the contrary, individuals can become quite attached to a fleeting relational partner for momentary emotional and cognitive support—all without extended commitment. At the same time, fleeting relationships can create a number of interactional ambiguities that create opportunities for social tension. Misperceptions or asymmetrical perceptions among relational players regarding the depth of a fleeting relationship can occur. For example, bar patrons can invest a great deal more time strategizing their management of a fleeting relationship with a server than vice versa, investing more significance in particular cues, such as a server's smile, than exist from the server's perspective. Ambiguities also manifest themselves when a fleeting relational partner is not recognized by his or her counterpart away from the place ("out of context") in which their interaction typically occurs. Moreover, the tacit rules to which relational players orient themselves in fleeting relationships vary tremendously by place. In some public places, conventions regarding "politeness" constrain those in a fleeting relationship from probing too deeply into conversational topics that stray beyond the immediate interaction.[71] In other public places, a fleeting relationship can take on the interactional characteristics of a more intimate personal relationship, as when people tightly embrace each other in a salutary hug at a bar.

Anchored Personal Relationships

Relationships in public also can be anchored in more durable emotional and behavioral interdependencies. Specifically, an anchored personal relationship involves recurring interaction and interdependencies that develop between individuals over time but are tied to a particular public place and a narrow range of activities that do not, or rarely, spill over into private households and other domiciled settings.[72] Illustrations of anchored relationships include regular customers of restaurants and bars, season ticket holders to artistic and sporting events who sit next to one another for years, "café" friends, and regular riders of commuter buses and railways. Examples of anchored relationships also can be found in popular television programs such as *Cheers* during the 1980s (a bar of the same name that acted as the hangout for a group of friends; a standing joke on the program was that the principals rarely returned to their households to be with their "intimates" because they were so wedded to their friends at the bar).[73] Peggy Wireman provides a general sense of what we mean by an anchored personal relationship: "[These] relationships . . . have the dimension of warmth, rapport, and intimacy normally connected with primary relationships yet occur within a secondary setting and have some aspects of secondary relationships. The dimensions are: intense involvement, warmth, intimacy, sense of belonging, and rapport; mutual knowledge of character; involvement of the individual rather than the family; a commitment that is limited in time and scope . . . ; consideration of public rather than private matters; and a preference for public meeting places."[74]

Even though anchored relationships have more limited time commitments and spatial constraints than typical primary relationships, they blur the boundaries between primary and other relations in terms of their significance and interdependence. Indeed, individuals can invest enormous emotional energy into anchored relationships, and, under some conditions, these relationships can compete with and even replace traditional primary relationships.[75]

MAINTAINING PUBLIC INTERACTION ORDERS

Our discussion thus far has only glanced at the social friction and tension that can occur as people conduct personal relationships in public. Fleeting relationships especially can appear frictionless because their transitory nature facilitates temporary avoidance or complete exit from interaction in the wake of threats to the interaction order. But avoidance, however covert it may appear to outsiders, is rarely a completely frictionless or emotionless action by the principals.[76] In relationships on a stronger footing—anchored and primary relationships—a good portion of conflict management in public may be devoted to what Goffman calls "remedial work" that attempts to repair fractures in the interaction order. In his discussion of remedial work, Goffman focuses on the behaviors that offending parties engage in to lessen the consequences of their transgressions and repair ruptures in the working consensus undergirding social interaction. From this perspective, offenders are concerned with keeping "normal appearances" that do not alarm an offended party (or surrounding audiences, particularly in public places) by proffering plausible accounts for their violations or apologies in the aftermath of problematic behavior or by making requests to the offending party "to be allowed" to engage in the offending action.[77]

In other instances, less privileged parties engaged in social encounters or fleeting relationships can flout the conventions of interaction to subvert the position of the socially powerful. Mitchell Duneier and Harvey Molotch analyze a poignant example of one such process—which they call "interactional vandalism"—in which poor, male African American street vendors intentionally undermine the conventions of public realm interaction by asking streams of questions or making "innocent" compliments to white female pedestrians even when they are ignored or actively avoided by the latter.[78] Under some conditions, such interactional violations take the form of overt public harassment, again primarily directed by men toward women in public places and realms.[79]

Offended parties are likewise motivated to maintain the interaction order and can take actions to sidestep, suppress, or repair its fractures through a variety of strategies, all in the presence of strangers or relational partner(s). Such strategies, especially among those who are "streetwise," are intended to minimize whatever transgression has occurred through toleration and social contact.[80] More active strategies can range from various forms of avoidance (e.g., the "silent treatment" or avoidance of particular conversational topics) to various forms of "voice" in which offended parties engage in negotiation or persuasion and, under some conditions, coercive self-help.[81] Aside from maintaining the immediate interaction order, remedial work can be used strategically to take the moral or symbolic high ground from relational partners (e.g., when a relational partner initiates negotiation in order to project an identity as a reasonable person).

Remedial work can also maintain "working" coordination in public and quasi-public groups that contain different types of personal relationships.

Under these conditions, personal enmities borne by partners in anchored or fleeting relationships can spill out into the group and threaten its social solidarity. Yet another factor in threats to public interaction orders is groups—such as street gangs—that lay claim to particular physical territories and enforce specific ground rules for public social interaction. Under these conditions, even streetwise actors may find it difficult to employ their usual strategies of toleration and may find exit (e.g., "duck and cover") their only option. These considerations lie beyond the purview of this volume, although a great deal of research on urban gangs and other forms of street-based violence has investigated the ground rules that undergird public interaction orders and personal relationships that turn less on toleration and remedial work than on aggressive confrontation.[82]

PREVIEWING THE STUDIES

Part 1 of this book contains three studies that investigate fleeting relationships across a variety of public and quasi-public places. In chapter 2, Lesa Stern, Mark Callister, and Lynn Jones explore the ways men and women position themselves physically and socially to encourage or thwart the creation of personal relationships as they work out in a college campus recreation center. What results from these attempts are fleeting relationships or, in some cases involving male initiators and female "targets," unwanted voyeurism and entreaties. Their chapter underscores both the pleasures and the social tensions in fleeting relationships, as well as the role that gender plays in such interactions. Irenee Beattie, Karen Christopher, Dina Okamoto, and Sandra Way report in chapter 3 on their study of public singles dances. Although the singles dances they studied ostensibly exist to encourage the development of long-term romantic relationships, the authors find that momentary encounters on the dance floor or transient personal relationships are more common among participants. Far from being meaningless, the dances draw many participants to return time and time again to experience the pleasures of fleeting sociality regardless of whether they meet the same partners. Part 1 closes with Joseph Massey and Trina Hope's study of "emotional labor" by female dancers in a strip club. For a dancer to be successful financially, she and her customers must co-create fictive personal—albeit fleeting—relationships that are both temporally compressed and highly visible during nude and seminude performances that occur at customers' tables. These processes translate into patterns of social exchange that both facilitate and constrain dancers' control over their efforts at work.

Part 2 contains studies that examine how anchored relationships unfold in public and quasi-public places. In chapter 5, Tyler Harrison and Susan Morgan investigate the anchored personal relationships that develop as teenagers "hang out" in fast-food restaurants, parks, and bus stops and on the streets. Rather than solely promoting juvenile delinquency, "hanging out" is a rich and complex set of behaviors that provides opportunities for the construction and maintenance of personal relationships, the development of gender identities, and resistance to adult control. Public hangouts are thus precarious contexts that youths must constantly work to create and protect. Alison Munch in chapter 6 then investigates the relational bases of a "floating" community that emerges among fans in an adult softball league. Although spectators rarely interact away from the games, they develop familylike relations with each other, looking after each other's children, sharing each other's misfortunes and triumphs, and ultimately developing a sense of collective identity with one another in the bleachers during games. The linkage between personal relationships and the "identity of place" becomes a central theme in chapter 7 with Lori Reid, Carolyn Karlin, and Michael Bonham-Crecilius's study of gay, lesbian, and straight bars. They focus on the social interaction processes that constitute gender and sexual identities via "territories of the self" as they are created, sustained, and violated in these places. Amy Ebesu Hubbard and Cindy White go one step further in chapter 8 to investigate how adults and children in postdivorce support groups come to grips with their intense anger and sadness in reaction to divorce. Nonintimate relationships in part constitute the quasi-public character of the groups and enable participants to express the intimate emotions linked to their former spouses.

Part 3 focuses on managing threats to the interaction order of personal relationships as they unfold in public and quasi-public places. In chapter 9, Christine Horne, Mary Kris Mcilwaine, and Kristie Taylor write about their observations of parents and children publicly managing fractures in their relational interaction orders. They situate their findings in an ecology of public places that vary by their permissiveness and strongly influence the interaction patterns that both spark and quell trouble among children and their parents. Jason Clark-Miller and Jennifer Murdock in chapter 10 focus on the remedial strategies that members of a right-wing political discussion group use to suppress personal and group conflicts in quasi-public meetings as they engage in political discourse. Members of the group join because their politically extreme views tend to isolate them from mainstream discourse and many other relationships. At the same time, these views create ideological strife within the group that constantly threatens members' personal relationships and attachments to it, thus prompting a range of conciliatory measures. In the final chapter, we reconstruct the larger picture painted by the contributors by discussing how personal relationships in public matter for everyday life and how various aspects of public places influence the likelihood, meanings, and dynamics of public sociality.

PART ONE

Social Encounters and Fleeting Relationships

TWO

Face Time

Public Sociality, Social Encounters, and Gender at a University Recreation Center

LESA A. STERN, MARK CALLISTER,
AND LYNN JONES

THE AIR IS THICK WITH the smell of sweaty bodies and the sound of loud rock music on a Thursday night in the workout room at Sunshine University's (SU's) student recreation center.[1] As on most weeknights, the workout room is filled to its 250-student capacity, with a long line waiting to get in. The entire room is in motion as young men and women move among the Nautilus weight machines on their "circuits"—routines that structure the use of the machines in particular orders. Not one of the two dozen exercise bicycles that line one of the room's long walls sits idle. Several large, square padded mats cover a relatively quiet part of the room surrounded by floor-length mirrors and an exercise bar at waist level. A dozen or more men and women sit stretching on the mats. Near a Nautilus machine stand two young men in T-shirts and loose-fitting shorts chiding one another about whether either of them will get the nerve to strike up a conversation with a woman in a two-piece orange spandex leotard who is stretching on the mats. After a few minutes, one of the men walks by her slowly. She looks up to watch him walk by, but they do not make contact. He then retreats to where the other man is standing. At another machine, a man and a woman who entered the room separately converse briefly amidst smiles and laughter and then agree to work out together on three consecutive machines before parting company. Throughout the room, loud grunts can be heard from the free-weight area as heavily muscled men bench press barbells loaded with metal disks. One of the weight lifters springs up from a successful lift to howl triumphantly and flex his muscles through a tight, partially ripped T-shirt. He then slowly strolls to the drinking fountain near the exercise mats while multiple pairs of eyes follow him. As he walks by a woman using a Nautilus machine, he lingers, smiles, and talks with her for a few minutes.

Scenes like these are increasingly common on American college campuses as multiuse recreation centers have become one of the prime public places where both acquainted and unacquainted undergraduate students socialize.[2] Here students engage in various forms of public sociality and, in so doing, manage complex and sometimes competing sets of interactional goals. For many students, these public interactions can be fun as they meet new people. Others, especially women, can find themselves vulnerable to hassling and other threats.[3]

In this chapter we explore aspects of personal relationships among college students that have largely been neglected by previous research. We pursue this issue in the context of SU's recreation center, principally its workout room. All members of the university community (numbering just over fifty thousand) have access (with a nominal fee) to the rec center, and nearly 70 percent of the twenty-nine thousand undergraduates use it on a regular or sporadic basis. Of those students who use the rec center, nearly two-thirds use the workout room, which is officially designed for workout activities of various sorts but is also known among students as a place to kindle personal relationships.[4] We pay particular attention to the dynamics of what students call "face time": strategies intended to maximize the likelihood of attracting interpersonal interest from previously unknown peers in quasi-public places. Such strategies are often cloaked in workout routines and the norms of public sociality. In most instances, face time results in brief social encounters or "fleeting relationships" (such as those illustrated above) that may last only a few minutes or a single visit to the rec center. But sometimes face-time strategies become annoying, threatening, or, as one student put it, "creepy." Virtually all troublesome instances involve face-time strategies used by men to target women.

In the following section, we conceptually situate our chapter with a brief discussion of public places and collegiate sociality as they relate to gender in the setting where we conducted our study. Next we present how men strategically use the norms of public nonintimate sociality to accomplish face time and how women ward off unwanted face-time tactics by men. Finally, we use our work to address broader theoretical issues relevant to social context and personal relationships, informal social control in public and quasi-public places, gender and public sociality, and, most speculatively, the future of collegiate sociality.

PUBLIC PLACES, COLLEGIATE SOCIALITY, AND GENDER

Public places—such as parks, sidewalks, plazas—are settings where there is broad social access and visibility. "Quasi-public" places exhibit more intentionally focused purposes—such as commercial, social, or physical activities—and somewhat less accessibility or visibility. Social interaction among strangers in North American public places typically displays an orderliness that suggests a set of loosely shared "principles." Such principles are organized around maintaining tacit social distance, physical motility, and a degree of social toleration of those with whom people have minimal social connections. Although the enactment of these principles varies enormously by locale and the social characteristics of those involved, they display a remarkable consistency across public places with broad social access and visibility.[5]

Quasi-public places introduce additional social expectations that can accentuate, compromise, or even violate the principles of stranger-stranger interaction. For example, visitors to bars and other nightclub settings often come to such settings with a variety of purposes that include escaping boredom, watching sports, and trying to create a personal relationship with another person of the same or opposite sex.[6] Some patrons, therefore, may want to be left alone and staunchly uphold nonintimate public sociality norms. Others may eschew those norms as they attempt to make new friends or "couple" with others. Health clubs and recreation centers illustrate other settings to which people come for a variety of purposes: some may come to work out, others to spectate, and still others regard these places as "interpersonal marketplaces" in the same way they would various kinds of bars.[7]

Interpersonal marketplaces pervade American college campuses, which are regarded as preeminent contexts to experiment with and establish personal relationships of all kinds.[8] As we noted earlier in this chapter, recreation centers are central to social life on many American college campuses because they bring large groups of students together in relatively safe, relaxed, and fun contexts. As in other public places, pure sociality—if only for a few minutes—can be a source of interpersonal pleasure.[9] Moreover, the public character of university recreation centers enables students to save "face" by camouflaging their relationally oriented actions amidst exercise and sporting activities.[10] However, such interaction can create social tensions and anxieties for those involved, particularly if the normative boundaries of appropriate public social interaction are crossed.

These tensions and transgressions are especially acute for women in cross-gender interactions. According to Carol Brooks Gardner, women are "situationally disadvantaged" in public because of the long American tradition of private *and* public discrimination toward them. Despite gains in a number of social domains during the past three decades, women still operate with "provisional acceptance" in public that assumes they have only "limited competence."[11] Unlike men, women in American public urban settings are often subject to various normative violations of public sociality. Some of these violations take the form of outward public harassment or physical harm, while other transgressions are more subtle, such as "interactional vandalism" that involves innocent-sounding communication embedded in violations of conversational norms.[12] The prevalence of such problems prompts many women to become accomplished in parrying the advances of men in a variety of ways. Drawing from Erving Goffman's work, David Snow and colleagues conceptualize these "interpersonal survival strategies" as a "cooling-out" process in which women attempt to deflect or extricate themselves from a troublesome public situation while reducing the humiliation or anger felt by the offending male party. Cooling-out strategies range from polite verbal refusals to engage in interaction, to nonverbal "repositionings" vis-à-vis an offender, to exit from the setting.[13] On American college campuses, these cross-pressures are further complicated by a heightened awareness (via campaigns and visible legal cases) about the possibilities for physical assault against women by men either outside or within existing relationships.[14]

This discussion points toward three interrelated questions that crystallized during our fieldwork and data analysis: How do students attempt to meet one another in quasi-public places? What normative violations occur during these dynamics? How are such normative violations, especially by men against women, handled by women?

THE REC CENTER

To pursue the questions posed above, we conducted fieldwork at SU's rec center for a total of thirteen months during 1996–98.[15] The rec center lies just beyond the south boundary of SU's campus and is adjacent to a secondary commuting artery. Built in 1992, the rec center complex consists of two acres carved out of a larger mixed urban area of small retail shops and private residences. As one approaches the rec center from the north, one can glimpse its three-story glass-walled facade and indoor open-air entrance. To the left of the facade is the main workout room with its large picture windows that enable pedestrians on the street to watch people riding exercise bicycles or lifting weights. The rec center's lobby has a large information kiosk at its center with another wall of glass directly behind it that enables entrants to see into the workout room. To the right of this window are glass-walled racquetball courts and a large lounge that leads to the outdoor pool area. Behind the information kiosk is the main corridor that runs the length of the building. Lining the sides of the corridor are the pro shop, locker rooms, basketball and volleyball courts, aerobics rooms, and main entrance to the heart of the rec center, the main workout room.

FACE TIME AND PUBLIC SOCIALITY

Almost without exception, all of the students we interacted with during our field research displayed a marked sensitivity to how public sociality could be used as a mechanism to accomplish face time. As one female student eloquently put it, face time is "exposure. Making yourself visible. Trying to increase your chances of seeing someone you're interested in, . . . being seen by others that you might be interested in but doing it in a way that blends in with the scene." To students, face time literally means having one's "face" recognized by another person or being able to see the face (or body) of a person whom one might be interested in meeting. "Blending in with the scene" is key in this process because it means cloaking one's face time in the principles of public sociality so that one treads a fine line between avoiding embarrassment and facilitating the possibility of transforming social interaction from a momentary encounter to the beginnings of a personal relationship. This interactional knowledge is apparent with regard to what we call "positioning," "strutting," and "timing" in the workout room. Each of these tactics enables one to accomplish face time without doing so too obviously. Below, we illustrate these tactics and discuss modal responses to them.

Positioning

One sense of *positioning* refers to the physical placement of one's body in the workout room so that it facilitates being observed or observing others. Our description at the outset of this chapter of the nervous Nautilus user who walked near a woman in an orange leotard on an exercise mat illustrates positioning. Indeed, one of the most effective areas in this regard is the stretching mat area, where people can linger before, during, or after a workout. While stretching or resting, exercisers can be ostensibly passive members of the social audience in the room. For example, an interview with a twenty-year-old undergraduate male revealed that he typically arrives thirty minutes early to the rec center before a regular "pickup" basketball game so that he can stretch and take a "tour" of the room. He notes: "I usually hang out on the stretching pads and then take a few laps around the [workout room] to check out what women are there. If I spot something good [a desirable woman] on the mats, I'll sit down near to let her see me and to see her too." He further explained that one can do this "without notice" since it's "expected" that people will "stare into space" on the stretching mats and that people typically walk around the room doing their circuits.

Other forms of positioning combine both placement of one's body and verbal interaction using various "opening lines." Both men and women mentioned that they might pick a weight machine near someone who was "attractive" in order to increase the likelihood that they could engage in conversation. The proximity of working out on adjacent weight machines can also facilitate a limited request for help, again within the boundaries of public sociality, as in this encounter between a woman and a man:

MAN: Let me help you with that [weight] plate.
WOMAN: Thanks.
MAN: Pretty crowded here now. It's better in the morning. You ever come in then?
WOMAN: I come in at a lot of different times depending upon classes.

The man later admitted he was involved in face time and had purposely moved to a machine near the woman and was encouraged when the woman accepted his offer of help. Despite this encouraging opening interaction, the woman focused her attention on using the weight machine after her last statement rather than continuing interaction. The man took the hint and turned his attention to an adjacent machine, which he set up for his exercising. The two did not speak again during their workout period, and we did not observe them interacting during later field visits. In a brief conversational interview, the man revealed that he prefers working out with free weights but that he uses weight machines if he sees a "good-looking woman" working out on a machine nearby. He also revealed that he enjoyed the momentary encounter with the woman but that "it was no big deal" that nothing more developed from it.

The illustration underscores the pleasure that momentary encounters can hold for those in the workout room and also the gender patterning of positioning. Specifically, women are more likely to engage in limited requests for help (again within the normative boundaries of public sociality) and men are more likely to offer limited help. For men, common opening lines include "Let me show you how this machine works," "If you do the sets this way, then you can work out [a particular muscle group]," and "What muscles are you trying to work on?" All of these lines focus on a task and either can be used as a springboard for further social interaction or can enable the male to blend back into the public scene without incident. Women's requests for assistance operate in the same way. One woman whom we frequently observed positioning and whom we interviewed about her tactics observed that if she were interested in a particular man, she would "go near the place he's working out. Like if he's on a [weight] machine, you could just use the one next to him . . . then you could, like, ask for help, or ask him if he's almost done, or something. If he doesn't want to talk or isn't interested, you haven't risked anything by asking a question."

Such encounters also embody the prospect of "cooling out" unwanted social interaction generated via positioning, thus enabling the parties to avoid public embarrassment. The woman's behavior exhibits a type of "studied seriousness" that involves "attention and energy [devoted to] an immediate, pressing task" rather than social interaction with another person.[16] Studied seriousness is typically coupled with nonverbal signals of lack of interest, such as avoiding the direct gaze of another and looking in any direction except toward the man attempting to initiate contact. Verbal signals of a lack of interest include quick allusions to one's "boyfriend" or a statement such as "Well, I gotta get back to my workout," followed by studied seriousness directed at one's machine. Very rarely did we notice men parrying unwanted face time via "cooling-out" strategies. Most often, men simply ignored the interaction directed their way by engaging in studied seriousness or occasionally repositioning themselves in the weight room.

Strutting

Whereas positioning targets another individual, "strutting" involves drawing a broader audience's attention to oneself through behavior or clothing in the hopes that such attention will lead to relational interaction with someone desired. The howling, flexing, strolling weightlifter we described at the beginning of this chapter nicely illustrates strutting. Of course, such behaviors can mean many things and may emulate behaviors found in famous public weight-lifting gyms such as Venice Beach, California, or even in televised body building contests. In the weight room at the rec center, however, these behaviors are tied not only to narcissistic displays of the body but also to face time. Listen to this account from a man who regularly uses the weight room: "Oh sure, guys try to draw attention to themselves with loud grunts, dropping a weight loudly, walking around flexing. Lots of people do it so it's no big deal. It can actually be kinda of fun—like a show." One of the intents of these behaviors, so this student argued, is to draw attention to oneself in the "hope" that a girl might "talk with you."[17] These "antics," as another women called them, "blend" into the weight room because exercisers are used to a variety of noises that people make while exercising: "People shout and grunt all the time, have their little rituals they go through, but people just tolerate it for the most part. It's funny sometimes even though it can be annoying. I mean, it is a public place." Thus strutters, like those engaged in positioning, benefit from assumptions associated with public sociality (in this instance civility toward diversity) that encourage toleration of their behavior.

Although we observed few female weight lifters strutting, we did observe several women strutting in the main areas of the workout room. An aggregate of women generally known as "hard bodies" contained a subset who strutted daily in tight-fitting bodysuits with thongs (G-strings) and "evening makeup" (that one would wear on a date) while working out. This woman's comments illustrate how aspects of attire are used to strut: "I want to look hot when I work out. I don't like to be watched in excess by any one individual, but I do like to be watched in moderation, particularly if there are cute guys around. I've never really met someone and dated them at the rec center, but I like to talk to the guys there. It's fun just to hang for a few minutes and move on."

In contrast to face-time positioning, which resulted in some social encounters, male strutting rarely, if ever, resulted in social encounters or the beginnings of personal relationships. Nonetheless, men did subtly try to create "openings" for social interaction through winks, nods, or gestures toward those they believed were watching them. Much of the time, women reacted to male strutters with concealed looks of annoyance or even mirth, but they rarely expressed these feelings such that a male strutter would see them. They then would engage in studied seriousness as they focused their attention back on their own exercising. Women strutters, by contrast, experienced more social encounters than male strutters. Women strutters initiated their encounters with the same wink or nod, or even a limited request for help. Men, on the other hand, most often reacted to female strutters by trying to position themselves to get a better look but often seemed too intimidated to initiate social interaction themselves. Listen to this quick conversation between two exercisers who spotted a hard-body female strutter they had seen before, but with whom they never interacted:

SHORT GUY: Was that her?

TALL GUY: Man, my heart is breaking. She's struttin' hot.

SHORT GUY: You better talk to her, man.

TALL GUY: Yeah, I know. I'll never get the nerve.

Timing

A final aspect of face time involves time itself, specifically the timing of visits to the rec center in order to achieve positioning or strutting with minimal risk and maximal effect. Visits to the rec center are constrained in part by the scheduling of classes and other university-related activities. Most classes are scheduled from eight in the morning to early to midafternoon, which, not coincidentally, is when fewer students are using the rec center and almost no one is in the workout room. When one *can* visit the rec center, however, is not the sole consideration for those engaged in face time. Many other weight rooms on campus are not filled to capacity during the late afternoons or evenings when the workout room is often overflowing. Indeed, students wishing to engage in face time visit the workout room *because* it is crowded during peak hours.

As is the case on a crowded city street or in a subway car during rush hour, the principles of nonintimate public sociality are both observed and relaxed during peak hours at the workout room. Individuals still practice cooperative motility to enable movement and civil inattention to achieve what Lofland calls "co-presence without co-mingling."[18] Yet the co-presence is intense. Bodies press up against one another as exercisers stand in short lines waiting for weight-lifting machines, stair-steppers, and exercise bicycles. During peak hours, students can engage in positioning more subtly with nary a "discovery" that they might be attempting to push beyond the confines of public sociality (unless they find a target who is mutually interested in doing so). Strutting is also enabled by crowding because of the bigger audiences available to strutters in the free-weight area and to hard bodies in the main part of the room.

The foregoing observations paint a picture of multiple interaction orders coexisting with relatively little social tension or friction. To be sure, those engaged in face time can experience personal anxiety, as underscored by the man who was afraid to interact with a female strutter. Other men and women displayed and expressed pleasure with momentary encounters and fleeting relationships. Moreover, women or men who face unwanted interaction initiated through positioning or strutting (in the case of women) can subtly distance themselves from their pursuer by simply not providing an opening for more interaction. By "piggybacking" their interactional purposes on the principles of public sociality, those engaged in face time minimize their potential embarrassment and are able to embed their behaviors in the public background of the workout room. However, there is a seamier side to face time that involves normative transgressions and their responses. As mentioned previously, all of these dynamics involve male face-time strategies aimed at women. It is to these dynamics that we now turn.

FACE-TIME TRANSGRESSIONS AND RESPONSES

At the core of the normative achievement of face time is one overarching principle: camouflage one's tactics within the normative boundaries of public sociality and the various activities associated with working out. At the same time, one must at some point partially come out from behind the occlusion offered by public sociality and/or workout activities to provide an opportunity for one's target to gain an inkling of one's motivations. This occurs in two ways, either during a moment of "disclosure" when an individual initiating face time enables the "object" of his or her tactics to become an interacting "subject" or via strutting when individuals create opportunities that suggest they are "open" to interaction with members of their targeted audience. Face-time transgressions occur when individuals initiating face time do not provide opportunities for targets to become interacting subjects, including the opportunity to be cooled out. Such offending parties remain in a purely voyeuristic role, even after they have been "spotted" by a target.

Throughout our research we did not uncover instances or stories of women engaged in normatively deviant face time. Many of the women we interviewed, however, were aware of the possibility of transgressions by both women and men. For example, one physically attractive, regular female exerciser commented that she is "always conscious about looking good. . . . I like to look presentable, but will not wear anything that will overly flatter my figure. I don't want to attract attention or have some guy

I don't know try to get to know me. Guys can be doing all kinds of weird stuff in there [the workout room] to get a look at women."

This same woman noted that some of the hard bodies "almost go overboard" with trying to attract attention but always seem to get right up to the point of crossing normative boundaries without doing so. Other women regarded the workout room as "scary"; as one woman put it, "It almost seems sometimes like you could get accosted by the guys in there because they're staring at you so hard." Men were also aware of deviant face time, particularly of men who spent too much time in front of the viewing windows or those who only "watched chicks" but did not work out. Even so, few men could tell more than a vague story about a face-time incident. By contrast, women had a developed an extensive vocabulary for talking about face-time offenders.

Transgressions: Stalkers, Roamers, and Lurkers

The term *stalking* evokes the threat that some celebrities experience from incidents in which fans intensely shadow them in public and private places; some of these have resulted in tragedy, such as the killings of the musician John Lennon and the actress Rebecca Shaeffer during the 1980s. In the workout room, stalkers move from place to place to shadow a face-time target during single or multiple visits to the workout room. Stalkers usually hang around a machine but do not use it as they pursue their targets. One woman provided a synopsis of her experiences with a stalker: "One guy used to always be here when I was, and he would kind of follow me. It was so obvious because he never used a machine or anything. He was just hanging out. He never said a thing. It was like he figured out my schedule and would be here the same times. Like he hoped I would miraculously start talking with him or something."

Roaming is similar to stalking in that the miscreant does not engage in the pretense of exercising as he moves around the workout room. Unlike stalkers, roamers do not target individuals. Instead, they wander around the weight room unabashedly staring at women or engaging in unsubtle forms of positioning. One roamer, for example, spent up to three hours in the workout room during a single visit sitting on the seats or benches of various weight machines intensely gazing at various women on nearby machines as they worked out. He periodically took a slow, measured stroll around the room, pausing to sit on a bench or lean up against the wall for a few minutes next to a woman or a group of women, but would never lift a weight or make contact with any of those whom he watched.

Lurkers differ from stalkers and roamers in that they find a vantage point outside the workout room, typically near a viewing window, to watch the activities in the room. The fact that such windows exist can initially camouflage their actions because many men (and a few women) stop by the viewing windows and watch exercisers. Lurkers also differ from the typical voyeur because of the time they spend watching and because they sometimes station themselves outside the exit of the workout room to get a closer look at those they are watching. At the rec center on any given day one could spot at least one lurker who moved from a viewing window to the main corridor as he watched women work out and then exit the workout room. At no time did we observe a lurker, stalker, or roamer pursue women outside the rec center. Women sometimes suggested implicitly or explicitly in interviews that they feared such spillover could occur, but they did not report specific incidents of this sort.

Responses: Studied Seriousness, Avoidance, Exit, Confrontation

Whether roaming, stalking, or lurking, face-time "deviants" rarely strike up a conversation with their targets. This may make the experience, from a female target's point of view, particularly unsettling because it is sometimes difficult to pinpoint what is exactly troublesome about a nearby man's behavior. Indeed, it can take quite a while in the workout room before a target realizes that she is being stalked or that she is in the roamer's path. Targets of lurkers may never know that they are being observed. In general, women respond to transgressions nonverbally, thus matching the nonverbal actions of the men they are attempting to parry.[19] Many of these initial responses mirror the strategies used to manage normative face time and are embedded in nonintimate public sociality. At the same time, they are enacted with more apparent emotion, including grimaces, raising of the eyebrows, or a stiffened posture, thus indicating some heightened anxiety.

The first line of response for women who experience stalking is studied seriousness, which we observed to be much less effective at deflecting face-time transgressions than when it is directed at unwanted normative face-time strategies. The strategy's lack of effectiveness may stem from the persistence of most stalkers and their misguided sense of how the norms of public sociality cloak their behavior as they pursue their targets. One women illustrated this problem by commenting, "Even though you ignore 'em [stalkers] and get into the workout, they can still be there. It's like they don't get the hint or they don't realize that their cover is blown."

Because studied seriousness is relatively ineffective, many women engage in a second-line set of tactics that involves avoidance. Here again, avoidance responses to normative face-time positioning—such as averting one's eyes to signal a lack of interest—do not function as well to handle stalking or roaming because there is little, if any, face-to-face interaction between those involved. As a result, women engage in avoidance by repositioning themselves in the workout room or, on occasion, by exiting. Examples of repositioning include moving to a different area in the workout room or, during peak hours, placing more of the crowd between oneself and a stalker. One such example occurred when a woman we observed being stalked for the better part of an hour abruptly finished using one machine and walked to the other side of the room to finish exercising. It took her a while to navigate through the crowd to get to her new area, and her stalker had an even more difficult time working through the crowd. Eventually he gave up the pursuit and left the room. Avoidance, however, is not without emotional or task-related costs because it can introduce a measure of anxiety into one's exercising and/or disrupt an exercising routine one has established. One woman, for example, noted that "she hates stalkers . . . they make working out a real drag because you have to change what you're doing to deal with them." Repositioning can also occur in response to roaming, only here the tactic requires that one place oneself out of the roamer's path as he makes his rounds. This response can be especially disruptive to a targeted woman because roamers often don't have a systematic route, which means removing oneself from a roamer's path may function effectively for only a few minutes at a time. Repositioning in response to lurking can involve trying to move to an area that is occluded from a viewing window, which again can entail some costs for the female exerciser and can be less than optimal in terms of avoiding an offending male.

Exit from the workout room occurs when women experience stalking, roaming, or lurking for extended periods of time or, as one woman put it, they experience a "repeat offender"—someone who engages in face-time transgressions with them over multiple visits to the rec center. As one women put it, "If I spot a guy lurking over a few workouts . . . staring at me through a window and then waiting to watch me in the lobby or something, I'm outta here." Another aspect of avoidance involves the use of timing, discussed in an earlier section, as a preventive strategy for either normative or deviant face time. Regular users who want to avoid face time as practitioners or respondents time their visits so that the workout room is the least crowded, or "dead." Under these conditions, one is less likely to find anyone using the workout room for face time of any kind. One woman commented: "It's really peaceful during off-peak. No hassles, no social scene, just people trying to get a good workout."

Verbal confrontations are the least likely responses to face-time transgressions because, as one regular exerciser notes, one must "initiate contact with [a] creep." Such interactions require the most dramatic departure from the dynamics of public sociality and can transform an uneventful navigation through a quasi-public place into an altercation. The factors that appear to account for verbal confrontations are (1) consistently close physical proximity between stalkers, roamers, or lurkers and their targets and (2) the length of time it takes for a transgression to unfold. The longer a target knows she is in the sights of a face-time deviant, the more likely a confrontation is between the parties involved. Beyond these general factors, the relatively focused attention that single targets receive from stalkers makes the latter most vulnerable to confrontations. The constant movement by roamers largely insulates them from confrontation unless their routes concentrate on multiple areas in the room. Lurkers proved most immune to confrontation; we never observed a confrontation between a lurker and his target.

When confrontation does occur, it appears as an extension of avoidance strategies and rarely approaches unambiguously the substance of an offending behavior. At no time did we ever witness a woman tell a stalker, roamer, or lurker to stop pursuing or watching her. Instead, lines such as "I'm trying to work out here," would be delivered using a cold or annoyed tone and were intended to signal that an offended party recognized a normative transgression and was annoyed by it. Questions delivered to stalkers in irritated fashion, such as "Are *you* waiting for this machine?" or "You gonna use the machine or just sit there?" serve similar functions. Although these lines are not delivered as politely as the typical cooling-out line aimed at men in public places as reported by Snow and colleagues, women in the workout room do draw upon the dynamics of nonintimate public sociality to reimmerse themselves in the larger social audience of the workout room and treat the interaction as largely uneventful.

DISCUSSION AND IMPLICATIONS

In this chapter, we examined how undergraduates engage in what they call face time—a set of tactics intended to facilitate opportunities for personal relationships in a quasi-public place on a college campus. Our examination of face time in the workout room at Sunshine University's rec center revealed several tactics that students use to accomplish it, including positioning, strutting, and timing. Students embed these actions in the dynamics of public sociality, thus reducing the likelihood of embarrassment either to those initiating face time or to those responding to it. These tactics, far from creating enduring personal relationships, typically result in momentary, pleasurable social encounters that quickly dissipate in public. We also uncovered a number of behaviors that cross the normative boundaries associated with face time. These actions include stalking, roaming, and lurking, which in turn draw various responses to deflect them. Aside from these specific findings, our chapter speaks to general issues regarding the study of social context and personal relationships, informal social control in public and quasi-public places, gender and public sociality, and, most speculatively, the future of collegiate sociality. We briefly discuss each of these issues below.

During the past decade, scholars have increasingly moved beyond a focus on relational dyads to recognize the importance of social context in the development, maintenance, and dissolution of personal relationships.[20] Steve Duck, for example, has argued that social context—which he defines as broad social, economic, and cultural structures combined with the "structuring effects of daily life"—profoundly affects the "realities of relational life" for individuals in contemporary society.[21] But a key aspect missing from such discussions, especially with regard to the structuring effects of daily life, is the mutual influences of nonintimate and intimate sociality as these play out in public and quasi-public places. What is clear from our limited research is that people do use aspects of nonintimate sociality in public in an attempt to initiate relationships. To be sure, much of the social interaction we observed does not ultimately constitute the kinds of personal relationships that have been the bread and butter of most relationship research. We did not observe, for example, enduring friendships or romantic liaisons emerging from face-time interactions. However, it is unclear whether the limited relational trajectories of the face time we observed are a function of the particular setting of our research or emblematic of a more general pattern. Research on heterosexual singles bars, for example, suggests that our findings are somewhat typical of such settings.[22] Enduring relationships are more likely to emerge from close-knit social networks organized around workplaces or communities than from "trolling" in bars. More generally, our research suggests the need to further investigate how interaction orders grounded in norms and dynamics of nonintimate and intimate sociality in public mutually affect one another and in turn affect the development of personal relationships of all kinds.

Related to the issue of context is the idea of treating "colleges," where much of the research on personal relationships occurs, as variegated places themselves. As Morrill and Snow argue in the opening chapter of this volume, a great deal of research on personal relationships "strips" them of the social places in which they occur. Morrill and Snow and other scholars criticize researchers for relying too much on laboratory and survey investigations of "college sophomores," who are taken out of the context of their ongoing circumstances. Our take on this problem is not to desert college campuses completely but to use them to study personal relationships among older adolescents and younger adults in a variety of public places. This strategy would not only help introduce context into personal relationship research but also give us more insight into colleges as important sites for the development of interpersonal skills and social relationships of all kinds.

Yet another implication of our research concerns informal social control in public places. Our findings are consistent with other studies of urban public places that find people largely left to their own means of informal social control when faced with troublesome incidents. Yet effectively deploying informal social control in a public context requires that people know more than the "etiquette" of face-to-face interaction, or, in our case, more than the rules of face time and nonintimate public sociality. Regular visitors to public places must become what urban ethnographer Elijah Anderson calls "streetwise." Being streetwise means knowing how to distinguish threatening from harmless situations, assess the probable intents of individual actors, and engage in social control in situationally appropriate ways. Such skills give people confidence and enable them to "feel a measure of control" as they negotiate public places.[23] For students at SU, then, enacting and responding to attempts at face time at the rec center occurs under safer conditions than in many urban public places. However, such interaction may have less to do with developing personal relationships than with developing and honing a quasi-street wisdom regarding the ways of cross-gender interaction in public places. Through the enactment, experience, and observation of face time, among other types of social interactions, students learn how to "read" actors, actions, and situations. But such wisdom is unevenly distributed among workout room regulars. Although all students in the rec center have some knowledge about face time and how it is accomplished, they exhibit different levels of social competence in enacting and responding to it. Future research needs to investigate how different experiences, the characteristics of quasi-public and public places (both on and off university campuses), and interactional dynamics constrain or facilitate the development of interactional skill in public places. For example, what impact did conducting our research in a largely homogeneous environment with regard to race have on the distribution of street wisdom among regular users of the workout room? What impact did being in a quasi-public as opposed to a more public context, such as the typical big-city sidewalk, have on the development and use of street wisdom among regulars?[24]

With regard to gender and public sociality, our research complements previous research on women's vulnerabilities in public places. Although we found that both men and women enjoy public sociality, women and men's experiences in public can be quite different because men have traditionally been more likely to initiate social encounters with women in public contexts. Thus this tendency increases the potential vulnerability of women in public. Regarding this vulnerability, our research suggests that men and women use the principles of public sociality in different ways. In the workout room, men typically embed "proactive" interactional tactics associated with face-time in public sociality, whereas women draw on public sociality as a "reactive" resource to deflect undesired face-time strategies aimed at them by men. One could argue that this implication crystallizes the gender patterning of social interaction in public places in that men are typically initiators of unwanted interaction and women typically find themselves on the defensive, protecting themselves. From another perspective, one could argue that the dynamics of public sociality provide women with a tacit source of power to parry untoward interaction from men. Like a judo move that draws the energy of the attacker against him or herself, streetwise women use public sociality to ward off men, at the same time protecting their sense of self. Women thus demonstrate resilience and resourcefulness as they tactically use the norms of public sociality to help reverse the social disadvantages they face in public.

Finally, we turn to the most speculative implication of our research. We began this chapter with the idea that American universities and colleges have long been thought of as hotbeds of personal relationships—or at least hoped-for personal relationships. If technological trends in higher education continue, the current decade will witness an unprecedented growth of "virtual universities" that have their primary presence online rather than on physical campuses.[25] While online campuses will not wholly replace physical campuses, we can expect virtual universities to alter the dynamics and expectations of collegiate sociality. To the degree that this occurs, we may also witness large groups of college students who no longer have the experience of honing their skills in public sociality at places like the workout room. Instead, they will develop new forms of public sociality and new forms of face time in online public contexts at virtual universities. This may represent one element of a new wave, not only of collegiate sociality, but also of public sociality more generally.

METHODOLOGICAL PROCEDURES AND REFLECTIONS

We collected data in three four-month "waves" during each of the study's three years. Our techniques included participant observation alone and in pairs; semistructured interviews with a convenience sample of university students ($n = 14$), employees ($n = 4$), and faculty ($n = 3$); and informal conversational interviews during the course of observations with dozens of patrons in the workout room and other locales at the rec center. Our data collection strategies thus enabled us to systematically vary the time of the school year during which we were in the field (spending an equal amount of time during fall and spring semesters), use earlier data collection efforts to guide our later forays, and observe longitudinal changes (if any) during the entire three-year study period.

Our observations focused on verbal and nonverbal interaction between "solo" men and women who did not appear to be "with" each other. We thus looked for evidence from a lack of "tie signs," such as handholding, arm locking, and proximity of body torsos, that two actors were unconnected.[26] Relational evidence from tie signs can be difficult to read. But our observational sense that two actors were not previously connected proved wrong only in a small set of instances, which we discovered during follow-up interviews or via eavesdropping.

Our ages (late twenties), mixed gender (two women and one man), and physical characteristics (in reasonable physical shape through previous years of working out) enabled us to blend in with rec center users. Our varied characteristics also enabled us to position ourselves close to both men and women. Because many people work out in circuits, we could all easily position ourselves to unobtrusively observe and eavesdrop as we worked out in our own circuits. Because it is not uncommon for exercisers to leave and enter the workout room numerous times during a single visit (e.g., to get water, use the restroom, or simply take a rest) and for rec center visitors to use the lounge areas for studying, it was easy to periodically exit the workout room in order to write field jottings and then return to the workout room for more observations.

Conversational interviews typically occurred after observations of various forms of social interaction between single exercisers. In these cases, we approached one or both of the parties to ask friendly questions such as "What happened there?" or "What was going on there?" These kinds of questions are typical in the banter of the room and were never met with objections by informants. We followed up such questions with additional inquiries regarding the typicality of the behavior in question and some background information on the informant. We balanced conversational interviews equally between men and women. Most of the informants we conversationally interviewed fell between the ages of nineteen and twenty-eight and were Anglo or European American in outward appearance, thus exhibiting more ethnic homogeneity than the ethnic composition of SU as a whole.[27] Conversational interviews with the students ranged from ten minutes to more than a half-hour. We discontinued our observations and interviews once we stopped discerning novel information from informants, which suggested that we had become "saturated" in the field.[28] Our semistructured interviews focused on the experiences of actors with social interaction among other single exercisers, including the types of interactions and their outcomes. Conversational interviews were recorded informally in field notes, while semistructured interviews were tape recorded and transcribed. We should note that we were unable to interview persons who engaged in normatively questionable actions because in each instance they scurried out of the workout room before we could make contact.

We first "open"-coded our field notes and interviews for broad categories of social interaction among singles, including types and extent of exercising done, workout attire, physical positioning of actors relative to each other, and verbal and nonverbal sequences of behavior between actors.[29] We used interviews and overheard conversations to understand what particular lines of action meant to the actors involved and as something of a "validity check" on our interpretations. As we developed particular themes, we focused our coding on what students described as "face time," the normative transgressions that some of these tactics involved, and the ways these transgressions were managed by those who experienced them.[30]

Our collective experiences also illustrate that multiple perspectives and types of field relations across different team members can help dislodge pre-existing beliefs held by any one member and control for researcher-based bias. Among the three authors, Lesa brought the longest history of rec center usage to the team during all hours of its operation. Mark regularly used the workout room during off-peak hours, and Lynn rarely used the workout room at all, instead using other facilities within the rec center. How and when we used the workout room prior to our research resulted in different preconceived notions regarding "what was going on" there. Lesa had the most developed sense of the workout room as a "social scene" based on her informal observations prior to the research and countless stories from undergraduates. Mark and Lynn were less aware of the workout room's place in collegiate sociality. For Mark, the workout room was typically quiet, with a few people using the machines and very few, if any, people conversing or interacting in any way. As he admitted later in the research process, he was "naive" to the workout room because of how and when he used it. Lynn, meanwhile, had little prior knowledge at all of the workout room. On the basis of her use of other facilities on campus and at the rec center, she explicitly questioned the assumption that an extensive social scene flourished in the workout room.

Our preconceived senses of sociality in the workout room translated into different fieldwork roles during data collection. Mark approached the field as a naive visitor attempting to "get a handle" on aspects of sociality in the workout room and as a "buddy researcher" also trying to get a workout.[31] In his cover stories to informants, he frequently mentioned how little he knew about the workout room "scene" and how much he needed to be "educated" about it. Informants proved quite willing to educate him the ways of face time. His observations and interviews during the first wave of data collection directly led to the first discussions with informants about face time as it was used in their lexicon. It also led to our concentration on face time as an aspect of personal relationships and public sociality during the second and third waves of fieldwork. Lynn approached the field as a "controlled skeptic" who communicated in respectful ways to informants that she doubted that either normative or transgressive face time pervasively occurred in the workout room. Her skepticism both motivated her to dig deeper into aspects of face time and motivated informants to tell her what they knew about it.

As the research progressed, a new potential bias emerged. Rather than being naive or skeptical about face time, we began to see every social interaction among exercisers as related to it. At this point we turned our fieldwork roles inward to examine how our own interpretations had evolved. Lesa's considerable experiences, Lynn's skepticism, and Mark's desire to be educated now became yardsticks with which to measure the consistency and validity of our own beliefs. Interviews by both Mark and Lynn facilitated this aspect of the research, as we mentioned earlier in the chapter, and enabled us to check with informants about the accuracy of our interpretations. As we came to understand our own fieldwork roles, we also better understood our coding choices, thus increasing our confidence in our findings and eventually the arguments we advanced in this chapter.

THREE

Momentary Pleasures

Social Encounters and Fleeting Relationships at a Singles Dance

IRENEE BEATTIE, KAREN CHRISTOPHER,
DINA OKAMOTO, AND SANDRA WAY

OPEN A DAILY NEWSPAPER IN any city in the United States or scan the television channels on any cable television network and one can find advertisements directed at "single" people. Some of these ads market services of an explicitly sexual nature, such as "1–900 chat lines" or "escort" services. Many services promise singles the chance to form "meaningful," long-term romantic relationships. Such services are part of a growing singles industry that includes matchmakers, personal ad pages, and other organizations that offer a wide range of activities, including dancing, sporting and artistic excursions, and travel.[1]

In this chapter, we investigate a typical site in this growing industry: a monthly "quasi-public" singles dance. This context differs from most matchmaker services and personal ad pages in that it occurs in highly visible group settings. It also differs from expensive singles clubs because it is relatively inexpensive and is accessible to diverse participants. The singles dance we studied therefore offers the opportunity to study a form of "designed" public sociability, one ostensible purpose of which is the formation of long-term romantic relationships. Although long-term attachments are possible outcomes for people who participate in this event, we find that ties of lesser social intimacy and emotional commitment are more common. Many of the participants initially come to the singles dances with the goal of finding a "mate" but return to the dances to enjoy what one participant called the "momentary pleasures" provided by the fleeting relationships and encounters at the dance itself. In addition to the enjoyment of pleasurable fleeting ties without the obligation of longer commitments, we argue that structural factors inhibit the formation of long-term relationships at the singles dance we studied and offer opportunities, instead, for fleeting relationships and encounters. First, the informal social organization of the dance encourages a sifting process through which participants briefly encounter many individuals during an evening with whom in most cases they have little subsequent interaction. Second, participants must manage various kinds of stigma associated with the singles dance that further constrains forming long-term relational ties.

Our chapter focuses on the social world of singles events, drawing from Erving Goffman's insights into the gaming aspects and potential identity threats in face-to-face interaction. The chapter concludes by linking our findings to the role of "overlapping premises," emotional expression, and social order in public places and the ways designed social contexts influence social interaction and relational formation.

HISTORICAL AND ANALYTIC BACKGROUND

During the past two decades, organizations and services catering to singles have proliferated. By the late 1980s, the International Society of Introduction Services Directory recorded over two thousand "dating services" in the United States.[2] In Chicago, for example, the number of listings for "singles services" in the Yellow Pages (e.g., matchmakers, activity clubs, and video dating services) increased from five to twenty-one during 1978 to 1991. Other large cities exhibited similar increases in listings for singles organizations during the same period. Personal advertising has also become more prevalent, as most major newspapers and magazines now incorporate it as a standard feature of their classified ad sections.[3]

One reason for the rise of the singles industry during the past two decades is the increasing demand for its services. The age at which people marry in the United States has steadily increased since the end of the 1950s.[4] The growing number of women entering the workforce and the sexual revolution that began in the 1960s have created a large singles population as more people spend their youths "finding themselves" rather than "settling down" in marriage.[5] The rate of divorce nearly doubled in the 1970s, further increasing the number of single individuals.[6] Both the 1980s and the 1990s featured a continued growth in the singles population, again due to the delay of marriage until a later age, a large pool of individuals deciding to remain unmarried, and a steady divorce rate in an increasing population. At the same time, many work, religious, and community institutions continue to operate under the assumption that marriage is a normative status for most people and that most singles are actively searching for marriage partners.[7]

Many academic studies of singles and singles organizations share these assumptions. Research on singles includes demographic trends in premarital cohabitation, sex ratios and the "marriage squeeze," and network ties linking potential marital partners.[8] When the focus shifts to singles organizations, researchers often view them as another factor that facilitates finding a marriage partner.[9] Examples of such perspectives include studies on how demographic characteristics and singles' self-presentation affect chances of attracting romantic partners at singles dances, in video ads, or through personal ads.[10]

By focusing on marriage as the primary goal of single people, previous research glosses over the varied experiences of singles at singles events and activities. Such experiences, for example, could include a broader range of meaningful personal relationships than long-term romantic ties. Previous research also glosses over how the social organization of singles events and the goals of singles themselves influence social interaction among participants. Finally, previous research ignores the changing role of women in the American society during the last quarter of the twentieth century, which, in turn, has led to the creation of alternative kinds of public spaces where single women and men can interact with one another.[11] Against this backdrop, we turn to the "Southwest Singles Dance," where we conducted our study.

SOUTHWEST HOTEL SINGLES DANCE

We conducted our study over a seven-month period during 1996–97 at the Southwest Hotel Singles Dance because it is the oldest continually occurring event of its type in the city where the research was conducted and enjoys a consistently large weekly turnout of approximately seventy people.[12] It also occurs in a public place as an explicitly public gathering with high social visibility and access to anyone willing to pay the nominal entrance fee. Southwest Dance occurs every Sunday night in the early evening for approximately four to five hours. Although Southwest Dance is advertised as being for "all ages," most participants range from forty to sixty years old, are Anglo (with a few Latinos and African Americans), and have varied educational levels. The female-male ratio at Southwest Dances is roughly 1.5:1. Men typically dress in jackets and ties, while women wear casual dresses.

The Singles Dance occurs in either a hotel ballroom or the indoor courtyard that dominates one side of the hotel. Chairs line the back and sides of the ballroom or courtyard, and tables are placed in the area next to the dance floor, where participants can sit between and during dances. Each setting—the hotel ballroom and courtyard—creates a different atmosphere for the participants, as the ballroom is a dimly lit 50 × 50 space, and the hotel courtyard is spacious (twice the size of the ballroom), brightly lit, and surrounded by tropical plants. Dawn, the organizer of Southwest Dance, notes that the events are "a comfortable, low-key service for meeting other single adults . . . we act as a stage with props. People come and they are the actors and actresses. What they do after they meet is up to them. . . . It is a good introduction for single adults who want to meet someone for a serious relationship or just want to enjoy the company of others in a public place."

THE SOCIAL WORLD OF THE SINGLES DANCE

Encounters and Fleeting Relationships

When one enters the ballroom at the Southwest Hotel for the Singles Dance, the first thing one notices is a kind of slow vortex of people dancing in pairs around the dance floor. Additionally, some people are standing or sitting on the sidelines (some leaning against a wall or table) looking away from one another, gazing in no particular direction. From time to time, those sitting alone interact, and various group members spin off from what appears to be a group of friends to interact with others in another group or those sitting alone. When people do interact in this manner it is most often in the form of an "encounter"—a brief interaction either on the dance floor or leading up to and immediately after dancing.[13] The following scene is representative of this type of interaction:

A "waltzable" dance tune sets the tone for the dancers on the floor. It is the first dance of the evening, and Ted, John, and Carol sit in some chairs along the back of the ballroom. They do not converse or appear to be sitting "with" each other. There is an empty chair between Ted and John on one side, and there are three empty chairs between John and

Carol on the other side. Ted stands up and heads toward the main exit door of the ballroom. Carol stands up immediately after Ted does and begins walking behind him. From all appearances, they have coincidentally stood up at the same time to exit the dance. As they walk, they gradually veer toward one another until they come together on the dance floor. During their dance, they clasp each other's hands tightly and stand very close to each other, occasionally brushing each other's torsos, but still do not converse. When the dance is over, they signal to each other a polite "thank you" for the dance but do not speak further and return to their respective seats.

As this encounter and others like it unfolded, we wondered how participants who were not sitting with each other in a group signaled to each other, without speaking or seemingly acknowledging the other person, that they wished to dance. We learned that the mechanism of communication is largely nonverbal, through subtle nods of the head or gestures with one's hands.

Another typical encounter from the Southwest Dance contains a greater range of interaction (including talking) and physical contact that leads up to dancing but still illustrates the often abrupt transformation of unfocused to focused interactions that is typical among participants:

Joe, a bald man in his fifties, approaches Kris, a women who looks to be the same age, for a dance. She accepts. As they walk to the dance floor, they hold hands and brush the sides of their bodies together. They hold each other by the waist, clasp their hands, and talk through their dance, occasionally chuckling. After the dance, Joe walks over to the wall by the bartender and Kris returns to her original seat. They do not interact with each other the rest of the evening.

Here again notice the ritual-like precision with which the actions leading up to, during, and after the dance occur. There is a formal "request" to dance; the dance unfolds with appropriate physical contact; and it ends with a proper "thank you" after it is complete. Also notice that Joe asks Kris to dance, rather than vice versa. We did not observe any woman asking men to dance (except during "ladies choice only" dances) and came to know the male prerogative to ask (and the rare female refusal) as a well-established norm of this setting. Other types of encounters also include brief conversations among participants in and around the bar or at tables. In all these situations, the interaction unfolds in relatively stylized ways, and only encounters that revolve around dancing include physical contact between participants.

When individuals engage in more sustained interaction with those they meet at the dance, they rarely develop the long-term romantic relationships mentioned in the ads and fliers for the events. Instead, most participants form what Lyn Lofland refers to as "fleeting relationships"—social ties of short duration and relatively shallow interdependence (compared with close friendships or primary ties).[14] Such relationships typically begin with an encounter on or near the dance floor and progress to a short conversation at a table in the ballroom. More often than not, these relationships begin and end during the same evening at the Singles Dance, with those involved rarely interacting again for any length of time, except perhaps for a short encounter on the dance floor. Dawn, the organizer of the Singles Dance, corroborates our observations by noting that personal relationships that develop from the event tend to be "short term [rather] than long term," adding that people who "come looking for a partner usually go away without one." Close to half of the participants we interviewed corroborated Dawn's observations and claimed they had dated people whom they met at the dance but that few of those dates had resulted in long-term relationships. Phil (a regular participant), for example, noted, "I've had dates with a few women from there [the Singles Dance], but those haven't turned into anything." We met two men, for example, who met their wives at the Dance many years ago, although both couples have since divorced. One of the few long-term "couples" who regularly frequent the dance also know of a few people who met and later married, but they emphasize that "coupling" is a rarity at these events because a lot of people "fail to find partners" at the dance. The most durable tie that many participants develop at the Singles Dance is with Dawn. She comes to know many of the regulars by name. On any given night, Dawn could be observed waving salutations to Singles Dance regulars and talking with a few singles at the tables scattered around the dance floor.

Aside from a fleeting relationship that may last an evening or result in a short-lived date, participants bring to the events friends that they have developed outside the dance. Members of such groups, or "cliques," as one regular participant called them, typically control tables at various places around the room and act as informal support groups for their members as they venture onto the dance floor or into conversations with singles who are alone or part of other cliques. On numerous occasions, we eavesdropped on singles who returned from an encounter to their clique and provided a shorthand account of their experience. In these instances, clique members would listen attentively for a moment and then quickly become occupied with other conversations or get up from the table to dance. On a few occasions, we observed cliques urging one of their members into an encounter.

Given these social dynamics, what inhibits the formation of long-term relationships at the Singles Dance? One answer could be that participants do not possess the relational competence to form long-term relationships. We experienced awkward encounters with some male participants that initially caused us to question the relational competence of men at the dance. At the same time, we did not notice a great deal of awkwardness among most women and men at the dance. Nor did it emerge as a central feature of our conversational interviews with participants. More importantly, our awkwardness diminished as we came to know the "rules" of social encounters at the dance. We learned that approximately half of the participants we interacted with claimed to have been in long-term relationships earlier in their lives. Although we cannot check these claims for their authenticity, the stories told by participants carried a ring of authenticity. More substantially, Dawn supports these stories by observing that she knows many participants who are "divorced or widowed." The existence of cliques also underscores a degree of relational competence among participants, at least for generating friendships.

Another factor that could inhibit the formation of long-term relationships is anxiety and face saving. Previous research on singles dances has emphasized the importance of face saving and impression management among participants.[15] Indeed, we felt anxious before and during our first excursions to the dance because of what we imagined to be the intense impression management among participants, the potential for rejection, and the sheer unpredictability of interaction. Add to these factors the avowed "official" goal of the dance—to facilitate the kindling of long-term relationships—and we believed that many participants could experience various sorts of anxiety that could negatively affect their interpersonal skills. After our initial jitters (similar to those experienced by many first-timers to the dance), we quickly did what most participants do: we responded to polite offers to dance and became accustomed to the scripted interaction on and off the dance floor, as illustrated in the two scenes described above.

A third factor that could constrain the formation of long-term romantic relationships is associated with the existence of the cliques. Here the argument would be that the social demands of cliques (and perhaps the added peer pressure of clique approval) could constrain an individual's ability to strike up a long-term relationship and then maintain it. However, we did not observe any differences in the abilities of clique members and nonmembers to create long-term relationships with other singles: regardless of whether one was in a clique, very few people formed long-term romantic relationships with those they met at the Singles Dance. Although our evidence is quite limited in this regard, we suspect that the supportive functions of the clique—similar to the supportiveness of social networks that generally nurture romantic dyads—can actually facilitate formation of long-term relationships with other singles, particularly if the clique strongly approves of the relationship.[16]

Relational competence, anxiety, and the deterrent effect of cliques are therefore less compelling as explanations of the lack of long-term relationships than they might at first appear. As our fieldwork and analysis progressed, we turned to two other factors that appeared more deeply tied to the prevalence of encounters and fleeting relationships at the Singles Dance: the act of dancing itself that helps to structure the "gaming" elements of the sifting and sorting that occurs among participants and the various kinds of stigma that participants manage at the Singles Dance.

Sifting and Sorting as Gaming

Although initial observations of the Singles Dance suggest an unfocused gathering, participant observation over time reveals a continual process of sifting and sorting as singles move from one dance partner to another. Unlike other singles events, such as matchmaking services, which claim to match applicants with compatible partners, the Singles Dance does not attempt to pair people. The onus is placed on the patron to sort through whoever comes through the door of the dance. Encounters and fleeting relationships therefore serve as sorting mechanisms; one dance or a conversation is often enough to determine that an individual is an unsuitable partner.

Consistent with the sifting and sorting is a "gaming" element that encourages quick interactions with individuals. From this perspective, individuals strategically maximize the number of potential partners, especially dance partners, with whom they interact.[17] Participants themselves use gaming metaphors to describe their experiences at the dance by referring to "the numbers game" of meeting as many other singles as possible, the "game" of presenting particular images of themselves to others, or the dance itself as a "game." Some participants become adept in choosing the tables where they sit in order to maximize their ability to "scout" out the floor for potential dances or "dates." Other singles become adept at choosing where to stand or "mill" around the dance floor or bar in order to maximize the number of dances they have with participants. During encounters, the game intensifies as singles size each other up.

Encounters and fleeting relationships are no less game oriented for the vast majority of participants who attend the dance with the goals of simply dancing or meeting new people. For these participants, the dance is still about sifting and sorting, but rather than being a means to an end (i.e., a means to find a romantic partner), it is an end in itself. The goal here is to maximize the number of dances one has with different partners: in essence, to experience the diversity and fun of human contact with a number of different partners.

Although most participants remain firmly within the local rules of "appropriate" interaction, some approach the game in a particularly aggressive manner and come to be known as "Casanovas." Dawn says that men earn the Casanova label who "get predatory and hostile and want to be king of the dance. . . . They are likely to compete with each other, especially when there are new young women at the dance." The following encounter illustrates a man known as a "Casanova" during an encounter on the dance floor:

> A gray-haired man named Ralph approaches a gray-haired woman named Alice and asks her to dance. Alice accepts and they head for the dance floor. It is a slower tune than usual—what regulars call a "slow dance." Ralph and Alice move close to one another, brushing their torsos against one another, each with one arm around the other's waist and the other arms in a classic right-angle dance position. Halfway through the dance, Ralph moves closer to Alice and begins kissing her on the cheek. Alice does not resist Ralph's kisses, but she does not do anything to encourage it. Alice's face remains placid, expressionless. Her body remains somewhat stiff, frozen in the "dance position," as she and Ralph move among the other dancers. Immediately after the dance, Alice breaks away from Ralph and bustles off to where she was sitting without further interaction with Ralph.

Subsequent to this encounter, Ralph danced with several other woman, occasionally exhibiting the same behaviors he did with Alice. In each instance, the women quickly moved away after their dance with Ralph was over.

At no time during any of our field visits did we observe women engaging in what the participants referred to as "inappropriate advances." Because women do not initiate contact with men and are only in a position to "receive" advances and propositions (to dance), they are constrained from enacting the "forwardness" that Ralph and other Casanovas exhibit. A woman's lot becomes one of positioning herself to be approached, rather than to approach, and being able to fend off any unwanted advances should they occur. The reputations that Casanovas develop at the dance can ultimately create situations in which women shun them by turning them down for dances or moving away conspicuously as they approach to request a dance. But being a Casanova is only one kind of identity threat that singles must manage at the dance as they sift and sort through the crowd. Far more common are identity threats that take on some of the characteristics of stigma.

Stigma

Stigma, as Goffman argues, involves the social construction of a "spoiled identity" that commonly exists in three forms: bodily stigma (e.g., scars, blindness, missing limbs), character stigma (e.g., immorality, particular kinds of political beliefs), or membership stigma (due to one's association with particular groups, including specific ethnicities, religions, social classes, and political groups).[18] Goffman further argues that stigma can constrain social interaction, making the development of sustained social relationships difficult. In other words, stigma can constrain the formation of social relationships because it discredits individuals and strains their interaction with others. As people exert energy to manage stigma, furthermore, they may have little energy or opportunity to develop other aspects of their interaction, especially long-term personal relationships.

We encountered each of the three types of stigma during our fieldwork at the Singles Dance. Although none of the participants exhibited the kinds of bodily stigma Goffman had in mind, we encountered people (including regulars) who believed that many of the individuals at the Dance were not as physically attractive as individuals in other public contexts where one potentially could meet long-term relational partners. Phil, for example, commented that he was "looking for a fit woman. There aren't many fit women here at the dance." Other participants pointed out other bodily stigma, such as people being overweight, having odd hairstyles, or having "body odor." Character stigma most strongly manifested itself in warnings from other participants "to stay away" from aggressive

Casanovas and other men who were known to overstep the carefully out-lined etiquette of the dance by asking "too many questions too quickly" during an encounter or perhaps engaging in inappropriate physical contact during dancing.

Bodily and character stigma both affect social interaction at the dance, but only for select individuals. For example, participants who are deemed "fat" or who have "bad body odor" face certain obstacles as they attempt to sort and sift. Casanovas, as illustrated in the previous section, face even steeper odds of turning an encounter into any kind of relationship, particularly if they are shunned by a number of women. Membership stigma, by contrast, affects any individual who attends the dance. This stigma rests on the assumptions held by Singles Dance participants, the wider public, and ourselves (at the outset of the research) that people who attend singles events are relationally incompetent. Otherwise, so the assumption goes, they would develop long-term romantic relationships through "appropriate" channels, such as friendship networks, places of worship, workplaces, or social clubs (with focal concerns other than facilitating long-term relationships).[19]

We noted above that many participants' relational histories include long-term marriages and other romantic attachments. Even so, attendees draw from the assumption that singles at the dance are relationally incom-petent as they talk about others at the dance. We heard participants use the term "losers' ball" to describe the Singles Dance as a whole. Some partici-pants admitted that their friends who do not attend singles events believe they are "kooky" or "weird" for attending singles events (including per-sonal ad and other singles events aside from the Singles Dance). Even Dawn commented that "most people might look around and think these people are losers." Membership stigma also stems from the character of the event itself. Participants mentioned that the event sometimes felt "unnat-ural" or an "odd pathway to a romantic relationship." Juan, a regular, observes, "The atmosphere at the Southwest Hotel does not feel natural because all the single people are thrown together, rather than coming together naturally like they do at the Juke Box [a bar he regularly visits on Saturday nights]." As participants navigate the dance, they manage these forms of stigma either in the foreground (especially if they are deemed to have bodily or character deficiencies) or in the background (because of the common assumption that many singles they encounter have potentially defective relational skills). It is no wonder, then, that participants adopt highly consistent, careful, and ritualized approaches to their encounters: this is a mechanism by which stigma is both minimized and managed.

Given the tensions of gaming and managing stigma that constrain the formation of long-term relationships, what brings singles back to the dance? One reason is simple: many people come to the dance with what can only be described as mixed motives. Some still hope to find a long-term partner despite previous unsuccessful outings, but they are also looking for the pleasures of the transient sociality, including dancing with multiple partners, short conversations, and people watching. Indeed, the pleasures of merely being in a place with other people who are circulating through a series of encounters is enough to bring many people back to the dance over and over. In the next section, we explore pleasure that singles take in fleeting interactions at the dance.

Pleasure and Safety

Listen to these representative accounts from regulars about why they return to the Singles Dance:

> There is something straightforward about going to a dance that is for singles only. I believe that people who attend are more honest about their intentions. No one is going to press any commitments on you. You can just enjoy the evening without hassles.
>
> It can sometimes be weird but also fun to meet a lot of new people.
>
> I like going alone or with friends. I come with my friends and mix.
>
> It's fun to get out of the house for a while and just be with other folks who you don't know.
>
> There are always a lot of different people to dance with. That can be fun rather than being stuck with one person for the whole night.

These statements suggest sentiments that there is fun, safety, familiarity, and enjoyment in the encounters and fleeting relationships at the Singles Dance. Just as people enjoy the conversational and observational "pleasures of the public realm" in bars and cabarets, on street corners, or in the lobby of the Southwest Hotel, many singles enjoy the pleasures of transient sociality at the dance.[20] We observed several indicators of pleasure at the Singles Dance, including people laughing while talking as they sat at tables or stood by the bar, smiling as they danced, and extending warm greetings to each other (especially Dawn). To be sure, their pleasure is mixed with the tensions discussed above and the highly bounded forms of interaction found at the dance. But pleasure exists side by side with these tensions. A regular named Linda, for example, noted that the pleasure in "human contact on the dance floor" was enough to bring her back to the dance. Although this statement could be read as having a sexual undertone (and in some cases it may well have such an aspect), Linda was careful to correct any misinterpretations of her statement by noting that she avoided certain dances that might invite "unwanted attention" from men (especially Casanovas) at the dance. Her account, then, illustrates what social scientists note as a fundamental condition of human well-being—physical touch with other humans.[21]

The boundedness of such contact, moreover, provides many singles with a comforting, safe predictability. Singles know that unwanted physical contact rarely occurs beyond the dance floor or during a dance (with a few exceptions). As we noted earlier, once one learns the interactional script at the dance, there is little awkwardness to the proceedings. Few people refuse other people dances or break these normative boundaries (except for those who achieve the "status" of a Casanova). There also is safety and comfort to be found if one comes to the dance in a group. We watched on several occasions as men and women returned from an encounter on the dance floor to a small group and begin recounting their experiences. There is thus a kind of esprit de corps among groups that brings people back to the dance.

CONCLUSION

Our ethnography of the Singles Dance reveals a social world in which people simultaneously experience a range of pleasures, sometimes mixed with tension and anxiety. Some participants come to the dance looking for romantic partners, but most seem drawn by the prospects of enjoying the momentary pleasures of nonintimate personal interaction with a series of different people. The formation of long-term romantic relationships, as either an intended or unintended outcome of attending the dance, is rare. Singles most often experience brief social encounters and fleeting relationships with those they meet at the dance. Moreover, roughly half of the singles who attend the dance do so with groups of friends who provide support and a base of operations. Thus most singles at the dance bounce back and forth between encounters and fleeting ties and their friendship cliques. These observations carry implications that speak to the links between shared goals and social order in public places and the influence of designed social contexts on relational formation.

In our observations and interviews with singles, we rarely learned of anything that we could label "trouble" or "conflict" except for the occasional Casanova's violation of the normative boundaries of interaction. Participants themselves find the dance to be a safe haven for personal interaction and often gave its safety as a reason for returning to it over time. At the same time, we noticed little formal regulation at the dances (except for the usual hotel security), particularly compared to most bars or other public events at which singles typically can be found. What explains the lack of trouble at the Singles Dance? One explanation is the light alcohol consumption or abstinence among participants, although we noted that more than a few participants (on the basis of their breath) appeared to drink beforehand or surreptitiously during the dance. Another explanation could be self-selection. Perhaps the dance attracts an especially "peaceful" or trouble-free crowd because the people are mostly middle-aged, belong to a homogeneous ethnicity (mostly Anglo with a few Latino and African Americans), and appear to be middle class in terms of work backgrounds. This is a difficult argument to confirm or support given that other public contexts that draw high numbers of people with these same characteristics are not always trouble free (e.g., sporting events, bars, public rallies).

A more compelling explanation for the orderliness of the dance can be found in anthropologist Robert Edgerton's analysis of social order on an urban beach.[22] He argues that order on the beach is tied to the way that people define the experience of going to the beach as enjoying the aesthetic pleasures of the locale. The common rituals of beach going—spreading out towels in a territorial fashion, maintaining physical distance from other beach goers, and generally not interfering with people who are not part of one's group—reinforce these assumptions and provide a sense of familiarity and safety for most people on the beach. In this sense, people on the beach are "alone" in that they do not have social relationships with other beach goers (outside of people they come with) but are "together" in that they share the same general physical spaces and social status as beach goers. Participants in the dance share more of the same physical space while dancing than do unattached beach goers. However, much of the time, dance participants return to their tables without those they have danced with, and many have a well-defined set of expectations about simply mingling with other people and enjoying "human contact" during a brief dance or conversation. Thus, as with beach going, the definition of the situation and the ritualized routines undergirding that definition instill an orderliness in the setting and help to minimizes trouble. Participants at the dance therefore illustrate somewhat different aspects of the co-presence/social distancing nexus described by Edgerton: dance participants are "together" in that they fleetingly commingle with one another (or may be with a friendship clique) but are "alone" in that the vast majority do not pair up with each other for any significant time. Moreover, many participants come away with small amounts of satisfaction and enthusiasm—what Randall Collins calls "emotional energy"—in the aftermath of successfully enacting ritualized interaction with other participants.[23] This energy also helps to socially integrate the dance, tying participants in interaction chains of transient sociality as it militates against interpersonal trouble.

A second implication of our study is consistent with this book's emphasis on the contextual constraints and facilitators of personal relationships in public places. Contextual factors such as social networks, ethnic communities, and wider institutions can significantly influence when and how people meet or how individual characteristics are interpreted by potential relational partners.[24] Our research adds another contextual feature to be considered by students of personal relationships: the unintended consequences of designed sociability. In most treatments, *designed sociability* refers to the ways in which physical environments are intentionally organized to facilitate public sociality.[25] In the case of the Singles Dance, a quasi-public social environment is designed to ostensibly facilitate the formation of long-term romantic relationships. The design feature is not physical but social and revolves around dancing as a core mechanism through which people initially interact with one another. Yet dancing itself, together with participants' shared definitions of the situation and interaction rituals of initiating and ending dances, unintentionally constrains the formation of long-term social relationships among participants. Because the dance itself is a punctuated social interaction that begins and ends with music, most partners tend to drift off from one another after completing a dance. Absent other mechanisms of putting people together for sustained periods of interaction (other than cliques of friends that exist prior to and outside the dance context), there are few other opportunities for previously unconnected others to meet and sustain their interaction. Ironically, then, the mechanism intended to facilitate the initiation of long-term romantic relationships militates against their formation.

In conclusion, our study underscores the strengths of ethnography for studying personal relationships in public places. Without the direct experience and observation that our team ethnography provided, the complexity, subtleties, and interactions at the Singles Dance would be impossible to access. Only through continued fieldwork in such settings will we come to have a full understanding of the range of personal relationships that are possible in public and quasi-public places.

METHODOLOGICAL PROCEDURES AND REFLECTIONS

Initially defining what we meant by a "singles organization" proved more difficult than expected because many groups offer social activities that are explicitly defined or can be construed as singles events. After a few weeks in the field, we developed a grounded definition of singles organizations as establishments that have as their primary goal the provision of services intended to facilitate the formation of long-term personal relationships among individuals who self-identify as single. This definition yielded a population of thirteen organizations that varied according to (1) whether they are nonprofit or not (nonprofits generally have nominal fees, while for-profit fees can be quite steep), (2) whether they cater to particular age or religious groups, and (3) the kinds of relationships they intend to facilitate among singles (long-term romantic or other friendship ties).[26] Some enterprises, for example, explicitly focus on providing opportunities to kindle long-term romantic ties among singles, whereas other organizations downplay these kinds of ties in favor of friendships or other people with whom to do "activities." Although some groups have rules that limit participants' dating of each other, all organizations have as a primary or secondary goal the facilitation of long-term romantic relationships among members.

We attended twelve Southwest Dance events during the seven-month period of our fieldwork. Although the absolute time we spent at the dance (approximately sixty hours) appears less than the field immersion typical of many ethnographic studies, two factors enhanced the depth and breadth of our fieldwork. First, we engaged in fieldwork as a team, which meant that every hour in the field could be multiplied by four as each author participated in and observed various aspects of the interaction at the dance. Second, the number of participants at each dance meant that there was a wide range of social interaction to observe and there were many participants (including both regulars and newcomers) with whom we could interact. While at each event, we posed as "interested" or "available" singles at the dances, which enabled us to both observe and participate in social interaction among participants. In addition to observations, we conducted conversational interviews with forty Southwest Dance participants. We attempted to maximize the variation in the participants we interviewed in terms of ethnicity, education, gender, and experience with singles events. We supplemented these data with a conversational interviews of the Southwest Dance organizer.

While in the field, we took notes on napkins and receipts, often excusing ourselves to the nearest restroom to jot down notes in privacy. We also pretended we were making phone calls from the pay phone in order to write down important key words that would spark our memories later. These practices (and the impracticality of secretly tape-recording conversations due to background noise) meant that it sometimes was difficult to record verbatim quotes from informants. If participants asked about our activities, we represented ourselves as either interested singles or graduate students working on a research project about singles events and organizations. At times our activities created ethical questions in our own minds about whether we were compromising participants' privacy. We agree, however, with John and Lyn Lofland's observations on this issue: "In our view, the fieldwork situation is no more (although certainly no less) difficult ethically than everyday life."[27] We take this to mean that many of the choices about whether to eavesdrop on a conversation or take note of social interaction among people unfamiliar to us exist as much in everyday life as in fieldwork. The choices between everyday life and fieldwork are especially parallel in our case because of the quasi-public nature of the Southwest Dance.

Aside from providing depth and breadth for our fieldwork, our team approach enabled us to adopt different roles and positions in the field. A portion of our team, for example, could participate in the event, talking with other participants, while another researcher could present herself as a graduate student asking for an interview with the event organizer. We also benefited from each other's strengths: one of the researchers was particularly adept at striking up conversations with strangers at singles events, while another researcher did not mind posing as an interested single because she was single and looking for someone to date. The multiple perspectives on the team meant we could "check" each other's observations at events and interpretations of the data. We also engaged in continuous checks of our data in return visits to the dance over the fieldwork period.

Our ages relative to the participants—all of us were between fifteen and thirty-five years younger than most participants—posed some challenges in the field. Some of the participants (especially women) initially wondered why such "young girls" were attending the dance. Moreover, our ages fed into some of our own anxieties about conducting fieldwork in this setting in the first place. At the same time, our age differences relative to the participants encouraged some to open up to us (particularly in interviews) to educate us about "how it really is at the [dance]." Through these opportunities, we learned about the importance of fleeting relationships to many participants, as well as other subtleties at the dance.

Our coding also assumed a team character. We distributed typed notes to each other and went through many iterations of open coding as we collectively decided upon important categories for initially organizing our notes. We then elaborated these initial categories by linking them to theoretically meaningful concepts.[28] Although this process did not always unfold without disagreement, we eventually settled on several categories during the latter half of our fieldwork: nonverbal and verbal social interaction at singles events, social relationships among participants, various kinds of stigma associated with singles events, safety measures fostered by singles organizations at events and perceptions of safety among participants, and participants' motivations and expectations for attending singles events.

Just as the single persons at the dance must constantly manage various sorts of anxiety in their endeavors to find a romantic partner, so too did we manage anxiety during our research. Although the anxiety we faced was more fleeting than that faced by our informants, it nonetheless affected us throughout the entire project. On our first trip to the Singles Dance, we all nervously called each other to confirm whether our "outfits" could be considered "proper attire" and to share our reservations about going to such an event. When we entered the ballroom at the Southwest Hotel, nothing could have prepared us to be several years younger than the other attendees. Prior to embarking on this research, none of us had attended any singles-related events, so we did not know what to expect. In our first several sets of field notes, each of us called attention to our feelings of anxiety, as illustrated by these excerpts:

Throughout the evening, I felt nervous about being asked to dance.

I realized later that I was using body language that was not particularly conducive to people approaching me (crossed legs and arms).

I found that entering this scene was difficult. I felt out of place initially, being so young, but when it became apparent that no one took any great notice of our presence, I relaxed and was more able to observe the scene around me.

Relaxing and acquainting ourselves with each new scene became the first order of business as we entered the field. We also found it useful to discuss our discomfort with one another ahead of field visits in order to prepare for potential discomfort that we might feel during fieldwork. Gradually, we realized that we felt more out of place than dance participants believed us to be.

Once we contained our initial discomfort at interacting with singles at the dance, we became concerned about our dual roles as "researchers" and "participants." How could we express our desire to find out about people's experiences without unintentionally conveying a romantic interest in them? Would singles believe that our cover story of doing an ethnography of a Singles Dance was simply a "line" in order to attract their interest? If we pursued a covert angle, could participants tell that we were doing research and ostracize us? Would we be kicked out of the dance even though we had previously talked with Dawn about doing the research?

Acting as we would in "normal" social situations became a useful solution to combat some of our uneasiness. As "normal" patrons in bars and in restaurants, many people "eavesdrop" on others conversations, watch others' activities, and strike up brief conversations with fellow patrons. These activities can convey further romantic interest, but the bulk of them do not. Despite our statements in the main text of the chapter, we continued to feel guilty about talking with people when we were merely interested in the data we could obtain from the conversation. This tension, often referred in the ethnographic literature as the "insider-outsider" dilemma, became particularly acute when we encountered many of the same people across field sites. One remedy for this anxiety involved openly presenting ourselves as researchers. This strategy yielded mixed results. People sometimes shrugged off our statements and continued to act as though we were potential dating partners. A handful became quite flustered and wanted to stop speaking with us. Generally, participants were interested in our research and happy to talk with us about their experiences. Most importantly, approaching participants in this way made us feel more comfortable about initiating conversations with people in these settings.

While researching singles events, we were also faced with the negative opinions of colleagues and friends; the stigma associated with singles organizations was strong enough to taint our status as serious researchers. After we submitted a presentation proposal for a conference, a reviewer wrote back, "Be honest. If you are using this research as an excuse to research dating, or worse yet, to go dating as researchers, it is not much of a program." Nowhere in that early proposal did the word *dating* appear at all. Many people immediately associated our attendance at singles events with the desire to eventually date participants. As one friend good-naturedly suggested, we "must be hard up for a date" to even want to participate in such events. A few friends wondered if we could give them advice about how to meet people.

We could only laugh these comments off, as they were indications that others were not taking our research as seriously as we were. No one accused our friends researching interaction and social control in bingo halls of using their research as a way to indulge in gambling. Similarly, a team of researchers in our qualitative methods seminar investigating the interaction rituals of public eating establishments, such as food courts and campus dining halls, were not chastised for using their research as an excuse to go "eating as researchers."

Over the course of the half-year that we conducted the ethnographic research for this chapter, we confronted our own anxieties about attending singles organizations, external discrediting of our research program, and our own as well as others' perceptions of the stigma surrounding singles organizations. We attempted to handle each of these in a reflective and proactive manner, rather than brushing them aside and ignoring them. What we learned, however, is that this subject area is rife with discomfort, no matter how one attempts to manage it.

FOUR

A Personal Dance

Emotional Labor, Fleeting Relationships, and Social Power in a Strip Bar

JOSEPH E. MASSEY AND TRINA L. HOPE

SOCIOLOGICAL RESEARCH ON STRIP CLUBS has long investigated the public dynamics of social interaction between female dancers and their customers. One branch of this tradition situates erotic dancing as a "deviant occupation" at the legal and moral margins of "mainstream" society. Of particular interest within this perspective are strippers' career paths and social identities and the social organization of strip clubs.[1] A second branch of interactionist research explores the lived experience of stripping, paying close attention to dancers' emotions and senses of self as they perform for customers.[2] Feminist scholars, in contrast to both these streams of inquiry, have confronted the power dimensions of erotic dancing within the broad context of gender hierarchies. Stripping is a key site at which women's bodies are publicly objectified and commodified, so feminists argue, which in turn helps reproduce male-dominated systems of sexuality and commerce.[3] A more recent trend combines interactionist approaches with feminist critiques of erotic dancing. What emerges from feminist-interactionist studies is greater insight into the social processes through which dancers ply their trade, as well as how social power is constituted, negotiated, and subverted through interactions between women and men in their respective roles as dancers and customers. Ultimately, such power serves men and feeds into male-dominated commercial-sex systems, but in ways unanticipated by purely feminist arguments.[4]

In this chapter, we focus attention away from the stigmatizing aspects of stripping and the personal experiences of performers to concentrate on social interaction and power dynamics between dancers and customers during "table dances"—nude and seminude performances that occur at customers' tables in strip bars. Table dancing is a core feature in many U.S. strip clubs and offers a strategic site to observe social interaction between dancers and customers. Our research specifically examines the creation and patterns of fictive "fleeting relationships" between dancers and customers—transitory socio-financial exchanges that are infused with an outward semblance of emotionality. The social structure of exchange that results from these patterns reinforces stereotypical notions of masculinity and femininity as it ironically facilitates dancers' capacities to exit from any one relationship they find unproductive or offensive. This structure increases dancers' potential for financial rewards yet can strongly bind them to the occupation and the club for their livelihoods. Table dancing can also heighten competition among dancers, further contributing to control processes undergirding economically successful dance clubs. The central contribution of our chapter is thus twofold. First, we offer additional insight into the nuances of fleeting sociality in a socially marginalized public place. Second, we suggest a new analytic path with respect to interactionist studies of social power and stripping by moving beyond dyadic analyses of dancers and customers to investigate the patterns of exchange relations in strip bars.

In the next section, we conceptually situate the chapter, drawing elements from previous interactionist studies of stripping, interactionist approaches to emotionality and emotional labor, and the social psychology of relationships in public urban contexts. Specifically, we combine social exchange and feminist-interactionist approaches on social power to conceptualize patterns of table-dance transactions between dancers and customers. We then turn our attention to the clubs where we conducted our fieldwork and our findings. We first delineate how individual dancers set the scene for table dancing via costuming and stage performances. At the dyadic level, we concentrate on how dancers cultivate fleeting relationships with customers via emotional labor and create the conditions for exit from such relationships. Finally, we examine the patterns of exchange relations that emerge among dancers and customers and their implications for what we call "local" social power in the clubs themselves. We conclude the chapter by discussing implications of our work for the study of local social power in strip clubs, public sociality and the social embeddedness of economic exchange, and the study of public sociality in marginalized settings.

SOCIAL EXCHANGE AND POWER IN STRIPPING:
EMOTIONAL LABOR, FLEETING RELATIONSHIPS,
AND MASCULINITY

Strip clubs, like retail stores and other types of bars, are quasi-public places in that they are accessible and visible to most members of the adult public but are set apart from purely public places, such as city streets or squares. In addition, quasi-public places typically have more focused activities and social control associated with them than purely public places. The focused activity of strip bars revolves around one overarching social exchange involving female dancers granting viewing access to their unclothed or semiclothed bodies in anticipation of exchange for money from customers. In many clubs, this exchange occurs via a twofold system. Customers pay a "cover charge" to see "reviews" and sex shows of various sorts presented on elevated stages. Interspersed with stage shows is a second system composed of nude and seminude dances performed at customers' tables or in private rooms. Table dances are generated entirely by tips from customers and unfold through a "pay-per-view" process in which the close-up view (and, under some conditions, certain types of touching) is of "breasts and hips and legs and bottoms all belonging to sexy women in various forms of undress."[5] In many clubs, dancers earn the bulk of their money from table dancing (as opposed to tips received from stage dancing).[6]

At table dances, performers *and* audience members directly participate in the "act." For the dance to be "successful" financially, customers and dancers must work together to maintain the definition of the situation as sexual and sensual (e.g., a sense that both parties, dancer and customer, are "turned on" and "having a good time"). Interactionist scholars argue that equally important is the creation of a sense of relational connection between a dancer and her customer. Such connections revolve around the "counterfeiting of intimacy" that gives off the impression of a personal tie. Customers are as much motivated to tip and tip more by simulated social intimacy as they are by a dancer's sexuality.[7]

The chief mechanism for achieving such connections is a type of impression management called "emotional labor" that includes stereotypical notions of gender deployed in commercial systems.[8] Concretely, emotional labor requires retail workers, when interacting with customers, to cultivate specific emotional definitions of the situation. Arlie Hochschild, in her pioneering research on emotional labor, argued that airlines train their flight attendants to communicate a sense of care and conviviality to passengers via behavioral cues, such as asking passengers if they need a pillow or blanket to make them more comfortable or smiling at passengers when they make eye contact with them. Emotional labor is not a one-way street—that is, something that flight attendants "do" to passengers—for it involves the co-construction of an "interaction order,"[9] to use Erving Goffman's term, in which passengers respond to flight attendants in ways that uphold the definition of the situation as caring, convivial, and safe. In general, emotional labor involves the "transmutation of emotional systems" from private to public contexts.[10] For strippers, emotional labor means creating a sensual interaction order that typically exists in private contexts. It is an order in which the customer feels that there is something more to the interaction than commercial sensuality—a sense, however ephemeral, that a dancer has "feelings" for the customer and that the customer, too, has feelings for the dancer.[11] Table dances, because they occur in public and are witnessed by other customers, also act as an anticipatory mechanism that creates customers' expectations for what an interaction will be like with a dancer. In this way, emotional labor contributes to an overall sense that a strip bar is a sexually *and* relationally charged context.[12]

The transitory sense of relational connection that successful strippers kindle with customers is in many ways akin to the fleeting "personalizing aspects" of many public retail economic transactions.[13] Such relationships build a sense of care and "human" connection between customers, softening the hard edges of material exchanges of money for food or services, sometimes even creating a sense of mutual obligation among those involved that moves beyond economic exchange. In many retail situations, fleeting relationships can last for a few seconds or a few minutes but can be built up through repeat interactions over long periods of time. In the case of table dancing, the typical fleeting relationship is built and abandoned in a three- to five-minute period with an individual customer. Although some dancers build a clientele who come in for dances on a "regular" basis or happen upon a "big spender" who lavishes them with tips during the course of a single night, most dancers move relatively quickly from table to table in search of new customers and tips.[14]

At an abstract level, the pattern that results from dancers moving from table to table can be conceived as a social structure of exchange, which carries important implications for social power in strip bars. Exchange structures are social relationships in which two or more actors trade valued resources of any kind. Resources may be material (e.g., money), service (e.g., stripping, representation in court), emotional (e.g., liking, anger, shame), or symbolic (e.g., deference, status) phenomena. From a social exchange perspective, social power results from actors' abilities to convert resource dependencies by other actors into authority, autonomy, or other forms of advantage.[15] Because dancers in strip clubs rarely depend upon solo customers for tips, they are able to preserve some autonomy if they can generate high volumes of tip payers. Particularly successful dancers may even raise the stakes of a table dance to the degree that they can "choose" which tables to approach for dances and which to stay away from. At the same time, dancers depend on the club to create the environment in which table dances can occur.

These structures of exchange occur against a backdrop of "caricatured" male-female role relations drawn from stereotypical definitions of masculinity and femininity.[16] One role relation relates to the idea of men as "providers" and women as "supporters." Although this role relation has been culturally and politically challenged in different ways during the past several decades, it remains current in contemporary American society and appears in exaggerated forms in strip clubs. For male customers, the exchange of money for table dances heightens the sense that the customer has the financial means to "provide" for women, at the same time signaling that women, in return, should provide a variety of nonpecuniary services to men, especially sex and emotional support. A second set of stereotypical role relationships paints male customers as "objects" of desire whom women cannot resist. This role relation turns the idea of woman as "object" on its head in that the man becomes the object rather than the woman (as in feminist critiques of sex work). Yet, in being objectified, male customers exert their "power of attraction" over women, again placing women in dependent and "powerless" positions. As we will discuss later in the chapter, these two sides of social power in strip clubs—characterized by patterns of exchange relations and stereotypical definitions of masculine-feminine role relations—play off of each other in unexpected ways.

This discussion suggests several research questions regarding social interactions between customers and dancers during table dances that we developed before and during our fieldwork: (1) How is emotional labor enacted before, during, and after table dances in strip clubs? (2) How do dancers exit the fleeting relationships they create through emotional labor with a minimum of social tension? (3) How does the exchange structure of fleeting relationships between dancers and customers feed into (a) performance strategies among dancers and (b) the social control of dancers? We turn now to a discussion of the field sites where we investigated these questions.

STRIP BARS AS FIELD SITES

In general, strip bars vary dramatically in their outward appearance. Some "high-class gentlemen's clubs" feature huge, Las Vegas hotel-like marquees that advertise guest performers or shows. These clubs are architecturally framed by grand entryways with backlit columns, huge searchlights "scanning" the night skies on weekend nights, and stretch limousines, hired by customers, parked in their vast parking lots. "Low-class strip joints," as some customers refer to them, typically display worn physical appearances, dimly lit facades, and decidedly poorer cars in their small parking lots. The patrons of clubs can be similarly differentiated. High-class clubs draw more professionals and groups of middle-class men out for parties and other special occasions, while lower-class bars draw more lower-income men and fewer groups. We chose five bars that fell somewhere near the middle of these extremes as field sites during the two six-month periods that we conducted our fieldwork during 1994–96.[17] To these bars we gave the pseudonyms "Tigress North," "Tigress South," "Seductions," "Erotica," and "Gates of Pleasure." Their physical plants were, for the most part, reasonably well kept up, and, although none of them had the grandeur of their higher-class counterparts, we did occasionally see a limousine pull up to their entrances. By choosing midstatus clubs, we ensured that our sites would be most similar to the vast majority of clubs both in the city where we conducted our research and elsewhere.[18]

All the clubs we studied displayed similar main barroom areas, with a large main stage, perhaps 40 × 20 feet, that dominated the "front" of the barroom and one or two smaller secondary stages on either side of the main stage. Mirrors lined the walls of the stages, creating the sense that the stages were twice their actual size and enabling customers to see dancers from multiple angles as they performed on stage. The main bars (with yet another wall-size mirror behind it) hung at the back of each barroom behind the bar, with one or two smaller bars located near the secondary stages. Dozens of black chairs, surrounding smaller round tables, filled the rest of the room. All four bars we studied opened at 11:00 a.m. and closed at 2:00 a.m. each day except Sundays, when they opened later and closed earlier.

One's first sensation on walking into a club is the deep back bass of loud pop music reverberating through the walls. The barroom itself is dimly lit, with red, blue, yellow, and green lights illuminating it with intermittent pulses in time to the beat. Between songs, an in-house DJ comes over the sound system to encourage the audience to applaud for the last dancers on stage ("Gentlemen, let's have a round of applause for Lela and Keisha!") and excitedly announce the dancers who will be performing on stage next ("On the north stage, put your hands together for the temptress from deep in the heart of Dixie, Billy Jo!"). Mixed with these announcements are advertisements for ongoing drink specials, most of which have some sexual innuendo connected to them, such as "For the next fifteen minutes, two-for-one shots of Sex-on-the-Beach [a rum-based concoction served in a large shot glass]!"

At any given time during a typical night, the ebb and flow of bodily movements in a strip bar includes three to five dancers performing on stage (alone or in groups), fifteen to twenty dancers performing at tables, cocktail waitresses scurrying back and forth between tables and the bars, bartenders rapidly mixing drinks, a few male overseers keeping close to the bar, and 100 to 150 vociferous men (with an occasional woman) in the audience. Also present are at least one "floor manager" who ensures that everything in the barroom runs smoothly, "security" men (who act as bouncers and may circulate between the barroom and the entrance depending upon size of the audience), and a "house mother" (who operates backstage helping the dancers get ready for their appearances and limiting backstage access to authorized personnel).

ENACTING EMOTIONAL LABOR AND FLEETING RELATIONSHIPS IN STRIP CLUBS

Setting the Scene via Stage Performances and Costuming

Strip clubs provide dancers with a contextual "script" in which they must fill in the specifics of their "acts." The raw resources of this script include the music, lighting, alcohol, and public visibility that dancers can marshal in their stage and table dance performances. Long before engaging in a table dance, a dancer begins to set the scene for table dancing through her costuming. At an analytic level, setting the scene is a way a dancer begins the work of creating a particular definition of the situation relevant to her performance that will be carried through during her stage performance and, more importantly, during table dances. Many inexperienced dancers pay little attention to costuming and wear only revealing lingerie or a bathing suit that can be easily removed. Such dancers, however, quickly find that such strategies are less successful financially and lead to fewer table dances and tips. For more experienced dancers, costuming can become more elaborate and involve creating the bare outlines of a "fantasy" character.[19] That character can then become the object of talk between a dancer and a customer leading up to, during, or after a particular table dance and can contribute to a deeper back story that dancers tell customers about why they chose their costuming, what their "interests" are, or how they became strippers. Examples of thematic costumes include a "college coed" wearing a football jersey and athletic shorts with local university logos on them or a "biker chick," wearing leather, chains, and spike-heeled knee boots and dancing to heavy metal music. At Tigress North, one dancer became well known for her "witch theme" because she dressed in a black cape and cobwebbed stockings and danced to 1970s pop songs with the words *witch* and *magic* in their refrains (e.g., Santana's "Black Magic Woman" and the Eagles' "Witchy Woman"). For many customers, their first impression of a dancer occurs during a stage show when she showcases her costuming, body, and "moves." Consider this excerpt from our observations of Billy Jo, an experienced dancer at Seductions:

Billy Jo begins the first of her two stage dances in her "farmer's daughter" costume—blonde hair in pigtails, a sheer, plaid, unbuttoned shirt revealing her breasts, and a pair of short, cutoff blue jeans. During the first song, a country western tune mixed with a loud, pulsating backbeat and alternating colored stage lights, she takes her hair out of the pigtails and flips it around so that part of her hair seductively covers her face. She then begins a series of pelvic thrusts punctuated with the removal of her shirt and the sucking of her right index finger, which she then uses to beckon customers to the front of the stage. She finishes the dance with a "bow to the crowd" in which she turns her back to the audience and bends over so that one can see her butt peeking out from underneath her shorts while she winks and smiles to the audience over her left shoulder. During the second song, Billy Jo slowly "shimmies" off her shorts to reveal a G-string thong and a red garter belt worn on her upper thigh. She then drops to the stage and begins slowly writhing on her back as she caresses her breasts and runs her hands over her butt and legs. Both dances draw smiling men to the stage waving one- and five-dollar bills in their hands. Every so often, she pauses long enough to invite a man to slip a bill in her garter belt or G-string, sometimes cupping her breasts in her hands while receiving the bill. As the music ends and the DJ calls for applause, Billy Jo exits the rear of the stage through a hallway that leads to the barroom floor. As she walks into the barroom—now clad in her unbuttoned shirt and G-string—she receives small patches of applause and hoots from nearby customers. She is all smiles and winks as she makes her way to a table where four men are gesturing for her to come over.

What this excerpt underscores is Billy Jo's attention to the consistency of her moves with her farmer's daughter costume—a bit "innocent" (as suggested by the pigtails) and a bit "shy" (as signaled by the "bow to the crowd"). And she embeds these moves in explicit sexual signaling, including pelvic thrusts, body caresses, and finger sucking. As the sequence above suggests, dancers showcase themselves via stage shows in relatively short periods of time, usually no longer than four to six minutes. For most dancers, the stage show, as one dancer put it, "whets the appetite" of the customer and is the first component of a much longer period of "working" the tables that can last up to an hour prior to a break. As a dancer exits the stage, she hopes to experience customers motioning her over to a table just as Billy Jo did. If she doesn't generate immediate interest, she will begin walking to tables that do not already have dancers at them and asking customers if they would like a dance. If a customer declines, she will typically smile and say something like "I'll check with you later" or "I'll give you a chance to settle in. Look for me later." Some dancers who are not immediately motioned over to a table after a stage show will sometimes sit down with customers and begin talking with them about a variety of "nonthreatening" topics, including the characters projected by their costuming. It is in these interactions that face-to-face emotional labor occurs.

Face-to-Face Emotional Labor before, during, and after Table Dances
Perhaps most striking about face-to-face emotional labor just before a table dance is the subtlety of nonverbal cues, such as winks, smiles, or enthusiastic nods by dancers in the direction of customers, amidst explicit sexuality. One could imagine that such subtlety would be lost on a man who is watching a near-naked woman walk toward him, but dancers report that these lead-in cues are key to quickly establishing a sense of connection to the customer in advance of verbal communication. As one dancer put it, "Most of these men in here [at Tigress South] want us to do more than

be sexy. You have to make them feel special, like you have a special little relationship with them." Those dancers who climb to the highest tipping brackets (earning $300–500 per night) mention the sexiness of their dancing as one of the *least* important elements of their success. As one dancer put it, "Sure, you gotta do the tits and ass stuff, but if you're not friendly, smile, make eye contact, they're not going to buy into the act and give you the money." A house mother from Erotica noted, "We like sweet girls here. You can always tell the ones who will be most successful. They understand how to make a man feel good about himself." Indeed, the best dancers (in terms of generating revenues) create, *with* customers, a context for customers to believe, if only for a moment, that there is some relational bond, however fleeting, between themselves and the customer.

If a customer has been properly "primed" for a dance, either from seeing the dancer's stage show or from watching her perform at neighboring tables, the dance will begin almost immediately upon the dancer's arrival to a table. If not, a dancer may talk for two or three conversational turns about her costume, about the customer's "attractive" physical appearance, or about any topic that inevitably leads around to a dancer asking the customer if he "would like a dance." Once a customer responds affirmatively, the dancer quotes him the minimum tip for a dance but may interject what a bigger tip can buy without getting too specific. Lines such as "It's $5 to start, honey, but for a guy like *you,* a little more gets *you* a lot more [emphasis by the informant]" typically draw hearty laughs about what "a lot more" means. Such lines also draw responses in kind from customers, such as "Well, for *you,* honey, I would spend more [emphasis by the informant]." Here, we begin to see the emotional labor of the dancer draw responses from the customer that help sustain the definition of the situation as involving not only a pay-per-view financial exchange but also a momentary relational connection between the dancer and her customer. Once a customer agrees to purchase a dance, it begins. Here's an example of a midpriced dance (about $20) performed at Tigress South:

> Randi—clad in a black G-string and a black, unbuttoned leather vest with a large Harley Davidson insignia on the back—is sitting at a table with three other men. The four laugh and converse about where they're from, where she got her "leathers" (i.e., her black "biker" vest), and what she likes about riding on a motorcycle. Although all three men participate in the interchange, Randi has clearly zeroed in on one of the men by scooting her chair close to his. When he talks, she leans toward him as if to listen and then laughs (appropriately) in response to various

comments he makes. After ninety seconds (it seems longer due to the intensity of the social interaction), Randi asks the customer nearest to her if he wants a dance. He agrees to buy one from her and spreads his legs apart, resting his hands on his thighs. Randi rises from her chair, slips out of her vest, and times the beginning of her dance to coincide with the beginning of a song to which a dancer is performing on the nearby main stage. Randi moves to a position between the customer's legs and, just before going into her routine, leans over to whisper something to him, cupping her hands around his ear. He smiles in response to her whisper. As she kneels in front of him, she moves her face and then her breasts close to his crotch. She begins grinding her hips as she moves up and down his body, never touching him. Occasionally, she caresses her upper body and breasts with her hands. He sits motionless, without much expression, transfixed until the song has nearly ended. Just before the song ends, she rubs her breasts slightly against his inner thigh and he moves his fingers to lightly touch one of her hips as she slithers by. The song ends with Randi in a kneeling position looking up at the customer with what can only be described as an adoring smile, bright eyes, and her arms gently resting on the tops of his legs. He quickly fumbles in his pocket and pulls out a twenty-dollar bill, which he bends over to place in her G-string. After receiving the bill, Randi looks in the direction of the other two men at the table and asks them if they want a dance. They decline. She smiles and, as she walks off, sweetly says, "I'll be back by here later. Will you be here?"

This episode displays multiple elements that illustrate how emotional labor, enacted by a very experienced dancer, unfolds during and after table dances to relationally color these interactions. In less than two minutes, Randi initiated a conversation among three men at a table by playing off her costume as a biker chick and asking the men where they "hailed" from. She nonverbally focused on one man at the table to whom she eventually sold a dance by moving closer to him and listening intently to his comments. Both of these cues communicated that *she* was interested in *him*, which in turn "primed" him to pay for a dance. Her "special touch" was the whisper right before the dance, which clearly provoked a positive response from the customer as indicated by his smile. The intent, as one dancer who engages in similar actions notes, is to make the man "feel as if he is the only one in the room you [the dancer] care about; tell him something like 'This is going to be a very special one [dance]' because of the way you [the dancer] feel about him [the customer]." The whisper move draws the man in close to the dancer, and for just a moment he and she metaphorically constitute an intimate island in a sea of booming back-beats, pulsating lights, and a multitude of tables with naked women in various stages of their routines.

Another important element to note in this sequence is the "know-how" exhibited by the customer's interaction with Randi before, during, and after a dance. Some of this knowledge is formally codified with posted rules about "not touching" dancers or "impeding" entertainment on or off the stages and with formal encouragements from the DJ to demonstrate one's "appreciation" to dancers for their "efforts." The public visibility of table dancing in the barroom means that tacit knowledge (e.g., spreading one's legs and sitting back passively) can be quickly gleaned by watching men at other tables who have bought table dances. With Randi, the customer made small talk as he might with a woman at a non–strip bar context in whom he was "interested." As soon as he agreed to buy the table dance, he sat back with his legs spread apart and allowed her "to do her thing." Although this customer appeared to "know what to do" in this interaction, some dancers report that they ask the customer to "sit back and relax and let [them] do the work." After the interaction, the customer quickly tipped Randi. Here again, some dancers have to remind the customer what is expected at the conclusion of a dance.

Randi's dance unfolded in rather straightforward sexual terms, with the usual stock grinds and self-caresses. It did, however, include one physical contact between herself and a customer. This is officially forbidden in all the clubs, but many experienced dancers we talked with considered slight touch between themselves and those for whom they danced essential for relationally (rather than sexually) "finishing" off a dance. Although touch can be slightly titillating for the customer, the more salient aspect of it, according to dancers, is that it communicates to the customer that they willing to "bend the rules" for customers with whom they have established a special "tie."

Finally, Randi's dance illustrates stereotypical definitions of male-female role relations that dancers strategically enact through a variety of tactics. During the conversation, for example, Randi asked questions of the four men and answered questions about herself but never made the interaction about herself. Instead, she fulfilled the "fantasy woman" role of a woman who is interested in what "her" man says and finds him funny. As one dancer put it, "You get *them* [customers] to feel that they're the center of the universe. You get *them* to think that they're funny, interesting, whatever. But you never expect anything in return—except, of course, money [emphasis by the informant]!" Randi's nonverbal positions during the dance also symbolically enacted these stereotypical role relations. For example, she began the dance on her knees so that she could look up at the customer and capped it off on her knees, this time looking back over her shoulder with a wide, adoring smile.

Exiting Table Dances

Aside from the emotional labor used to create a sense of connection between themselves and customers, dancers must create contexts in which they can leave their fleeting relations with customers in ways that reduce the potential for social tension and trouble. As illustrated in Randi's table dance above, the conclusions to songs provide natural opportunities for dancers to pick up and leave. At the same time, however, several intense moments directly precede exit during which dancers work hard to create a sense of relational connection with a customer. What a dancer does not want to do, according to one house mother we spoke with, is "to completely break the spell and leave the guy feeling as though she walked out on him." This concern may seem overblown because of the illusory nature of the relational connections during table dances. Moreover, a hallmark of fleeting relationships in other public contexts is relative ease of entry and exit from social interaction.[20] In strip clubs, however, transitory social relations are laden with other cultural elements that can create trouble for dancers and customers, especially stereotypical cultural definitions of male-female relationships and the underlying dynamic of financial exchange. Because dancers play off the role relation of "men-as-providers" and "women-as-receivers," men can develop a sense of exclusivity with regard to dancers. What this means, from one experienced dancer's perspective, is that the dancer has perhaps been "too good" at giving an impression of being relationally interested in a customer. For most customers, such feelings are only momentary and are usually appeased by dancers with stock lines that leave open future possibilities for more dances. The same lines— "I'll check back with you later" or "Will you be around here later?"— used in conjunction with winks and smiles to exit from an interaction with a customer who does not want a dance are also used to frame an exit from a fleeting relationship in order to move on to a different table. According to one customer we spoke with about this strategy, "You can tell a dancer who really cares about the people she dances with. She enjoys interacting with them and wants to do it again." Most customers we watched and interacted with, however, plainly recognized the fictive nature of the fleeting relationship between themselves and a dancer and did not want to "make waves" or "embarrass" themselves by appearing too "into" the dancer after a lap dance.

Nonetheless, trouble with regard to exit occasionally arises when men, as one dancer put it, come to believe that they "own you [a dancer]" or become too "emotionally invested." Of course, this orientation creates no problems if the customer continues to pay for table dances. Some dancers told tales of big spenders who spent several hundred dollars of tips on them through the course of a long night. The problems arise when a customer wants to retain exclusive "rights" to a dancer without continuing to pay, goes beyond the minimal touching that most (if not all) experienced dancers allow customers to engage in, or attempts to cross the boundaries of public sociality by badgering a dancer to, as one dancer put it, "go out with him on a romantic date" or engage in sex with him either on or off site. Exit from these situations is less graceful and can involve an abrupt, brisk walk away from a table to the sanctuary of the dancers' dressing room or moving closer to where security personnel and managers stand near the bars. Dancers, however, minimize removing themselves from the table-to-table flow of dancers because this interrupts their table-to-table rounds, thus reducing their opportunities to generate revenue. Exit strategies that enable dancers to move from table to table without constraint are far more common. It is to these interactional dynamics that we now turn.

Patterns of Exchange among Dancers and Customers

Until now, our ethnographic gaze in strip clubs has consisted of narrow-angle views of individual stage performances or dyadic interaction at table dances. We gain a different perspective on the "action," so to speak, by expanding our gaze to a wide-angle view. The excerpt below represents such a view on a weekend night in the barroom at Gates of Pleasure:

> From our vantage point near the back of the barroom, we count four dozen tables with nearly 150 men seated at them in various combinations. The front row of tables nearest to the main stage contains several men, each sitting alone: "pervert row," in one dancer's words. These men sit close to the stage for most of the night, impassively gazing at dancer after dancer on stage. They rarely buy a table dance, rarely tip a dancer on stage, and slowly sip their drinks. Behind pervert row is a second set of tables, each of which contains groups of six to ten men. This is the row of bachelor parties, college fraternity functions, and groups of colleagues partying together. Behind these tables lies yet another row that contains men sitting in smaller groups of two to four

individuals. We occupy the last row that has a few groups and singles. Amidst this seating architecture, there is a continuous flow of dancers from the stage (via the back hallway) to the barroom floor. Once on the floor, they move from table to table like bees slowly flying from flower to flower. Some move faster than others. Some stop and sit before moving on, while others talk to customers as they slowly, almost languidly, stroll through the barroom in search of customers who want to buy table dances. Very few dancers visit pervert row, while a few "light" for extended periods of time with one of the groups seated just behind pervert row. These tables are the most active, with one or two men typically the focal objects of table dances by solo or paired dancers. At these tables, the other men watch and shout encouragement. A few dancers service their "regulars" who are sitting toward the back of the barroom near us. Some of these interactions last a half hour or more. The dancer sits and converses with a solo customer, periodically rising to do a table dance for him and receive her tip, and eventually exiting with stock lines that create a vague sense of hoped-for future interaction.

As the scene above underscores, dancer motility is highly fluid in the barroom. Because most dancers have a "hit rate" of four tables contacted for every one that buys a table dance, they need to continuously circulate among tables and customers to remain financially viable during the course of a night. As dancers hone their skills at emotional labor and exiting from particular interactions with individual customers, they also develop skills at "working the room." As one dancer observed, working the room involves recognizing what ultimately leads to financial success: "This business is all about gettin' the man to pay. . . . Look, I'm sweet to them 'cause they're giving me money [for a dance]. If I ain't gettin' money . . . , I gotta move on to the next table. Girls [dancers] have to learn how to move around the room to get customers who wanna pay for dances."

Dancers develop various strategies for generating such volume, which we gleaned both from our interviews and observations. One of these is "scanning," the constant surveillance of possible opportunities for table dances. Although the lighting makes it difficult to scan while performing on stage, some dancers are able to scan while table dancing (even as they appear to be focused on the man for whom they are dancing). Most dancers scan during their constant tours of the barroom in between stage performances. Another strategy involves a more purposive search for particular types of men who are likely to buy table dances. One type is the "party man," a member of a group that has come to celebrate a special occasion. These men, according to one dancer, "come to spend money, so they might as well spend some on me." Another type is the "lonely heart" who, as one dancer articulated it, "has something missing in his life." These men typically sit alone, slightly slumped over, heads bowed (except for an occasional glance at a dancer as she walks by or dances on stage). They nurse their drinks and do not sit near the main stages, preferring instead to be out of the mainstream of the barroom. Some dancers risk volume for "working" a lonely heart in the hopes of generating several dances and tips from a single table.

Out of these dynamics develops a system of competition among dancers to find "good bets" among customers to buy table dances. As one dancer noted, "All the girls want to find guys who will pay [tip]. The girls [dancers] who do the best aren't always the ones with the killer bods or the sexiest moves. They know how to find guys who will pay and get there before another girl does." Undergirding competition among dancers is an informal normative system organized around a simple rule that new dancers quickly learn and older dancers assiduously follow: never offer a dance at a table that another dancer is already working unless explicitly invited to do so by a dancer or a customer. There is also informal coordination and exchange among dancers. Some dancers, for example, will team up for a "twosome" table dance for well-paying solo customers or groups (e.g., bachelor parties). Other dancers occasionally help their colleagues by pointing out a customer who wants a dance but whom they cannot service because they are already involved with another table.

Because dancers constantly float from table to table looking for tips, they rarely become dependent upon a single customer for their revenues. Some dancers, as the excerpt above illustrates, develop regular customers who may ask for them on a consistent basis. But such relationships are in the minority compared to fleeting ties that develop with "one-shot" or single-night customers. As a result, most dancers escape the "power dependence"[21] that can develop when actors can obtain a valued resource only from one other actor. In this sense, both dancers and customers can exit their exchanges and typically engage alternative exchange partners. To be sure, customers can withhold tips and thus ultimately exercise power over a dancer's financial success. Dancers can also withhold particular moves or emotional labor cues as a signal of what one dancer called a "protest" against a man who offers small tips. Moreover, slow nights can limit the number of exchange partners available to dancers. On busy nights, in contrast, customers outnumber dancers by as much as ten to one, which becomes a source of asymmetrical social power for dancers as they pick and choose those customers they believe will yield the best tips. Ironically, then, as dancers symbolically enact stereotypical subordinate roles in their table dances with men, they also enact and experience local social power as a result of the pattern of exchange relations in table dances.[22]

A more subtle aspect of the structure of exchange among dancers and customers involves the "valences" of their exchange relations. At an abstract level, in "negatively" connected structures, exchange in one relation decreases exchange in another. In "positively" connected structures, by contrast, exchange in one relation increases exchange in another.[23] The pattern of exchange relations among dancers and customers is decidedly positive. A successful table dance by one dancer, in which men are visibly "having a good time" or are "turned on," typically leads to other dancers enjoying similar successes at other tables. One possible explanation for this pattern comes from the "attention hypothesis" developed in interactionist-feminist studies of stripping. This hypothesis plays off stereotypical definitions of male-female role relations and the quasi-public nature of strip bars, in which most activities are visible to others in the club. The argument is that men enjoy being seen by other men as desirable, which is symbolized by their being attended to by a dancer playing the role of the sexy, caring woman. Visible table dances act as contagions that constantly diffuse through the barroom with more and more men wanting similar treatment from dancers, as well as desiring their experience to be witnessed by others. In turn, the attention hypothesis and dancer-dancer competition combine to feed into the overall success of strip clubs, which, as we noted earlier, generate their revenues from alcohol sales and cover charges. A floor manager implicitly supported this perspective when he stated, "We want all the girls out there doing their thing so that everybody gets involved and everybody sees everyone else having a good time. That keeps people coming back to the club, paying the girls [for table dances], and buying drinks." In the end, then, the enactment of local social power by dancers through their emotional labor and patterns of exchange ironically helps to reproduce the broader system of female subordination in contemporary society.

CONCLUSION AND IMPLICATIONS

This chapter addressed dancer-customer social interactions in strip bars at the individual, dyadic, and group levels of analysis. Against the backdrop of the quasi-public context of the strip club, dancers use costuming to set the scene for the emotional labor they engage in during table dances. While on stage, dancers begin their emotional labor as they mix explicitly sexual moves with nonverbal cues that correspond with their particular fantasy character. During table dances, they use emotional labor as they cultivate fictive fleeting relations with customers. Aside from the emotional labor itself, dancers develop skills at exiting table dances without provoking social tensions with customers. At the group level, the motility of dancers through the barroom in search of customers who will buy table dances creates a dynamic structure of social exchange relations. This structure of exchange includes competition among dancers for "tipping" tables, normative rules, and some forms of cooperation among dancers. As dancers fulfill male fantasies that play off and reproduce stereotypical patriarchal conceptions of male-female role relations, the structure of exchange offers alternative exchange partners and thus sources of social power for both dancers and customers. On crowded weekend nights, dancers can convert their exchange opportunities into social power by picking and choosing customers they believe will tip the best while avoiding "cheap" tippers. Finally, the quasi-public nature of the barroom ensures that table dancing is highly visible to most customers, which in turn facilitates the demand for table dancing and creates positive patterns of exchange relations among dancers and customers. Aside from these findings, our work suggests implications for four areas of research: quasi-public places in urban settings and the changing nature of public visibility of table dancing in strip clubs, social power and control in strip clubs, transitory social relationships and the social embeddedness of economic exchange, and the importance of studying personal relationships in marginalized contexts.

Our ethnography of five strip clubs portrayed them as quasi-public spaces similar to other kinds of retail contexts that one can find in any urban setting. Of course, strip clubs differ from most retail contexts in that their focal activities revolve around explicit sexuality that involves watching naked women's bodies framed by patriarchally charged emotional labor. The visibility of table dancing, however, ultimately provides limited local social power to dancers as they work. During the past few years, however, private rooms and alcoves (sometimes called "VIP" lounges) in which table dancing can occur out of sight of the main barroom areas have become increasingly common in many strip bars. Such lounges first appeared in only the highest-end "gentlemen clubs," some of which are owned by corporations that control a wide variety of sex-work enterprises.[24] Access to lounges is controlled by dancers working closely with club personnel. If the space in strip clubs becomes increasingly privatized in the sense that social interactions among dancers and customers becomes less visible to broad social audiences on the barroom, then the limited exchanged-based local power that dancers enjoy in clubs organized similarly to the ones we studied could diminish.[25] Indeed, one might speculate that "private" lounges are, in part, a strategy by clubs to reduce the social power and autonomy that dancers wield on the barroom floor, at the same time increasing clubs' formal control over interactions between dancers and customers. Moreover, lounges provide opportunities for clubs that want to engage in illegal activities on their premises, such as prostitution or drug sales, and keep them hidden from public audiences. We urge future research on stripping to examine changes in the balance of private and public space in strip clubs with an eye toward social power.

Our research also carries implications for the study of social relationships and economic transactions. As early as the 1950s, Gregory Stone observed how clerks drew customers back to their retail stores by treating them in a "personal, relatively intimate manner".[26] More recently, economic sociologists—echoing earlier arguments by the historian Karl Polanyi—argued that economic exchange is "embedded" in social relationships that both constrain and enable markets of all kinds.[27] Our study suggests another way that economic exchange plays off social embeddedness through fictive fleeting relationships. Emotional labor in all retail contexts embeds economic transactions in fleeting social relationships, thereby creating a sense that there are other motivations at work in any particular social interaction other than hard-edged exchange. Fleeting relationships between dancers and customers in strip bars are not as dissimilar as one might initially believe from the fleeting relationships established by flight attendants, waiters, or other retail and service workers to sell goods and services. Fleeting ties, like more durable social relations, should be added to the economic sociology research agenda. An important question along these lines might be: What are effects of fleeting relationships on economic transactions for one-shot and repeat exchanges?

Another implication suggested by our chapter addresses another aspect of our previous point regarding social embeddedness. As relationship researchers continue to explore the various ways that "context"—including cultural definitions, social networks, racial and gender hierarchies, and social institutions—affects personal relationships, we suggest that they explicitly add economic transactions to their agenda, particularly as they begin to mine how personal relationships unfold in public settings.

Economic transactions can certainly be socially embedded, as we suggest above. Economic transactions can also be the occasion for starting or ending personal relationships. Future research should address how economic transactions constrain and enable personal relationships of various sorts, paying particular attention to the often blurred and negotiated boundaries between "purely" economic and social relationships.

Finally, this chapter underscores the need for conducting research on public sociality and personal relationships of all kinds in marginalized settings. Such settings, by dint of their social position relative to mainstream society, present particular challenges to those who attempt to conduct personal relationships in them. Urban ethnographers, for example, have long chronicled the difficulties with which homeless people, those engaged in illegal activities, and low-income Anglo and minority families struggle to maintain meaningful relationships under the harshest social conditions imaginable.[28] Other researchers have focused on the effects of being gay and lesbian on the maintenance of long-term personal relationships.[29] These works strongly suggest that socially marginalized conditions profoundly shape the vulnerability of personal relationships to dissolution, at the same time providing important building blocks of social integration, meaning, and personal identity. Our research has addressed one aspect of fleeting relationships in a setting where dancers face multiple challenges: specifically their work in an occupation stigmatized by large portions of society and their engagement in behaviors that feed into a male-dominated commercial and sexual social system. While our chapter has not investigated the stresses and strains that these conditions create for durable intra- and intergender personal relationships, or investigated the relationships among the dancers themselves, we hope future research can address these issues. Particularly important along these lines would be investigations of how different forms of marginality—that is, marginality based on ethnicity, religion, class, gender, or normative difference—affect the emergence and maintenance of personal relationships. Only by expanding the contexts and places in which we study personal relationships will we be able to examine the broad ways that close ties of all kinds emerge, take shape, and operate.

METHODOLOGICAL PROCEDURES AND REFLECTIONS

During our fieldwork, we visited field sites together or alone, spending nearly eighty hours in them. Our visits to the clubs varied by time and weekday but concentrated in busier periods on Thursday, Friday, and

Saturday nights. We supplemented our observations with conversational interviews with several dancers and semistructured interviews with ten dancers (drawing at least one dancer from each site).

At each location, we paid our cover fee and made our way to a table to begin observing. As long as we ordered drinks, no one questioned our presence or purpose.[30] Our observations first took a "wide-angle" perspective as we become accustomed to the "scenes" at each club. As particular themes emerged in our research (see the next paragraph below), we focused on the interactions between dancers and customers during table dances and the movement of dancers between tables. Like previous researchers on stripping, we found most dancers willing to talk with us as they took breaks between stage or table performances.[31] When we approached dancers, we informed them of our interests as researchers and assured them of the confidentiality of their responses. By contrast, customers proved largely off limits to us, first because men were unwilling to talk to us as we attempted to make conversation with them and second because of formal restrictions imposed upon us by some club managers. In a couple of instances, dancers approached management to tell them of our attempts to talk with customers, which resulted in a floor supervisor asking us not to "disrupt" the audience. Their concern, as we later learned, turned on the possibility that we might disrupt the flow of cash from customers because our conversations would distract them from buying dances and drinks.[32] As a result, we confined our data collection on customers to observations and a few overheard conversations (although the booming music in the clubs made eavesdropping quite difficult). Conversational and semistructured interviews targeted much of the same information regarding dancers' backgrounds and work experiences, dancers' perspectives of customers, the strategies dancers used to effectively present themselves to customers and "work the room," and the reasons they chose stripping as an occupation. Interviews also provided opportunities for us to "check" our interpretations with dancers, which in some cases caused us to rethink how we were conceiving of some behaviors we witnessed in the clubs.

Both authors took field "jottings" during or immediately following observations and interviews with dancers, which we later typed as field notes with initial analytic ideas and methodological asides (e.g., about accessing customers). Early in the fieldwork, we began to treat our field notes as an emergent, holistic "data set" by reading and rereading our earliest notes—line by line—in relation to later sets of notes and interviews. By doing this, we constructed patterns and themes that cut across field sites and types of data. We then used these emergent themes to guide our later observations and interviews. After several weeks in the field, we also began writing short analytic memos that selected examples from the notes to illustrate emerging themes and to link conceptually to relevant literatures on the sociology of erotic dancing, sex work, exchange, and public sociality. As a result, our data collection, coding, and writing processes were in dialogue with one another and various literatures as we developed the grounding for our "ethnographic story" of dancers and customers.[33] We also brought very different experiences and assumptions about strip bars that initially influenced our fieldwork and interpretations as we made sense of our field data.

Joseph Massey

I had been to strip bars before we set out to systematically study relationships in them, so I felt I knew something about strip bar activity beforehand. This knowledge was useful in that I knew generally what to expect, but I do believe it colored my thinking about some of the issues we studied. This is where my research partnership with Trina proved useful because she had virtually no experience with the strip club world and frequently raised questions about taken-for-granted assumptions concerning dancers and customers. Ultimately, Trina and I agreed on the interpretations we formed about most of our observations, but it was still useful to me, and, I believe, to the research we produced, to talk about our different expectations, anxieties, and experiences in the club. Indeed, it was the opportunity to talk to a person who had experienced the same field setting at the same time as I had—a team member—that was most beneficial during the research process and write-up.

Let me give you an example of one of the ways our conversations benefited the research we produced. Going into the research, I was sure of one thing: dancers were the ones with the power in interactions with customers. They literally "made" men pay for whatever they did and, in so doing, controlled the situation. Trina entered the field with a very different view based on her general sense of strip bars as exploitative sex work (which it is) and her generalized knowledge of deviant occupations from the criminology and the sociology of deviance literatures. Our first set of conversations—really more arguments—set up the limited social power of dancers as something of a hypothesis to be confirmed or disconfirmed by our observations. Once Trina began to engage in direct observation of strip bars, she began to see ironic aspects of what we ultimately called the local social power of dancers. Our discussions then turned completely away from the exploitation thesis to the patterns of social exchange and social power between dancers and customers. Ironically, I began to notice some of the more exploitative aspects of the clubs and began to wonder whether we had swung too far toward the micro. What was the relationship between what was going on in the bars and the larger social cultural and social environment? This is where we began to talk about how to blend our senses of the different levels of analysis both within the bar (what we called the individual, dyadic, and group levels) with the broader cultural definitions of stereotypical male-female role relations.

Trina L. Hope

Like all the contributors to this volume, I started and completed most of the research for this chapter as a graduate student. Also like many of my female (and a few of my male) colleagues in graduate school, I was (and still am) quite a feminist. I'd always found the idea of women dancing half-naked for lust-crazed men very disturbing. (As I write this, I realize that my choice of adjectives—"half-naked" and "lust-crazed"—reflects my sense of strip bars as exploitative on several different dimensions.) At the same time, I'd never actually been in a strip bar and was academically interested in deviant behaviors/occupations. It seemed like an interesting setting both to test my strongly held "exploitation" hypothesis about what "really" happened to women in strip bars as they encountered men and to find out something about a stigmatized setting.

When I originally approached Calvin Morrill and David Snow about my idea (within the context of their qualitative field methods course), they weren't too sure how it would turn out, but they agreed to let me proceed on the condition that I find a male research partner for both perspective and safety. On the one hand, I was glad they were concerned about my welfare. Another part of me felt that their concern was a bit overblown, perhaps a bit too paternal with just a dash of patriarchy thrown in—the girl needs a chaperon to study the nudie bar. The first male graduate student I asked to work with me was eager to join in (perhaps a bit too eager in retrospect) but told me the next day that his wife wouldn't let him do the project. Joseph's wife, however, was a bit more understanding, so I had my male research partner. As Joseph mentioned in his reflections, I went into the bars expecting to be outraged at such a bastion of oppressive patriarchy. I still believe the existence of strip bars (and the fact that women can earn more taking off their clothes than they can teaching school) is linked to societal subordination of women in American society. But as Joseph says, in the bars themselves, especially in social interaction with customers, dancers exercise social power. How they exercise that power and how their local power ironically helps to reproduce their social subordination in the broader society became our chief concerns.

As I think back on it, pairing a man who had been in strip bars before with a woman who had not turned out to be fortuitous because it brought to the surface (via our conversations) many of the preconceived biases we held. Joseph had the eyes of someone experienced, while I saw everything for the first time (including my own feminist beliefs subjected to empirical inspection). Meanwhile, Joseph had his analytic and social consciousness expanded. Long after I had bought into the local power theme, he began to bring up broader concerns about exploitation of dancers and women's subordination. At times, I felt as though our roles and perspectives had been reversed.

Two things most surprised me. First, I was surprised by how little attention my presence (as a woman) received and the way dancers approached their work. We saw only two other women in the bars who were not dancers or waitresses, and, unlike other female researchers in strip bars who have drawn attention from customers, I felt invisible most of the time.[34] In fact, one night I was sitting alone at a table (Joseph was talking to someone at the bar), and one of the dancers came up behind me and asked me if I wanted a table dance. As I turned around to answer her, she realized I was a woman and her eyes widened, her mouth dropped opened a bit, and she immediately apologized. I told her I wasn't really in the mood for a table dance, but I'd love an interview. Unfortunately, I think she was too embarrassed at mistaking me for a man, so she hurried away.

I was also surprised at how practical the dancers were with regard to their jobs. They had no illusions about the work, themselves, or the customers. I found it a fascinating reversal of traditional gender roles. Here was a place where women were rational, calculating, and only interested in making money in order to generate the most "exchange relations" they could with customers. Yet, as we detail in our chapter, they did so by enacting stereotypical subordinate gender roles during their fleeting relationships with men. Many of the customers, meanwhile, acted in what seemed to me to be very irrational ways—spending hundreds of dollars to buy table dances in the hopes of buying a little fleeting intimacy and a close-up look (maybe a little feel) of a naked woman. I left the strip bar not worrying about the women but feeling the same thing many of the dancers felt for the men—a mixture of pity and disgust. For me, what used to be an exotic and somewhat intriguing setting is now mundane and uninteresting. I think all women should visit their local strip bar: it's really quite enlightening!

PART TWO

Anchored Relationships

FIVE

Hanging Out among Teenagers

Resistance, Gender, and Personal Relationships

TYLER R. HARRISON AND SUSAN E. MORGAN

IT IS EARLY SATURDAY EVENING, and small groups of teenagers chat as they lounge in the booths at Burger World. Burger World evokes a vaguely nostalgic 1950s malt-shop image. Neon stripes and 45 RPM records decorate the walls, punctuated by movie posters of James Dean, Marilyn Monroe, and Rock Hudson. On the sidewalk outside Burger World, four teens—two boys and two girls—casually talk. All of the group wear much the same style of clothes as the teens inside Burger World, including dark-colored baggy T-shirts that reach nearly to their knees and baggy jeans slung low around their hips. One of the girls in the group sneaks up behind a boy and pulls his underwear up as high as she can, shouting, "Wedgie! Wedgie!" He grimaces and begins chasing her down the sidewalk, laughing. He catches her and puts her into a playful headlock. The two wrestlers grapple and cackle on the small lawn outside the restaurant until they let go of each other and run into Burger World, where they begin chasing each other by rapidly walking between various tables and booths. After a minute or two, the girl spies two friends, who greet her, and she plops down in a booth to talk. Her pursuer gives up the chase as well, sitting down at another booth crowded with teenagers. Another guy joins that booth, slapping high-fives and greeting everyone sitting there.

This scene illustrates what many teens at Burger World call "hanging out," "kicking back," or simply "chillin'." From an adult perspective, teens often appear to be "doing nothing" as they hang out.[1] As we observed it, hanging out often occurs in a variety of public contexts, including city sidewalks and fast-food restaurants. Although teens can hang out by themselves, it is more common to do so in an informal group. From a teen perspective, hanging out involves a variety of social activities, especially talking, eating, and various kinds of play-fighting. Other activities, such as watching television, smoking cigarettes, drinking alcohol, taking drugs, or engaging in sex, can accompany hanging out, but they are ancillary to the casual interpersonal interaction that is primary to hanging out. Rarely is there a concrete goal articulated by teens who are "hangin'."

The topic of hanging out among teens closely aligns with a reemerging interest among social scientists in youth culture that departs from strict concerns with developmental issues on the one hand and gangs on the other. The developmental literature focuses on the ways in which youths "develop" into adults by internalizing adult mores and roles. In this perspective, youth culture is an imperfect version of adult culture, which adolescents must grow out of as they learn the roles and normative expectations that will transform them into "functioning" adults.[2] The gang literature paints youths as more active than the traditional developmental view but concentrates on understanding how hanging out provides contexts for youth deviance and crime[3] or, less often, how hanging out unintentionally reproduces adult class differences among youths.[4] Contemporary work on youth culture picks up where the youth culture literature in the 1960s and 1970s[5] left off by analyzing how youths actively participate in developing their own interactional competence, emotional expressions, and cognitive constructs through daily peer interaction, even as they navigate and resist adult authority of all kinds.[6] This perspective views youth and adult culture as somewhat bounded, somewhat permeable contexts that are mutually influenced by each other. Because of the disparities in social power and control inherent in these influence processes, however, youths constantly must carve out cultural, social, and physical spaces for themselves in the larger adult culture.[7] Our chapter aligns closely with these latter strains of work by concentrating on everyday aspects of hanging out.

We conceptualize hanging out as an interaction order that simultaneously reflects and resists aspects of adult interaction orders. Within their interaction orders, youths manage personal relationships that are "anchored" primarily in the social and physical contexts in which they hang out. At the same time, the public places where youths hang out are often officially designed for other purposes and defined in part by various forms of regulation that impinge upon youths' activities. Our work therefore confronts the interactional processes by which youths suspend, in Erving Goffman's terms, the "deference" and "demeanor" they express toward adults and, by implication, rebel against adult authority more broadly.[8] Finally, our research considers issues related to the influence of sex differences on interpersonal interaction among youths.

In this chapter, we explore these themes as they unfold in a variety of public and quasi-public places to which teens typically have access, such as fast-food restaurants, shopping malls, bus stations, and sidewalks. We focus on the ecology of public teen hangouts, especially the regulatory nature of the places in which teens hang out and the relationships they conduct while in public. We conclude with implications for understanding hanging out as "everyday resistance" and relate these ideas to the stereotypical sex differences we observed in teens' relational interaction.

THE ECOLOGY OF PUBLIC TEEN HANGOUTS

We conducted our fieldwork over an eight-month period during 1996–97 in Southwest City, a rapidly growing urban area of approximately three-quarters of a million residents.[9] Initial forays into the field ultimately led us to develop an "ecology of teen hangouts" across the city's main geographical areas.

Teen public hangouts in Southwest City comprise three types of sites that have different levels of formal social regulation: (1) *unrestrictive public places* (to which any teen has access: e.g., sidewalks, street corners, deserted parking lots in business areas after hours, open-air city plazas), (2) *marginally restrictive public places* (to which almost any teen has access but that have various municipal restrictions in terms of how long teens can stay continuously at the site: e.g., bus stops, bus kiosks, city parks), and (3) *restrictive (quasi) public places* (to which any teen with a generalized status as a "customer" or "student" has access: e.g., fast-food restaurants, football games, all-ages dances). We derived this typology from our own observations and informal interviews with youths who explicitly make distinctions of places with respect to the "hassles" of hanging out.[10]

Southwest City's primary geographical areas consist of "Downtown," "Northside," and "Southside." Again, this typology was derived from youth experiences with these regions and our own knowledge (from personal experience and fieldwork) of each region. Downtown is generally known as a "mixed-use" space, containing a preponderance of office buildings, public works, vacant buildings, and a various retail establishments. It attracts teens from all social and cultural backgrounds and contains a high density of unrestrictive public places where teens congregate. The "Downtown Celebration," a street fair held twice monthly, proved to be an especially rich context for observing and interactions with teens. Northside is known as one of the wealthiest areas in town, boasting mainly single-family dwellings and expensive condominiums, golf clubs, and upscale shopping centers. It contains a few fast-food restaurants and unrestricted places (such as dry riverbeds and washes) at which middle-class teens typically hang out. Southside is known as the least wealthy part of town. It is separated by the rest of the city by a series of rail yards and factories. It contains fast-food restaurants and unrestricted places that attract youths from lower-income and poor families. Northside contains fewer restrictive places than either Downtown or Southside due to having fewer fast-food restaurants and more open space along river beds and between houses or on the margins of golf courses. Moreover, Downtown and Southside displayed a greater police presence than Northside, which meant that youth who did carve out an unrestrictive place to hang out in were on the constant lookout for the authorities.

REGULATION, RESISTANCE, AND RELATIONSHIPS WHILE HANGING OUT

Regulation and Resistance

To teenagers, the differences between the regulation of public places becomes readily apparent as soon as they start to hang out. At the Downtown bus plaza (an unrestrictive place), for example, teens can meet and sit for long stretches of time. On most nights, no one bothers teens hanging out until nearly midnight, when an officer from the local police department may decide to enforce the city teen curfew and disperse anyone at the station who looks "under age." During the Downtown Celebration (a biweekly street fair), the density of teens increases at the bus plaza, and they fill nearby streets with small conversation groups. Jill commented on the Downtown Celebration: "You can find all kinds of people down there to hang with on those [Downtown Celebration] nights and just kick back without getting too hassled."

By contrast, restrictive public places, such as fast-food joints, present far more challenges for teens wishing to hang out. The activities we described at the outset of this chapter seem harmless enough, although to workers, managers, and adult diners at Burger World they are annoying and require intervention. Consider this excerpt from our field notes taken at another restrictive public place:

> Since three p.m., a group of a dozen or so Anglo and Latino teens (most female) have been sitting in the Downtown Wienerburger's main eating area. A few minutes before five p.m., a middle-aged Latina worker appears with a broom in the doorway to the back kitchen. She has been watching the group for some time from behind the service counter. She says in a firm, loud voice, "You all have to leave now! You've been here long enough!" No one moves, but some complain loudly in reply: "We just got here, man!" "We bought something!" (with a drink or food item held aloft as "evidence"). Faced with the group yelling at her nearly in unison, the worker retreats back to the kitchen, only to reappear in a few minutes with her broom and dustpan to begin cleaning up cigarette butts left by the teens on the floor. She sweeps close to the edge of the wall that borders the dining area, occasionally brushing quite close to the teens still lounging on the restaurant's tables and chairs. She says loudly again, "You all have to leave now! You can't sit here for two hours!" No one moves toward the exit, but many begin to argue with her about whether they will leave or not. One boy reads the time off a receipt he picked up off the floor a few minutes earlier. The time on it "proves," he shouts, that the teens have only been at the restaurant for fifteen minutes. Some teens again hold up sodas and others yell that they "bought" something when they arrived. The worker listens stone-faced and again retreats toward the kitchen. She hesitates and points to another group of teens sitting at the tables, angrily spitting out these words: "They hadn't bought nothin'."

This incident illustrates the rhythm of authority and overt teen resistance in restrictive public hangouts. At restrictive hangouts, the process takes on a ritual-like nature as it unfolds. A small group, perhaps three to five, begins hanging out. They are joined by friends until a group of ten to twelve is firmly established. After the group forms, perhaps forty-five minutes to an hour lapses until workers and managers begin staring at the group and perhaps talking in hushed tones behind the counter among themselves, occasionally looking over their shoulders at the group. These behaviors usually precede a retreat to the kitchen and then verbal attempts to disperse the teens, provoking verbal ripostes by teens and exaggerated allusions to the conventional demeanor of a customer ("We bought something, man!").

Restrictive places that are regular teen hangouts also have various sorts of signage intended to limit teen access. Signs at the entrance restrict hanging out during school hours or to a particular time period (e.g., one hour after purchasing something). Although we never witnessed it, teens also believed that restrictive places (particularly fast-food restaurants) had thresholds, the crossing of which would trigger the intervention of police. The trigger for police action, so Mitch (a key informant) argued, typically involved direct "intimidation of customers or workers," damaging physical aspects of the restaurant (e.g., chairs, tables), or "fighting that got way out of control." Teens also claim that if a fast-food place becomes a regular teen hangout, the threshold can lower, making the likelihood of police intervention higher on any given day. In marginally restrictive places, all of these processes existed in more muted forms and were typically temporally bound. For example, security officers or police officers would "sweep" the shopping mall in advance of closing time, dispersing various teens who were hanging out. The interstate bus station would make teens (along with homeless people) leave if they looked like they might stay the night on a bus bench.

Aside from overt resistance, there is a more subtle side to teen resistance that manipulates and colors the normative boundaries of a restrictive hangout. Jill (another key informant) explains:

> You can nurse a soda for a long time or put some leftover food from someone else so you can, um, say that you bought something or whatever. If the workers are nice to you, you could even help clean up the mess that the other people left. When you been there for a while, you could leave and then come back. The people workin' have to treat you like a new customer so they can't hassle you even if they recognize you from before. You can also act like you just didn't know stuff because you're kid, you know what I mean?

All of these actions occur simultaneously during the full participation of each teen in the informal conversations, teasing, and play-fighting that constitute the core of hanging out. At an analytic level, these strategies combine Goffman's observations about how mental patients conform to the official normative order of total institutions, all the while creating alternative arrangements that enable them to survive the oppression of the asylum.[11] Like inmates, teens subvert formal authority by ritualistically conforming to it, yet creating and maintaining an alternative normative order within hanging out that they themselves control. At the same time, they reflect Gary Alan Fine's assertions about how teens occupy a liminal social terrain between being children and adults and are thus able to access repertoires of everyday knowledge and accounts for their behaviors from both social worlds.[12]

When teens are forced to leave a regular hangout, they simply go someplace else to hang out. In other instances, the group will disband until the next opportunity to hang out arises. Some forced removals, moreover, engender more resentment than others. Teens resent being removed from an unrestrictive place (e.g., the Downtown open-air bus plaza or a street corner) more than they do being asked to leave a restrictive place. This difference relates to the tacit assumptions built into the ritual-like precision of resisting authority while hanging out in restrictive public places. In such contexts, the rules of the game are familiar to both teens and official authorities (i.e., workers, but not necessarily other adults or teens unfamiliar with the place). As Mitch explained:

> It's kind of a game [in restrictive places]. . . . Yeah, we're [my friends] cool with it. I mean [the police and employees] are dicks, but I guess we have to leave. What really pisses us off is when a dick [an adult in authority] decides to hassle us even though anyone can be hanging out where we are. Like in a park or in the desert. Like they act like we don't belong anywhere except at home, school, or work.

In unrestrictive places the rules of the game permit hanging out, and teens resent it when rules that seem more appropriate for a restrictive place are applied to hanging out in an unrestrictive place. An element of normative "pollution" thus occurs in instances when teens view the application of rules from restrictive places as "spoiling" the normative order of unrestrictive places.[13]

Despite the regulation teens can encounter in public places, they face far more potential for regulation in private places, such as their homes, classrooms, or workplaces. At the same time, most teens have limited resources in terms of places available for hanging out, money, and time, which means their options can be limited. This is why hangouts are often close to high schools or major transportation lines. Street corners, bus stations and stops, open spaces (such as the sides of riverbeds or lakes), fast-food restaurants, and malls are popular for these reasons. The more restrictive the place, the harder it is to carve out the social space to hang out.

We also witnessed more encounters between police and teens in Downtown or Southside than in Northside, which may be a function of the greater density of fast-food restaurants and the higher profile of police patrols in the former two regions. Moreover, we observed far more calls to the police or attempts to disperse youth in Southside and Downtown restrictive public places than in similar settings in Northside.

The Importance of Personal Relationships While Hanging Out

As teens engage in overt and covert resistance to regulation in their public hangouts, they conduct their personal relationships. A common way of defining a personal relationship in the scholarly literature turns on the deepening of emotional commitment and an increasing behavioral and/or cognitive interdependence between individuals over time.[14] The teens we spoke with agreed with this general sense of personal relationships, describing their "relationships" with peers (they typically did not include the "personal" qualifier) in terms of the emotional, cognitive, material, and behavioral consequences for their lives. So influential are these consequences that personal relationships while hanging out constitute the center of the universe for many of teens we talked with and observed. On any given day in the field, we observed teens gossiping, debating, planning, decrying, and worrying about various aspects of their personal relationships with peers. And many of the relational activities teens recounted and engaged in occurred within the social spaces they created in public places. In this way, such hangouts become safe places (relative to other contexts) for teens to constitute and explore relational interaction and interpersonal competence away from the regulation of their families, schools, and workplaces.

As mentioned previously, the personal relationships developed by teens while hanging out largely remain anchored to that social space and focus on activities accomplished while hanging out. Moreover, such relationships are conducted largely on the public stage, so casual observers outside a teen group can watch. Because hanging out is typically a group activity, teens conduct much of their personal relationships in small gatherings embedded in larger groups. In larger groups, these smaller gatherings appear quite fluid as they form, break apart, and reform on a continual basis during a stretch of hanging out (reminiscent, in some primordial sense, of adult cocktail parties). This dynamic means that much of the interpersonal competence that teens develop while hanging out in public places has a self-conscious performance quality to it. Teens are keenly aware of how they and others "are doing" in a group, both during a particular gathering and over time. Of particular importance is the management of same- and opposite-sex relationships, which is not surprising given the uncertainty and curiosity many teens experience as they explore their own and others' gender identities during adolescence.[15] It is to these issues that we now turn, first for same-sex and then for opposite-sex relationships.

Same-Sex Relationships

Although both boys and girls in our study talk about same- and opposite-sex relationships, girls do so more often and more explicitly than boys, often directly talking about which girls in their groups are friendly or "upset" with another. Jill commented, "With a girl, you can talk about how you feel, you know, express your feelings." Boys talk about relationships between themselves and others as well but do so in somewhat oblique ways, commenting, for example on who is "riding shotgun" next to whom (i.e., who sits next to the driver of a car on the passenger side; nearly always a privileged position indicative of a relational tie). Occasionally, boys speak very directly about their relationship with another boy, usually referring to the other as a "friend" or "someone I hang out with."

Both boys and girls experience and construct much of their emotional dynamics through very different types of physical actions toward one another. As Jack Katz argues, such processes are "corporeal" in the sense that they occur via the body rather than wholly through discourse.[16] At a Downtown high school football game, for example, we observed seven girls sitting in front of us who were talking among themselves in pairs and as a larger group. They were seated away from the football game, not paying it much attention. As they talked with each other, they often leaned toward one another, occasionally brushing each other's bodies, and engaged in a great deal of touching of each other's shoulders, arms, and torsos with their hands. Two girls in particular paid a great deal of attention to each other, with one stroking the other's hair as she spoke with another girl in the group. These kinds of behaviors were common among girls across the field sites we studied. Girls commonly hugged each other or did various "dance moves" together (often bumping hips or arms) to celebrate the successes of members of their group at video games or when interacting with boys.

The boys we observed would express their personal relationships through very different sorts of physical actions, including various kinds of play-fighting and other informal contests. A central theme in much of the physical contact among boys was one's reputation for being "tough" and "cool," which is a consistent theme found among boys in urban public places.[17] For example, at football games and on a street corner where we were regular visitors, we observed boys routinely "high-fiving" each other until recipients grimaced in pain and did not want to continue the exchanges. Ultimately, one boy would emerge who had bested all of the others, signaling his winning by raising his hands high over his head. Yet Mitch explained that such physicality is not always about the informal pecking order among boys; sometimes it expresses pure sociality:

> Guys do all kinds of stuff when they know each other: Some guys fight each other because they're having fun and they know each other. Head buttin', slamming chests, or whooping where you run around all crazy stomping the ground and over whatever is there [e.g., outdoor benches or trash cans], making a racket until you get tired and you just collapse. Sometimes it matters who wins. Sometimes it doesn't. Sometimes it's just guys having fun who like each other and just hanging out with each other. Girls talk or hug; we [boys] fight.

Here Mitch underscores the sociality of activities that from afar might appear to be violence and coercion in the conventional sense of the terms. Moreover, he underscores the gender differences we observed between boys and girls with respect to discursive and corporeal emotional expression.[18]

Opposite-Sex Relationships

The play-fighting and physical bravado characteristic of same-sex male relationships sometimes carries over to male-female relational interaction. At a Northside high school football game, we watched a group of teens engage in various forms of play-fighting as they hung out on a grassy hill at the far side of the football field away from the crowd. Boys feigned punches or slaps toward girls, while girls lightly hit the boys if the latter made contact with them. We observed one pair play-fight for quite a while until the boy lightly hit the girl in the face. She and another girl gasped loudly as she began to rain light blows on his shoulders, back, and stomach. He curled up in a ball on the ground laughing as he tried to block the blows. Later on, he chased her in the area where the two were hanging out with other teens. On occasion, we also observed girls resisting the play-fighting of boys or behaving aggressively toward boys themselves. One such incident occurred when Jill quit play-fighting with boys on a Southside street to berate them for their actions and to correct them for not having taken her seriously when she had talked to them earlier about an upcoming public event in Downtown. We noted with interest the response by the boys in this situation. With raised eyebrows, they either ignored Jill or walked away from her to another group of teens nearby. Jill explained,

> I don't take shit from nobody, male or female. But if it comes to it, I can fight the boys. With girls, you can talk about what you're feeling or fight, but with boys, you have to just fight. They [boys] get freaked out if they're fighting a girl, but that's what you have to do.

We also observed relationships that indicated deeper emotional attachments than those typically conducted while hanging out. At Wienerburger, for example, boys and girls would sometimes pair up on one side of a table with their arms around each other, occasionally kissing while the other members of their group milled around or talked on an opposite bench. After a few minutes, the couple would separate and join conversations with other teens in the group. As we questioned various teens about this pattern, we learned that boys and girls in romantic relationships often continue to hang out well into the time they are a couple. Mitch explained some of these dynamics in an interview with both authors:

MITCH: Like my girlfriend, she's best friends with Brandon so she hangs out with us . . . the three of us are always together. And then the rest of them [other people who hang out with them] I don't know, if they're out . . . we'll just meet them somewhere. . . .

TYLER: So do you ever go on dates with your girlfriend, just you and she?

MITCH: No, not really, we have like maybe once or twice.

TYLER: Is it just hard because of driving and stuff?

MITCH: No, she drives, we just don't, I don't know.

SUSAN: Do you ever go to dances?

MITCH: Well, we've gone a couple of times . . . not like the two of us individually, like a group of us.

SUSAN: Do you hang out with your other [male] friends and their girlfriends?

MITCH: Pretty much.

SUSAN: Do you like that or would you rather just hang out with your girlfriend alone?

MITCH: No, it's cool, 'cuz I'm usually friends with them too.

Personal relationships among the teens we studied, then, are as much anchored in other individuals as they are in the informal groups with whom teens hang out. We do not mean to imply that teens never differentiate themselves from the groups with whom they hang out. We observed multiple instances where teens opted out of group interaction by citing other activities with another peer. For teens who routinely hang out in public, however, such differentiation is not a social priority in their lives. The priority is to maintain ties to the group with whom they regularly hang out. Publicly anchored relationships of this type can also facilitate the management of competing loyalties among teens. Anchored personal relationships provide an opportunity to explore how romantic relationships and friendship can be managed together.[19] By integrating romantic relationships into the group and anchoring them in public places, teens are able to develop competencies in romantic relationships while sustaining their ties to other people.

DISCUSSION AND IMPLICATIONS

As our observations and illustrations suggest, hanging out involves far more than "doing nothing." As teens overtly and covertly resist regulation, they learn about how formal authority functions and how to subvert it. They also learn how to construct and maintain interaction orders in places that they have appropriated for hanging out. Our fieldwork also details stereotypical sex differences in verbal and nonverbal relational interaction among teens as they hang out. Girls talk more directly about their relational connections to those they hang out with and nonverbally often engage in various forms of physical touching with their same-sex peers. Boys, by contrast, resort to relational metaphors or speak in offhand ways about relational interaction with their friends and often engage in physical contests of dominance with other boys. The same bravado that emerges in boys' same-sex interaction also emerges in opposite-sex interaction. Finally, teens who regularly hang out become as attached to the group as to any individual in it. These findings provide the context to discuss theoretical implications related to resistance to everyday routines and the prevalence of stereotypical sex differences among the teens we studied.

The places where teens hang out have established interaction orders to them. People typically come to fast-food restaurants, for example, to buy food, perhaps consume it on the premises, and then leave. Most people on sidewalks and in bus stops attend to their business and move on. Where they hang out, teens suspend the typical demeanor and activities expected of an individual in most public places. In this way, hanging out provides an "escape route"[20] or, perhaps more accurately, an "escape island" that suspends the routines of everyday life with which adults map their personal lives. When youths directly confront adults while hanging out, the lack of deference by youths briefly compromises part of what it means to be an adult (i.e., to expect deference from youths). As Goffman noted, "When a [person] fails to receive anticipated acts of deference, [that person] may feel that the state of affairs which he has been taking for granted has become unstable."[21] This may explain why adults become especially annoyed when teens hang out in public places not designed for such activities. Hanging out disrupts the basic sense of status and order in adult lives. (At the same time, some adults look back nostalgically at the "fun" of hanging out, perhaps suggesting a hint of boredom in their everyday lives.) Hanging out is about relational interaction for the moment; there is no plan, no collective goal except the protection of an existential space where the hangout can be constructed and sustained.

The irony of this seemingly romantic paean to hanging out is that much of the resistance to everyday authority enacted by teens takes on a ritual character that all of the principals involved can predict fairly accurately. Even more ironic, although some relational interaction among teens is about pure sociality (as underscored by Mitch's comments about some of the fighting among boys), much of it conforms to stereotypical gendered routines in which boys favor dominance and autonomy while girls favor care and connection.[22] Resistance to adult interaction order thus falls on its own sword. While teens are busy resisting the everyday rituals and routines of public places, they enact gendered routines that they will reproduce as adults. Our findings on sex differences also are consistent with other research on stereotypical behavior in adolescent relational interaction.[23] Why might this be? Why do teens exhibit such stereotypical sex differences in their relational interaction while hanging out? One explanation could be derived from psychologist Carol Gilligan and linguist Deborah Tannen, who argue that sex differences in relational and other forms of interaction result from primary socialization into different "gender cultures."[24] Such cultures tend to develop early in childhood via sex segregation and are particularly strong during adolescence. Although primary socialization can be modified in adulthood, proponents of the gender-cultural perspective argue that it continues to exert enormous influence over men and women through their life spans. Unexplained in these arguments is why particular behaviors are associated with men and women in the first place.[25] Gender-culture proponents either provide little response to this question or imply that sex differences are deeply embedded in the nature of society and the biological substrata of males and females.

A more relevant explanation for the gendered routines we observed could derive from the primary themes of relational interaction between boys and girls and the public nature of the places where they hang out. We observed that the dominance and play-fighting among boys in same-sex interaction carried over to opposite-sex interaction, such that boys tended to enact the same dominance games with girls as they did with other boys. In this way, the stereotypical sex differences we observed can be viewed as "rehearsals" for the strategies boys will use as men to maintain interactional power over women in their personal relationships, which is consistent with findings from other contexts involving young adults.[26] But what does the public context of place have to do with these relational dynamics? Again, we note the tenuous nature of hanging out. Teens are always mindful of the potential collapse of the social spaces they create to hang out in, especially within public places that are explicitly designed for particular purposes (e.g., fast-food restaurants, retail stores). Such tenuousness creates enormous ambiguities for all teens, but particularly for boys in opposite-sex relational interaction as they simultaneously participate in struggles to maintain control over their hangouts vis-à-vis external regulation and attempt to maintain control of girls within their hangouts. Couple these situational ambiguities with the developmental ambiguities associated with adolescence relevant to the continual exploration of personal identity and sexuality more generally, and the conditions are ripe for boys to pervasively use shorthand gender stereotypes (taken from a variety of sources available in popular and adult cultures) to guide their relational interaction with girls.[27] Moreover, these explanations fit with atypical interaction we observed in which girls (such as Jill) turned the tables on boys and aggressively addressed them. In these instances, boys typically responded to girls by ignoring or avoiding them. In effect, these instances violated boys' expectations about girls and rendered useless their typical ways of dealing with girls.

A final implication of our research pertains to the broader contexts in which youth hang out, specifically spatial class contexts in Southwest City. As we noted earlier, our ecological mapping of the city's regions ultimately revealed how public places available for youth to hang out in varied. The tonier Northside contained fewer restrictive places and less likelihood of youth being rousted from unrestrictive places by the occasional police visitation. In Southside and Downtown, by contrast, youth were constantly wary of the increased police presence (even though police did not target them with great frequency). In this way, the conduct of anchored personal relationships among youth is both shaped and shapes the broader sociospatial contexts in which they are embedded.

In sum, our research reveals hanging out to be a rich context in which to study the ways teens negotiate adult interaction orders attached to public places and construct their own alternative orders yet reproduce stereotypical gendered routines in their personal relationships. At the most general level, our research argues for an approach to adolescent relational interaction that pays serious attention to the processes by which youths construct their personal relationships in contexts of regulation and resistance, as well as the conditions under which gendered routines constitute personal relationships among youths.[28]

METHODOLOGICAL PROCEDURES AND REFLECTIONS

Using the ecological scheme outlined earlier in this chapter to structure our fieldwork, we focused our fieldwork on eleven sites, five restrictive public places (a fast-food restaurant in each area and Downtown and Northside high school events, respectively), two marginally restrictive public places (the interstate Downtown bus station and a large shopping mall straddling the boundary between Downtown and Northside), and four unrestrictive public places (a Northside dry riverbed, a Downtown street site, a Southside street site, and the Downtown open-air bus plaza). Aside from distributing our fieldwork across these sites, we visited the same sites at different times (either solo or as a team) to capture temporal and activity variation.

After a few months in the field, we still found it difficult to visually identify the social class of teens on the basis of their appearance unless we interviewed them.[29] We obtained some clues as to their regional origin due to their ethnicities. Youth from Southside were more likely to be of Mexican descent (and Spanish speaking) than those from Northside. Downtown contained a wide range of ethnicities. Whatever their gender or ethnicity, most of the teens we interacted with adopted the same baggy style described in the vignette that opened this chapter. More importantly, we found few differences in the basic activities that composed hanging out in public across areas of the city, regardless of the region. Wherever teens publicly hung out, they tended to engage in similar behaviors organized around casual interaction. Moreover, we came to understand that personal relationships, whether shallow or deep, constituted the core of "hanging out" for the teens we studied.

We observed and talked with a total of fifty teens during our fieldwork. In our initial visits to the field, we talked with any teen who would talk with us. We would generally tell a teen that we were from the local university and were interested in what teens do when they hang out. The public access to most of the sites we studied created a great deal of social fluidity such that most teens simply accepted us at face value. Thereafter, we talked with those with whom we enjoyed rapport. We developed close relationships with two informants—Mitch from Northside and Jill from Southside, who also frequented Downtown—on whom we came to rely for in-depth commentary on the hangouts we studied. We selected both of these informants because they had a wide range of contacts at our research sites and appeared to know a great deal about the teen "culture" of hanging out. Nonetheless, we carefully used the information they provided, cross-checking its validity with other informants as much as possible. We also tape-recorded four formal interviews with these informants.

Many teens ultimately accepted us as a part of the "scene," although most responded unfavorably to direct questions about their backgrounds or their activities. Some even became suspicious when we asked them where they lived in the city, for fear that we might be "undercover cops" ready to "bust" them. Most of the verbal data we collected, therefore, derived from a technique called "interviewing by comment," through which the interviewer substitutes direct questioning for indirect comments that elicit information from informants.[30] We used comments intended to demonstrate puzzlement ("I'm not from around here; I wonder what they're doing"), humor ("He looks like a pig trying to smoke that cigar"), and moral outrage ("I can't believe the Burger World manager kicked you out!"). Once we established rapport with several teens, we collected a great deal of information via eavesdropping on conversations with teens while they were hanging out. We employed many of these same techniques with the fast-food restaurant employees, police officers, high school officials, and bus drivers with whom we talked about teens and hanging out.

Our data consisted of field jottings from our conversational interviews and observations and the tape-recorded interviews. In most field situations, one of us periodically excused him- or herself to steal off to a private place to make a few notes. The fluidity of the settings again facilitated these opportunities. At the end of each day in the field, we elaborated our field jottings into full-length field notes, which later became the basis for our analysis.[31]

We first organized our data in categories composed of specific field sites (e.g., restaurant, bus stop, sidewalk), reactions between youths and formal authorities (e.g., restaurant managers, police), and youth interaction among themselves. As the fieldwork progressed and our theoretical interests sharpened, we developed the ecology of places described earlier and linked our initial categories to substantive concerns in relevant literatures on adolescent behavior and regulation and resistance. The illustrations used in the chapter elaborate these themes and represent typical situations and dynamics we observed while hanging out with teens.

Although we were hardly "old" by "adult" standards while we were doing this research (our mid- to late twenties), we were certainly far older than the teenagers we studied. Even so, we often felt out of place and highly conspicuous. We tried to diminish these feelings of awkwardness by reducing the number and magnitude of our differences with those we studied as much as possible. We did this through dress (T-shirts and jeans, no skirts or jackets), by manner (always casual, although we are sure we often appeared overeager to talk to the teens around us), and even by adopting some of the habits and mannerisms of the groups around us. This sometimes led us to do some foolish things that accomplished exactly the opposite effect from what we intended. For example, one night we found ourselves at a Downtown Celebration hanging out at the bus plaza with nothing to do but watch, when we suddenly felt a desperate need to "do something" with our hands. We bought a pack of cigarettes and even though neither of us smoke, we awkwardly (and with more than a couple of coughing fits) smoked the whole pack in a couple of hours. We felt especially sheepish when Jill began making fun of the "yuppie kids" in another school district who pretended to smoke like the "cool" kids did. We felt like the "posers" Jill made fun of and had a sudden anxiety attack. Was she really talking about us? Could she see through us? Was she fronting us about everything she told us about hanging out?

Our anxieties and senses of being strangers to teenage culture ran deeper than what to do with our hands while we watched street life Downtown. We found it discomfiting to be confronted with the fact that no matter how familiar being a teenager seemed to us, teenagers still viewed us as the "other"—as adults, and as part of much of what they overtly or covertly resisted on a daily basis as they hung out in public places. We were adults, and for the first time we were on the wrong side of the divide between youth and adulthood. Even when the behaviors of teens described made us want to run and tell their parents or, at the very least, offer a lecture on the dangers of, say, drug and alcohol abuse or unprotected sex, we worked hard to give the impression of been nonjudgmental lest we betray the informant's confidentiality and trust in us. As we wrestled with the ethical dilemmas these situations posed for us, we consulted with two of the editors of this book to make sure that we did not knowingly stand by as a teenager self-destructed. Fortunately, we can assure the reader that at this writing the teen we most worried about has done extremely well during the years since we completed the fieldwork for this chapter.

As we think back on our research, we ask ourselves how we will treat our own teenage children in the future when they hang out with their peers. Should we fear hanging out as the "devil having work for idle hands" and as a context in which sex-difference stereotypes are rehearsed for adult life? Or should we embrace hanging out as a social space of autonomy carved out by teens as they make their way in the world? Perhaps what we have learned through our fieldwork is that we will have to live with the tensions and contradictions of hanging out, much as teenagers live with the tensions and contradictions of growing up.

SIX

Everyone Gets to Participate

Floating Community in an Amateur Softball League

ALLISON MUNCH

IN HIS BEST-SELLING BOOK *Bowling Alone,* Robert Putnam argued that "at the conclusion of the twentieth century, ordinary Americans shared a sense of civic malaise" as they experienced a pervasive weakening of community.[1] His voice joined a chorus of scholars and pundits who have decried the state of Western community for the past two centuries.[2] Putnam argues that "the collapse and revival of American community" (the subtitle of his book) depends upon the waxing and waning of "social capital." Unlike material capital (such as trains, shovels, and computers), financial capital (money), or human capital (individual skills and capacities), social capital is constituted by interpersonal relationships arrayed in social networks.[3] Social capital provides valuable social and economic resources, as well as moral restraint, for individuals and carries aggregated effects for groups and societies. Healthy communities, according to Putnam, are webs of social capital that "entail mutual obligation and responsibility for action."[4]

Chief among Putnam's concerns are indicators of individual-level participation in various civic domains; for it is participation, through face-to-face interaction, that builds patterns of reciprocity, trust, and mutual obligation. During the 1990s, Putnam found declining rates of participation in political associations and forums, local institutions (such as neighborhood clubs, unions, professional societies, and PTAs), philanthropic/volunteer activities, and informal ties outside the household. Whatever the public or quasi-public activity, Americans, it seems, are "doing" less and "observing" more. In effect, Americans are becoming passive spectators rather than engaging in activities themselves. Nowhere is this more evident, Putnam argues, than in sports spectatorship. He notes, for example, that all major professional sports (baseball, basketball, football, hockey, and stock-car racing) experienced steep growth curves in per capita attendance that outstripped population growth in the last forty years. If one includes television and radio audiences, the growth of spectating over this period is even greater. From a social capital perspective, Putnam claims that sports spectatorship is not a "dead loss." Sitting with friends to root on a professional or amateur team can certainly foster sociality. But he repeatedly argues that sports spectating—by definition, watching games played by others—is more passive with regard to building community than actually playing the games with others.[5]

This chapter offers a modest caveat to Putnam's claims by investigating an *active* community among a sports audience who followed the "Astros," an amateur men's softball team in Southwest City.[6] In the audience I observed, the vast majority of spectators enjoyed family ties with one or more players but began each season with fewer bridging connections among themselves (and across families). Over the course of a season, ties between Astros fans (either previously known or unknown to one another) strengthened and, by midseason, took on characteristics associated with primary relationships typically found in private contexts. At the same time, these ties remained firmly *anchored* in a public place: that is, Astros spectators who were not in the same family had little contact with each other beyond the bleachers. By season's end, spectators formed a community organized around an ethic of mutual care. In this sense, *not* playing softball enabled fans to devote their social energies toward building meaningful personal relationships among themselves that ultimately resulted in community bonds in the bleachers.

In the section that follows, I discuss analytic leads for characterizing community and the social processes that constitute them. I then turn my attention to the site where I studied softball spectators. I unfold my findings temporally by discussing the integration of new spectators into social relationships among long-time fans, then focusing on the dynamics of personal relationships among fans, and finally presenting some of the collective properties of the Astros spectator community. My chapter concludes with implications for studying personal relationships in public places and the contemporary variability in community.

In his study of sports spectators, Allen Guttman argues that sport was once considered to be a "civilizing process" in Western culture through which players and spectators learned the values of fair play, cooperation, and self-sacrifice.[7] He further notes that over the course of the last century conduct at sporting events—especially professional events—became increasingly *un*sporting. Taunting, drunkenness, hooliganism, and full-scale riots have, in places, become the order of the day.[8] In addition to its "deviant" tendencies, one could argue that much of mundane sports spectating approximates what Lyn Lofland calls the "public realm," in which sociality is dominated by stranger-stranger interaction.[9] That is, a great deal of social interaction in everyday sports spectating involves brief, impersonal encounters or fleeting relations among strangers in which actors share limited segments of themselves.[10] Like brief encounters on subways or city streets, such interactions hardly suggest the sorts of conditions likely to foster networks of mutual obligation in Putnam's social capital depiction of community.

The barriers for creating community among spectators become even higher if one moves beyond Putnam's characterizations to embrace a less individualistic, more holistic perspective. For example, Robert Edgerton argues that community is "a collectivity of people who feel personal involvement and intimacy for one another, who share a moral and emotional commitment not only to one another but to their way of life, and whose way of life exhibits social cohesion and continuity over time."[11] In this definition, Edgerton picks up strands of Putnam's approach by identifying the personal relations that constitute the social structures of community. He also introduces elements that are less emphasized or ignored in the Putnam scheme, such as the idea of community as a collectivity, which, in turn, suggests more than webs of social capital. Communities, in this view, ultimately involve groups, collective identities (a sense of "we-ness"), and moral boundaries that both define appropriate expectations regarding community members' behavior (i.e., a "way of life") and differentiate members from nonmembers.[12] Moreover, Edgerton emphasizes temporal and affective elements in his definition of community, which deepens the social ties that bind people to the collectivity.[13]

In light of Guttman's observations about contemporary sports spectating and the implicit challenges put forth by Putnam, Lofland, and Edgerton, an argument linking contemporary sports spectating with community may seem especially untenable. Spectating at local, amateur sporting events, however, may be qualitatively different from watching professional events. Local amateur settings may indeed produce commitment, mutual care, emotional intimacy, and moral boundaries (the primary elements of Edgerton's community) among spectators. For example, Gary Alan Fine argues that Little League baseball games are attended only by those who are *emotionally committed* to the game and its players: "I was an unrecognized adult, a stranger whose presence did not "make sense" within the established community of parents. There is 'no reason' for outsiders to be present, as Little League is defined as an activity that does not have sufficient intrinsic interest to warrant the attention of anyone not emotionally committed to attend."[14] Indeed, a key difference between professional (or even many high school and intercollegiate) and local, amateur sports spectating may lie in their stakes. Local, amateur sports—such as park leagues and most youth leagues—are less a means to a material end than an end in themselves. That is, few people can gain wealth or fame by playing or directing such teams. I do not want to romanticize amateur leagues as the perfect context in which competition without stakes occurs. Such leagues can carry enormous stakes in terms of winning and losing on the local level, personal reputations, and self-esteem, as some of the uglier incidents involving youth sports can attest. But these leagues come closer to the ideal of sport for sport's sake, as opposed to the business of sport. Attendance at games played at the local, amateur level may imply (as the quote from Fine underscores) a predisposition toward personal involvement with the players and perhaps among spectators themselves. As the density of such personal involvement increases (in Putnam's terms, as webs of social capital intensify), the likelihood of community in Edgerton's sense (a cohesive collectivity with moral boundaries) increases. It is a floating community, to be sure, as it does not exist in a neighborhood or residence but "floats" across times and locations, occasionally anchoring itself to particular public places—in this case, the bleachers during softball games.[15]

Nonetheless, community must be achieved interactionally if it is to exist at all, even if spectators come to local amateur games holding "good" feelings about what they are about to watch or whom they are about to interact with. How is this accomplished? How do spectators accomplish durable, anchored relationships, especially in public contexts, necessary to build a floating community in the bleachers? What is the relationship between the floating community among spectators and the game itself? How does knowledge of spectator communities contribute to our understanding of personal relations in public contexts?

My interest in these questions took me to the Southwest City Parks and Recreation men's fast-pitch softball league, where I gathered field data during the 1992 season.[16] The season extended from preseason games in the summer to the league's championship series in the early winter. Southwest City boasts nearly three hundred days of sunshine per year, and the city's amateur baseball leagues ("park leagues") have existed for decades. The adult city league softball program consists of 184 teams organized into a number of leagues by style of game and skill level. Each league's games occur in the evenings in one of twelve different city parks.

Two other factors bear mentioning about the players and the geographical location of the league. The players, like Southwest City itself, were nearly equally divided among "Anglos" and those of Mexican heritage. Some teams in the league were "Anglicized" or "Hispanicized" in that they contained players of only one ethnicity, but most were integrated in almost equal proportions. This fact introduced cultural diversity not only into the teams but also into the bleachers among the fans. With regard to the league's geographical context, pundits have often noted that the culture of baseball and softball spectating varies tremendously by geographical region. In northern regions, where baseball and softball are played only during the summer, spectating is more fervent and focused and more tied to the games themselves. In the American Southwest, the climate permits baseball throughout most of the year, so spectating unfolds at a more leisurely pace. Baseball writer Roger Angell follows up on these general impressions with his observations of a major league spring training game in the Southwest: "[Southwestern] baseball is slower, sweeter, and somehow better fixed in memory. For one thing, there seem to be more young children in attendance at the western parks: the stands are stuffed with babies and toddlers—or else I just notice them more. In Phoenix one afternoon, a small barefoot creature came slowly and gravely up the aisle behind the home dugout wearing nothing but a Pamper. Six- or seven-year-old home-team batboys are already veterans of two or three . . . seasons."[17]

All of the games took place on Tuesday and Thursday nights at a downtown park, which was old but well maintained. The park carried a reputation for being unsafe, and the city had stopped scheduling women's games there after a series of attacks on women and children in the park's restrooms and parking lot. Screams, sirens, and the rumble of helicopters frequently pierced the hot, dusty night air, and a thumping stereo bass was nearly incessant from cars parked in the nearby parking lot. A few hundred feet from the bleachers where the games took place, a constant stream of individuals sauntered into the park, casually conversed with those they found sitting on the grass or on a park bench, and then moved on. The atmosphere under the lights was warm and congenial. Children played under the bleachers, and some people sold home-baked goods. Transients chased foul balls for money or beer, while others just slept on the bleachers or talked to themselves.

Most of the Astros players were of Mexican descent and in their thirties, with a few players as young as twenty and one as old as sixty. Team members represented a wide variety of occupations, including a lawyer, a civil engineer, a police officer, a construction worker, a university graduate student, a high school coach, and an unemployed grocery stocker.

The bleachers at an Astros game could contain as few as a dozen and as many as one hundred spectators (for the late-season championship games). On most nights the crowd hovered around thirty (including children and adults). With the exception of girlfriends and close male friends, the vast majority of fans were players' family members, including parents, wives, siblings, nieces, cousins, and children. Some of the Astros had played together before, and consequently some of their wives, girlfriends, and children knew each other. However, new team members brought with them new spectators, most of whom did not know any of the preexisting Astros fans. As I came to know the fans, my observations concentrated on seventeen adults who regularly attended Astros games over the course of the season. These fans reflected the demographics of the team in terms of their ages and occupations, although they evinced more diversity with regard to ethnicity: of the seventeen fans, six identified themselves as Anglo.

FROM NEW FACES TO FLOATING COMMUNITY

In the sections that follow, I trace the creation of personal relationships and community among Astros fans over the course of a season. I start by discussing how social capital, in Putnam's sense, is constructed by the integration of "new faces" (fans new to the Astros bleachers) into relationships among "old-timers" (fans who know each other from previous seasons), which, in turn, initially result in "fleeting relationships"—social connections that evoke recognition and some level of emotional connection between people.[18] I then concentrate much of my attention on "anchored relationships"—personal relations that evince some aspects of a primary relationship in terms of their emotional interdependency, sharing of multiple aspects of the self, and temporal durability but that are tied to particular public contexts.[19] Finally, I discuss collective aspects of the Astros floating community by focusing on the fictive kin and home symbols they use to demarcate the moral boundaries of the group.

New Faces

At season's onset, new spectators largely conformed to the normative expectations for behavior in the public realm. A new spectator might greet other spectators upon arrival but would otherwise practice some semblance of "civil inattention"—head nods to indicate recognition and lack of threat, but then various tactics of physical and social distancing.[20] In the bleachers, for instance, new spectators generally sat within speaking distance (three or so feet from each other) but not so close as to be able to engage in verbal interaction without slightly raising their voices. New spectators with children typically required the children to sit nearby, which also created something of a physical and social boundary between small groups of spectators. In addition, new spectators did not typically share refreshments or blankets (for warmth as the summer turned to fall) with strangers. The following scene, which I observed early in the season while sitting with one of the old-timers, Mickie, illustrates this pattern:

> An Anglo woman with a young baby girl in a pram and a dark-skinned, dark-haired, Hispanic-looking boy arrive and sit on the opposite side of the aisle, but also down on the lowest bleachers. Mickie nods to the woman and briefly turns to me to comment how much the baby has grown since the last time she saw her but does not introduce me to the woman. The woman, who is dressed in jeans and a brightly colored T-shirt, sits quietly watching the game. The boy is talkative but sits in one place. The woman interacts with the boy as she watches the game and attends to the baby in the pram. The boy offers a sharp contrast to Danny [Mickie's own son] and his group of little boys, who are playing tag all over the bleachers. During the entire course of the game, I never saw this boy leave the side of the woman.

I later learned that the Anglo woman, call her Carol, was married to one of the Mexican American Astros players who had recently joined the team. Mickie had seen Carol at an earlier game and so had seen the baby once previously. All three—Carol, her son, and her baby daughter—were new faces from the perspective of old-timers. As such, it was common for Mickie, as an old-timer, to treat Carol as what might be called a "familiar" stranger—a stranger that one vaguely recognized but did not have a relationship with, such as someone at a bus stop or in a city plaza.

Fleeting Relationships

By the third week of the season, the divisions between new faces and old timers began to dissolve. One of the key elements in the dialogues that began this process was the tacit understanding among spectators that people in the stands were not there to watch the game per se but rather to support a player or players. Therefore, the first step in creating relationships among fans often turned on ascertaining the tie between a spectator and a player. Early in the season, for example, a fan asked me:

FAN: So are you Marc's [an Astros player] girlfriend?

ME: No, Warren's.

FAN: Warren? Who's Warren? What's his first name?

ME: That is his first name. His last name is Mills.

FAN: Warren Mills? That sounds like two last names to me. So are you a Mills?

ME: No.

FAN: Do you wanna be?

During the conversation, I began chuckling, as did a couple of other fans who were eavesdropping. Even though the conversation was painfully annoying, it proved fortuitous because it allowed another fan, Lucy, to begin to figure out who I was and thus ultimately provided the foundation for our interactions.

Initially halting and hesitant, a first conversation among spectators could become intimate in minutes. Undoubtedly, the game itself contributed to spectator sociality because its slow pace lent itself to easy sidebar interaction. While paying sufficient attention to the game, spectators could easily get wrapped up in their own conversations. For example, after Lucy and I figured out how each of us was connected to the team, we turned to a discussion of her recent vacation, aspects of her job, including how her boss annoyed her, and her benefits package. Over the course of watching the game, Lucy turned the discussion toward having another child:

LUCY: If we [she and her husband] get pregnant again, I hope I can still take disability leave.

ME: Are you guys thinking of having another child?

LUCY: We've been trying really hard. It took six years to conceive our first child, and we've been trying ever since our first child was a couple of years old.

Lucy went on to describe intimate details of the anxieties of fertility in between clapping for an occasional out recorded or good play performed on the softball field. Although Lucy and I did not sit next to each other every game, we always exchanged warm hellos upon arriving at a game and would often walk from where we were sitting to each other to talk a few minutes.

Anchored Relations among Spectators

Gradually, fleeting relationships could become more anchored, durable, and purposive. At first, the differences between fleeting and anchored relations among spectators could be somewhat blurred. Over time, such differences crystallized as the depth of people's interdependence increased. Here is an example of one such interaction in a relationship that began during the season and by midseason had become quite close:

A friend of Mickie's named Manuela showed up in the third inning of a game and sat between us with a slightly guilty smile (almost a grimace with the corners of her mouth slightly turned upward) sent my direction. The smile seemed to apologize for her sitting between Mickie and me and let me know that she "had" to talk with Mickie about something. Mickie and Manuela had met early in the season when Manuela's boyfriend joined the Astros. I overheard only bits and pieces of their conversation because they spoke in hushed tones, turning their bodies toward each other and slightly bowing their heads so that their voices would not carry. It was difficult to hear what they were saying even though I was only a couple of feet away. At one point, I heard them distinctly discuss intimate feelings in their "relationships" and how certain things that their husbands "did" made them feel.

From talking with both women and other spectators, I learned that they used the game as an opportunity to "talk privately" (although they were in a public place) about very personal matters. Both women felt quite secure using the game for this purpose because they could conduct their relationship while they supported their husbands, and they "trusted" the setting.

As relations between spectators developed, sharing not only of intimate feelings but also of other things, such as food, beverages, clothing, and referrals to various repair services, occurred on a regular basis. It is not surprising that as the nature of social exchange became more intimate, the items shared took on more personal meanings as well. For instance, on a particularly chilly evening I recorded the following social interaction:

> I approached Fidel, who is an older spectator and sometime player, to ask him if he would get me Warren's coat from the dugout. (Spectators are not allowed into the dugout during games.) Fidel graciously agreed to get me Warren's coat, but as he was getting up to walk to the dugout, he saw me slightly shudder, and turned around to offer me his own coat. He said, "This isn't Warren's coat. I'll get it if you want; my coat's probably warmer."

One could explain Fidel's actions as a straightforward function of which coat (his or Warren's) was warmer, but in reality both coats probably would have served. Another explanation might couch the interaction as a function of stereotypical gender relations in public. Feminist scholars have argued that publicly unaccompanied women are particularly accessible to men because of Western patriarchal cultural perspectives that paint women alone in public as incomplete without being attached to a man. Much of this accessibility can result in interpersonal hassling, but some of it can take the form of chivalrous impulses to "take care" of a woman who is perceived to be unable to secure a male companion or whose male companion is unavailable at the moment.[21] Perhaps my status as a "woman temporarily alone in public" did, in part, motivate Fidel. But he extended his care, as did many spectators, to men and women alike. Indeed, he took particular pride in attending to the needs of all the fans he sat near and would sometimes remind me and other spectators (young and old, male and female, Anglo and Mexican) to bring coats to the next game if the weather looked like it was going to turn "bad." On the basis of my overall understanding of personal relations among Astros fans, I interpret Fidel's actions as an exemplar of the collective expectations of the group—in a sense, what it meant to be an Astros fan.

Yet another aspect of the dynamics of the anchored relationships among Astros fans revolved around how spectators who were parents allowed their children to play as a group at the end of the bleachers. The children became a collective responsibility, safe and secure under the supervision of an increasingly interdependent collective of trusted adults. Here is an example I recorded about six weeks into the season:

> I arrived at one game early to be greeted by a player, Bobby, whom I had met just a few times, and his daughter, who was about nine years old. Right as the game was about to start, Bobby walked up to me and said, "This little girl says she wants to sit with you. Do you mind?" I didn't. Since there were no other children there that night, the little girl sat with me for the duration of the game, cheering occasionally for her father and holding short conversations with me about a range of topics.

Ordinarily, however, the children of Astros spectators played together in a group (sometimes segregated by sex) at the end of the bleachers. Adults were careful not to allow children to go too far past the end of the bleachers (down either the right or left field foul lines) because they would lose the protection of the backstop and could be hit by a foul ball. Just seconds after this was explained to me, an Astros batter fouled a ball down the right field line beyond the backstop. It headed straight toward a group of six little girls, who looked to be no more than six to eight years old. Bertha, an Astros fan sitting nearby, yelled, "Watch out, *mi hitas!*" As she defined this expression (and as I heard other Astros fans use it), it means "little sweeties." In addition to protecting the children (none of which were her own), Bertha was expressing her affection for them. Such expressions of affection in both English and Spanish commonly occurred among Astros and other teams' fans. By midseason, most spectators treated all the children who came to the games as if they were their own.

In addition to sharing information, material resources, and responsibility for children, personal relations among spectators were marked by various "tie signs" that communicated the type of relationship among those interacting.[22] At the center of the most socially intimate tie signs were children, especially female children, who received the most hugs and kisses from adult spectators. On numerous occasions, I witnessed little girls holding out their cheeks expectantly, or even verbally demanding a kiss, from a passerby whom they knew by name. If a girl did not request a kiss from an Astros spectators, her mother would often do it for her, as illustrated in the scene below:

> During one game, José, the father of one of the Astros players, walked by and made a special point of greeting me. Mickie, who was sitting next to me, whined to Joe, "You haven't kissed Maria yet." José stooped to

kiss her on the forehead, smiled sweetly, and moved on to another location in the bleachers. José walked over to talk to Mickie three times during the course of the game, and each time he made it a point to kiss Maria.

José and Maria were not technically related, but Maria's father, who played for the Astros, was quite close to José, and José considered Maria something of a "granddaughter." For male children, other gestures were more commonly exchanged with adults, such as a pat on the head or a "dab," which was like a handshake but required the two parties to grasp only each other's index finger rather than the entire hand.

Adult spectators, meanwhile, exhibited similar kinds of tie signs that varied somewhat by gender. Women would sometimes kiss one another on the cheek upon greeting and perhaps exchange a brief hug when leaving the bleachers after a game. Men, on the other hand, shook hands in a variety of fashions and sometimes patted each other on the back at the close of a game. During games, fans constantly circulated through the bleachers to make sure they said hello and interacted with other fans. Although some fans revealed their personal dislike for some of their colleagues, I never encountered any outward conflict. Spectators who did not like each other merely said hello and moved on.

Although I did not formally measure how many fans regularly interacted with each other, it was clear that by the middle of the season nearly everyone who routinely came to the games knew one another by name and many had exchanged some sort of resource or limited information about themselves. These multiple exchanges created what anthropologists generally call "cross-cutting" ties—social relationships that reached across aggregated actors to involve multiple contents and social obligations.[23] Cross-cutting ties also facilitated the convergence of shared expectations about dyadic interaction and the collective identity of the group. It is to these collective aspects of the floating community among spectators that I now turn.

Moral Boundaries

Much of the social interaction I have discussed in the previous sections seems quite close to the interpersonal webs of social capital that Putnam describes as the bedrock of community. At the same time, Astros spectators developed aspects of community that extend beyond the interpersonal level. As Edgerton suggests, community involves various collective expectations, which I earlier referred to as moral boundaries. Such boundaries defined not only what it meant to be an "upstanding" member of the Astros community but also who was excluded from the group.

Among adults, the key symbolic markers of the community were fictive kin terms that were extended to both men and women. Since most teams contained a few players from the same families, it was not uncommon for children to have an uncle on a team. But the title of *uncle* or *tío* ("uncle" in Spanish) eventually extended to all of the players and male spectators of a particular team. Here is an excerpt from my field notes that underscores this pattern:

> As the Astros prepared to take the field, Lucy, the sister of one of the players, informed her nine-year-old daughter, Brittany, that "Uncle Ray" would be pitching tonight. "Do you remember Uncle Ray?" she asked. Brittany did not. Since Brittany did not remember him, I guessed that he was not an uncle but a close friend of the family. Later during the game, Lucy told me that Ray used to pitch for the Astros but was not actually related to her or Brittany. As we watched the game, we noticed some of the players spitting tobacco as they waited to bat or in between plays as they stood on the field. Brittany asked her mom why the players spit. She told Brittany how "gross it was to stick a bunch of tobacco into your mouth" and that she should never do it if someone gave her some. I commented in Brittany's direction that Warren never did that [chewed tobacco]. Lucy picked up on my comment, pointed to Warren, and said, "Look, Uncle Warren doesn't do that. Neither does Uncle José."

Lucy extended the *uncle* moniker to both Warren and Joe even though neither was actually related to Brittany. The words *aunt* and *tía* ("aunt" in Spanish) were similarly used. Such markers underscored the core values of the community: care, support, and respect. That is, children were supposed to respect their "uncles" and "aunts" and follow their (positive) role models. Adults, meanwhile, were supposed to exercise care and support toward one another, as in a "real" family.

The treatment of regular fans who were not directly related to Astros players also helped mark the moral boundaries surrounding Astros spectators as a whole. For example, several homeless people frequented the park and set up small camps in its physical margins near a wash. One homeless man, call him Fred, adopted the Astros as his team and attended most, if not all, of the Astros' games during the season I observed them. Most Astros fans knew Fred by name, and Carl, the Astros coach, made Fred the "acting ball boy" for the team. Every game, Carl paid Fred a few dollars to chase foul balls. After each foul ball he would return to the umpire, Astros fans would sometimes give him quick round of applause and an "atta boy, Fred." Between innings, Fred could sometimes be seen chatting amiably with players and fans as he waited for the next foul ball to chase. Indeed, as long as Fred performed his role as a ball boy and did not disrupt the game or fans, he was embraced as part of the community. Yet he was never afforded the title of *tio* or *uncle*. Rather, fans tended to treat him like an older child. They shared food with him and sometimes offered him a blanket during the game on a cold night but did not entrust him with the care of children as they would anyone who bore the title *tio/uncle* or *tia/aunt*. On those few occasions when some of Fred's friends heckled players or fans, the group quickly closed ranks both symbolically and physically by avoiding the hecklers or even shouting at them to "move on" to another part of the park. Fred, for his part, sometimes asked the hecklers to "cool it" during the game and would appear as exasperated as the fans by the untoward behavior.

My presence underscored the moral boundaries that demarcated the collectivity of Astros fans. Though I linked myself to a player, I was atypical of spectators in several respects. I was unmarried, lived alone, had no children, and was not a native of Southwest City. On the one hand, I was a full member of the group (as indicated, among other things, by the number of Astros fans who entrusted me to look after their children either alone or with other fans with whom I sat). On the other hand, my "lifestyle" away from the bleachers gave some fans cause for concern. Consider this scene:

> During one game, Bertha (an old-timer) asked me if I had heard about the college girl who had been abducted from her Southside apartment and later found murdered. I replied that I had read about it in the newspaper but hadn't kept up on the details of the case. Bertha leaned over and smiled warmly as she wrote her home number on a piece of paper and gently put it in my jacket pocket. "Take this," she said, "in case you ever need anything." After she gave me her number, she pulled me close to her and lectured me in a serious tone for five minutes about the dangers of trusting people when one is living alone. She ended our "conversation" with a hug. The next game she again sat near me and gave me one of her "famous" bean burritos, insisting that I get some "good home cooking" in me.

Here we see parts of what could be called the "double edge" of moral boundaries. The social control associated with moral boundaries can both motivate behavior (in this instance care and concern about my welfare) and attempt to respond to behavior defined as deviant within the borders of the community. Bertha's actions certainly manifested the ethic of care that pervaded fan community. At the same time, the tone of her lecture was as much about trying to convince me to "change my ways" as it was about care. Her warnings strongly suggested that my actions away from the stands could lead me to "trouble" or in themselves be trouble. Indeed, other fans wondered why Warren and I simply didn't "move in," if for no other reason than for safety.

A stronger indication of the moral boundaries of the Astros community occurred one night during a game in which a girl was attacked away from the field where the Astros were playing:

> Fifth inning. The Astros center fielder shouted out to the left fielder that he "thought" he heard a girl screaming "rape" beyond the outfield fence behind some public restrooms in the distance. I turned to José's wife, Bobbi, who was sitting next to me, and said: "Did he say he heard a girl screaming rape?" To which Bobbi replied, "Yeah well, what was she doing *back there* [emphasis by the informant]?" Nobody on or off the field made a move to see what was happening despite the fact that Bobbi, other fans and ballplayers, and I could now clearly hear a terrified-sounding scream. I asked her if she would come with me to see if "anyone is hurt." She replied, "No way! It's not our business." Just then, a boy who looked to be high school age ran from the restrooms toward a pay phone at the entrance of the park. We could see him anxiously digging in his pants pockets for coins for the phone. After he finished with his call, he then ran back toward the restrooms yelling something about the possibility of him "getting killed." Suddenly, several similarly aged boys ran out from behind the restrooms in all directions. A couple of adults gathered the children together into a tighter group. I could hear sirens getting louder as police cars pulled into the park's main parking lot.

As I talked with fans in the aftermath of this incident, I came to interpret it on several dimensions. First, people were clearly unmotivated to see what had happened or to help whoever was in need. Some of this inaction emanated from fear of what might happen to them if they did interfere. An additional clue to the fans' inaction could be found in Bobbi's question:

"What was she doing *back there?*" "Back there" referred to the victim's being partially responsible for her behavior by being out of place—that is, beyond the boundaries of appropriate behavior as defined from the perspective of Astros fans. By being out of place, the victim was also beyond the boundaries of collective responsibility for the group, which did not extend to that part of the park or to people uninvolved with the Astros. Finally, the only moves made by adults were to gather the children into a tighter group. Here, the group closed ranks to protect its most vulnerable (and valuable) members, once again highlighting the normative contours of the Astros community.

Other telling markers of the moral boundaries of Astros fans and fans from the other teams whom I interviewed were expressed in continual references to the bleachers as a "second home" for their "way of life." One long-time fan of another team commented:

> The whole thing is like a family. You can have a team on which multiple brothers play or fathers and sons and daughters, and even some mothers play (in Jack and Jill leagues). You can have a team where no one is related. It doesn't matter because softball brings generations together to play. Everyone gets to participate, whether you're on the field or in the stands. People in the stands are as much a part of the action as the players.

In this quote we also see how those on both sides of the foul line—on the field and in the stands—were considered "participants." The participation on the field focused on the game being played, and in the stands participation was about sustaining the community of fans.

The dual meanings of participation also enabled Astros and other softball fans to draw distinctions between their spectating practices and intercollegiate and professional spectating. Here again, references to family, an ethic of care among fans, and commitment to teams during entire and multiple seasons were continually cited as reasons why being a softball fan in Southwest City was "so different" from attending most live sporting events at other venues. Whereas fans of intercollegiate and professional teams could develop some aspects of community in terms of collective identities or mutual care, Astros fans pointed to the "depth" of their commitments to one another and to the players (family and nonfamily members) on the team.

A final aspect of the norms that bound the Astros community concerns the line drawn between interaction at the park before, during, or immediately after a game and interaction completely disconnected from the games. Simply put, most fans (who were unrelated by birth or marriage) did not interact with each other away from the bleachers. Some fans—even those who routinely shared intimate feelings or information with one another—did not know each other's last names despite interacting with each other over the course of multiple seasons. Indeed, there was an ethic that constrained fans from becoming interactionally and emotionally close to one another outside the parameters of the games. As one fan put it, "Our back porch [is] the stands. We come from all over [the city] to play and meet each other, but we don't hang out much in each other's homes. Maybe that's why people keep coming back year after year."

CONCLUSION AND IMPLICATIONS

This chapter sought to document how fans constructed and sustained the floating community among spectators associated with a single team, the Astros, in a local amateur softball league. My findings covered how new and old fans became integrated, how fans enacted fleeting and then anchored personal relationships in public, and, finally, how cross-cutting ties among fans facilitated the development of a collective identity and moral boundary around the group. These findings suggest that spectating can produce some forms of community, in contrast to Robert Putnam's arguments that sports spectating is a largely passive or shallow social activity.

Given the questions raised earlier about the difficulties of creating and sustaining community among fans, one might wonder what conditions might promote the dynamics I observed among Astros spectators. Although it is difficult to isolate causal factors given my research design, I can speculate about some of the conditions that appeared to be salient for the present case and could help focus future research. Among these conditions were the preexisting family ties between fans and players, which, as noted earlier in the chapter, created a predisposition toward personal involvement in the games. These ties also created a sense of trust in fans regarding cross-fan interaction that helped ease the creation of new ties while sustaining previously formed connections. Another factor that played a role in these dynamics was the continuity of involvement with the league enjoyed by many players and fans. Although players might switch teams or styles of games from season to season, one longtime league official estimated that up to 50 percent of the players and their fans had participated in the league for five years or more. This suggests yet another factor, durable institutional support, which continued to provide the orga-nizational backbone of spectator communities that followed the teams. Not only the league's durability but also its adaptability helped spectator communities to flourish. During the 1970s, the league expanded its style of play to include coed leagues. The league also had plans to expand its fast- and slow-pitch styles to include all-female leagues. Moreover, some men's teams occasionally allowed well-versed female players (typically former intercollegiate softball players) to play on male teams. Finally, one might point to ethnic homogeneity as a facilitator of community among Astros spectators. The majority of Astros players either were originally from Mexico or claimed Mexican heritage. Sociologists have long argued that cultural and social homogeneity facilitates community because it introduces a degree of shared assumptions about personal relationships, family, and social interaction itself.[24] Despite this seeming cultural homo-geneity, the Astros players displayed a great deal of diversity in terms of occupations, incomes, primary language (i.e., all spoke English, but not all players claiming Mexican heritage spoke Spanish), politics, and the part of the city where they lived (some lived in predominantly Mexican parts of town, while others lived in predominantly Anglo parts of town). What the players and spectators importantly shared, more than some iron-clad col-lective sense of ethnicity or social class, was a set of shared expectations about the meaning of softball playing and spectating. Through their social interaction at ball games, ballplayers and spectators continually produced and reaffirmed these meanings. By doing so, they reproduced their float-ing community. In addition to my findings and speculations about the conditions under which a floating spectator community can emerge and be sustained, my chapter also carries implications and suggests future lines of inquiry relevant to personal relationships in public places and the nature of contemporary community.

My findings are consistent with this volume's thesis regarding the com-plexity and multifunctionality of personal relationships in public, as well as the blurred differences between primary and secondary relationships. Although spectators typically did not engage in interaction with each other outside the park, their interaction inside the park was warm and intimate. It appears, then, that Astros fans did not substitute fan-to-fan support and intimacy for family intimacy. Instead, the Astros floating spectator com-munity complemented and helped support kin ties. Like Little League baseball, the Astros community appeared to integrate actual families into the public context.[25] The cross-cutting ties that developed across individual fans and their families, moreover, led to a strong sense of shared expectations, collective identity, and social obligations. At the same time, one could imagine a situation in which the time spent in a floating community and at home could operate as a zero-sum game (especially if part of the family did not come to the park). Future research should delve more deeply into these issues by exploring the linkages between "quasi-primary" relations anchored in public contexts and primary relationships situated in private contexts. Under what conditions are such relationships complementary or in tension with one another? How do individuals manage the demands of both types of relationships?

A second implication of my work concerns the multifaceted nature of contemporary community. Sociologists of community argue that prior to the twentieth century, communities in urban Western cities were largely sustained by men who met in public places for social purposes and, on occasion, to engage in collective political and economic projects. The density of interaction and accessibility of public places (e.g., pubs, cafes, parks) increased the likelihood that men would find friends or friends of friends with whom to talk. Although some women ventured into public in "respectable" contexts, such as churches and civic groups, the vast majority of women operated in private as "kin keepers." It was women who kept relatives connected and offered primary sources of social support across and within households. During the late nineteenth and early twentieth centuries, the separation of work from neighborhoods and residences, and then the massive entry of women into the labor force during the past thirty years, created the conditions for communities to retreat from public places. Ironically women, so this line of argument goes, have largely been expected (by men) to maintain their earlier roles as domestic managers (e.g., responsible for cooking, cleaning, children) and kin keepers.[26] Barry Wellman argues that these changes have wrought the "domestication" of community. Communities are now organized around households and kin relations embedded in unstable personal networks that can span large geographic distances. Moreover, "community keeping has become an extension of kin keeping," with women shouldering the primary responsibilities for both.[27]

My findings certainly fit with some of these trends. Women played key roles in cultivating the Astros spectator community and in constituting it as a fictive family. One could even make the strong argument that without women the floating community I studied could not be robustly sustained. One could also argue that the social structure of the Astros community did not rest on personal relations among individuals (as Putnam might argue) but on exchanges of support among household representatives. On the other hand, the Astros floating community is interesting in that it eschewed domiciles. Instead of retreating to people's homes, the group stayed on the public stage in the bleachers. The Astros community also included men as community keepers who operated as caretakers of both of children and adults. Finally, it exhibited more stability, as indicated by the enduring ties to the league and to each other that a substantial portion of players and fans maintained.

Although one might dismiss the Astros floating community as anomalous or atavistic, it might be more useful to treat it as a point of departure to study the diversity of community types that exist. This orientation assumes that community is not a monolithic phenomenon that waxes and wanes over time. Neighborhood communities, personal communities, kin-based communities, spectator communities, and so on may all coexist to one degree or another in contemporary Western society and may serve very different functions for their members and society. Among the relative questions to pursue are: How and when do different types of community emerge, grow, and decline? How do different types of community contribute to political, economic, and social institutions? What roles do different types of communities play in individuals' lives? What are the relationships between different types of communities? Under what conditions do they undermine or reinforce one another?

This last implication suggests that different types of communities can provide people with meaning in their lives—in one sense, a larger purpose for living. For Astros fans and players, their larger purpose revolved around mutual care and a way of life that unfolded game after game, season after season, on the ball field and in the bleachers of Southwest City parks. It was a way of life that they could accomplish only together and that raises questions about whether social capital actually is declining in the United States or whether old forms of social capital are being replaced by new forms that have yet to be fully understood.[28]

METHODOLOGICAL PROCEDURES AND REFLECTIONS

My field methods consisted primarily of "hanging out" with the people who came to the Astros' games, getting to know as many of them as possible, and learning what being a spectator was like for them. Although I began the study as something of a "peripheral member"[29] of the Astros fans in that I knew little about what it was like to be a fan and was not particularly committed to the team, by the end of the season I became a "complete member"[30] of the Astros' spectator base in that I shared many of the same feelings and concerns regarding my fellow fans and the team as others who followed the team.

The slow rhythm of games facilitated note taking on interactions among the fans as we watched the games. Immediately following each game, I turned my "jottings" into more elaborated field notes. Although I did not then have the words to articulate what I was doing with regard to my notes, my later understandings of the ethnographic literature suggested that during the first half of my forays into the field I was in what Robert Emerson and colleagues call a "writing mode" as I attempted to get as much down as I could into my notepad without attending to my writing style or the analytic complexities of what I was observing. As the season wore on, I began to enter into what they call a "reading mode" in that I went back to read my early notes as I composed more current ones.[31] This process led to my first attempts to code my notes into broad thematic categories of "topics of conversation" and "gestures of affection." These categories further evolved into more finely honed categories related to the interactional dynamics among fans based on further observations, semistructured interviews with spectators, initial write-ups of my study, and further reading in relevant literatures. In this way, my "dialogues" across multiple empirical and conceptual domains became more interdependent and frequent as my fieldwork and write-ups progressed.

My interviews provide an interesting case in this regard. The longer I watched the games and talked with and listened to Astros spectators, the more I came to have a feel for how they themselves characterized being a spectator, what it meant to them, and how they regarded the games. But I became curious about how the fans of other teams saw themselves. Had I just stumbled upon one special niche of spectators in a sea of anonymous fandom? As a result, I created a semistructured interview that contained questions about background experiences as a park league spectator, what it was like to be a spectator, and various aspects of the significance of different strands of social interaction. My eventual sample of seven spectators of other teams was not random, although they represented a mix of ages, ethnicities, genders, and occupations, and all regularly attended league games. What I found interesting was that my interview data overwhelmingly dovetailed with my field observations, which suggests that the experiences of Astros spectators were similar to those of other spectators in the league.

As I reflect back on my research, I realize that a team of ethnographers could have conducted the research presented in this chapter. This approach, as is illustrated by the other chapters in this volume, carries many advantages, including the possibility of comparing multiple perspectives, built-in reliability checks, mutual support during the research process, and field safety. I could imagine how another researcher would have expanded both the depth and breadth of the research by being able to gain different perspectives on Astros fans or even enabling a comparative study of different teams, leagues, or similar leagues in a different city. In some sense, adding a teammate could have expanded the theoretical scope of the study itself.

Yet my project also underscores some of the challenges posed by team fieldwork. A team of researchers working together among Astros fans might have had the opposite effect. Because I was alone and friendly, players and spectators considered me approachable, perhaps even adoptable. Thus my emotional connection with the group that undergirded much of my writing about it might have been muted or at least altered by my belonging to a team. My interaction with Bertha underscored this and also made me aware of the relative impermeability of group boundaries. Like many communities, the Astros spectator group was somewhat suspicious of outsiders whom they "did not know." The rape incident illustrated how the group could quickly "close its borders." A team of ethnographers could have threatened the community or, at the very least, experienced difficulty developing the same level of access I was able to achieve.

Even more intriguing are aspects of my fieldwork experience with respect to my emotional experiences of safety and violence. Under the bright lights of the field and the stands, all was safe. But even the distance from the parking lot to the field or the parking lot itself could be threatening after dark. My recounting of violence away from the field during a game provoked in me (as it may have in some fans) a sort of "existential shock" about whether "this was really happening."[32] Ethnographers of warfare and other forms of violence have often noted that existential shock in the face of violence committed either against them or among those they are studying can provoke insights into informants' emotions, culture, and social structures. Certainly this was the case for me. The existential shock of a girl crying rape during a game helped to galvanize my sense of the Astros as a tightly bounded community, yet at the same time distanced me somewhat from the group since I wanted to investigate what had happened. Had I been a part of a team ethnographic effort, I might have felt safer and have been helped emotionally by being able to talk about the incident with others. But I might have gained less insight into what the group meant to Astros fans and how their community was sustained over time via tight moral boundaries and tight-knit personal relations. What I learned from this experience was that both solo and team ethnography pose challenges and opportunities. The trick is to understand some of the trade-offs entailed by each style of field research in relation to the context one studies and the research questions one pursues.

SEVEN

Inclusion and Intrusion

Gender and Sexuality in Gay, Lesbian, and Straight Bars

LORI L. REID, CAROLYN J. AMAN KARLIN,
AND MICHAEL D. BONHAM-CRECILIUS

THE REFRAMING OF MASCULINITY OR femininity as being "accomplished" through social interaction, rather than as being an essential individual attribute, stands as a useful turn in sociological research on gender.[1] From this perspective, gender is the management of one's comportment, dress, and bearing relative to the "sex category" (male or female) for which one is attempting to pass and be recognized.[2] "Sexual identity" (e.g., being identified and identifying oneself as a heterosexual, gay, lesbian, or transsexual) further complicates these processes, for it need not tightly map onto gender. At the same time, one accomplishes sexual identity in much the same way as one accomplishes gender—through social interaction that is oriented to various institutionalized normative conceptions about what it means to be heterosexual, gay, lesbian, and so on. Thus gender and sexual identity are as much institutional processes as they are functions of interpersonal interaction.[3]

Appropriate ways of enacting gender or sexual identities vary considerably across social contexts. In many public places, such as city streets, gender and sexual identity often turn on tacit and explicit norms about heterosexual masculinity and femininity.[4] Other public places, especially bars, can vary considerably in their tacit assumptions about gender-appropriate behaviors and sexual identities to the point that particular genders and sexual identities are associated with particular places. In this chapter, we ethnographically investigate how interpersonal dynamics signal gender and sexual identities in bars. Bars have traditionally been an important terrain on which a number of social relationships are worked out that fall somewhere between the primary ties of the family and the impersonal and fleeting ties of many public places.[5] Across straight, gay, and lesbian bars, sexual and gender identities often figure prominently in social interaction as men and women explicitly attempt to categorize one another along these lines, thus constituting the groundwork for communicating their own and others' potential availability for personal relationships.[6] Our research specifically compares how patrons in heterosexual, gay, and lesbian bars interactionally create what Erving Goffman calls "territories of the self"—personal spaces and preserves that are maintained during face-to-face interaction with others. Such personal spaces become part of the "displays" through which people not only communicate how they feel about themselves and those they interact with but also add up to an entire "scene."[7]

In the next section, we flesh out Goffman's perspective on territories of the self in public and quasi-public places as it relates to gender and sexuality. We then discuss where we conducted our research. Our findings focus on the interactional tactics through which heterosexual men and women, lesbians, and gays manage their territories of the self. We conclude with implications regarding the study of gender, sexual identity, personal relationships, and social power in public places.

TERRITORIES OF THE SELF, GENDER, AND SEXUALITY IN BARS

In *Relations in Public,* Goffman outlines various ways people interactionally establish and maintain territory as their personal "preserve" in public places.[8] Conceptually, Goffman suggests that individuals mark both physical and purely symbolic territories of the self. In his nomenclature, "stalls" are "well-bounded space[s] to which individuals can lay temporary claim, possession being on an all-or-none basis." In bars, examples of stalls could include a particular table, booth, location at a bar, or piece of equipment (e.g., a billiards table). Another type of physical territory is the "sheath," which is an individual's skin and clothing. "Informational" and "conversational" preserves constitute more symbolic territories but can involve physical boundaries reinforced by the demarcation of physical spaces. An informational preserve controls access to information (about oneself or another), whereas a conversational preserve restricts access to particular interchanges between oneself and others.[9]

At an interactional level, individuals use various strategies to carve out and maintain territories of the self. These strategies include verbal actions that explicitly communicate the boundaries of one's territory but more often include subtle nonverbal gestures and bodily positionings that signal the control of space, information, or conversational access. One of the key mechanisms along these lines is "tie signs" through which individuals designate other co-present individuals as part of their territory and, in so doing, communicate a particular relational identity with an associated degree of exclusivity.[10] For instance, holding hands or putting an arm around another person can function as a tie sign that suggests individuals are in a close personal relationship with another and thereby excludes other individuals from access to interaction. Other tie signs—such as an arms-length hug in which the individual drapes his or her arm around another individual with torso contact—can communicate less exclusivity in public. Although tie signs can be a source of information to an observer (or to oneself) about the relationships present in a public setting, "reading" what they specifically mean and how they function can be ambiguous. For example, when two men embrace in a bar, does that indicate a close relationship, a ritualized form of embrace appropriate for that particular bar, a joking relationship, a unilateral claim by one man on the space of another, or some combination of all or parts of these actions? As such, tie signs are complex and often nuanced displays that must always be interpreted in context and with some sense of what the action(s) means to those involved.

Violations of personal boundaries offer one way to gain more information about how territories of the self operate in public. In bars, the most relevant violations involve forms of "intrusion."[11] Intrusions into a territory of self include defilement of another's sheath through touch; unwanted eye contact, glances, or staring; and the "ecological placement of the body relative to a claimed territory" such that it encroaches on another person's territorial preserve.[12] As with tie signs, an understanding of territorial violations requires knowledge about the local contexts in which they occur. Defilement in one context, for instance, may not be defined as a violation in another context.

Goffman argues that territories of the self, apart from signaling relational identities, facilitate the communication of "fundamental codes" associated with sex categories and sexual identities.[13] Territories of the self can thus be enacted with an eye toward how they will be evaluated as "womanly," "manly," "gay," "heterosexual," or "lesbian" in the local context. If a particular place contains consistent patterns of social interaction that are identified with avowed sexual and/or gender identities, that place can come to be identified in explicitly sexual or gendered terms.[14] Thus how territories of the self are enacted can help mark whether a place is "straight," "gay," or "lesbian." These arguments also suggest that patterns of territories of the self in particular places can shed light on the dynamics of interpersonal social power and their linkage to gender and sexual identities. That is, how personal space is constructed and maintained can provide insight into the power dynamics that undergird personal relationships across gender and sexual identities.

Our discussion of territories of the self, gender, and sexuality informs three primary research questions that emerged during our fieldwork and data analysis and frame our research: How does ongoing social interaction constitute public places that come to be recognized as "gay," "lesbian," or "straight"? How do territories of the self affect the potential for personal relationships in these places? What implications do territories of the self hold for the exercise of interpersonal social power in public places? These questions suggest a comparative ethnographic strategy capable of examining territories of the self across gay, lesbian, and straight bars. In the next section, we discuss our research sites and how we selected them.

THE BARS

We engaged in fieldwork for nine months during two different points in time: the fall of 1992 and the spring and summer of 1996.[15] During these periods, nearly 150 bars, nightclubs, and lounges operated in various parts of the metropolitan area where we conducted the study.[16] Bars near the city's large public university, for example, primarily attracted college patrons. The west side of town contained numerous strip clubs (catering to both men and women) and "outlaw" bars, including those with reputations for "biker" and/or "criminal" clienteles. The north side of town was home to several "upscale" bars and lounges, connected either to freestanding, top-end restaurants or to resorts that attracted out-of-town tourists and local "high rollers." Finally, the east side and downtown contained a mixture of bar types, including comedy clubs, sports bars, lounges, wine bars, strip clubs, and dance bars oriented toward straight, gay, and lesbian patrons.

We restricted the pool of potential research sites to bars with dance floors because of our interest in observing public interaction between large numbers of people. Because people tend to stand and move about more in dance bars than in bars without dance floors (where people spend the majority of their time sitting at tables), we believed dance bars would facilitate our observations of interpersonal interaction. We also chose to concentrate our attention on the downtown dance bars because they were all roughly the same size (drawing about three hundred patrons on a heavy night), this was where all of the gay and lesbian bars were, and we could "bar hop" easily across field sites on the same night to experience multiple contexts. Thus all five bars selected for our project contained at least one dance floor and were found (in initial outings) to exhibit significant motility among patrons in the bar.

In 1992 there were a limited number of gay dance clubs in town, and at the start of the project there were no lesbian bars. To observe lesbian and gay interactions, we chose to focus on "Club Satyrn," the city's most popular gay dance club. Club Satyrn billed itself as a "men's club" but exhibited an approximate 2:1 ratio of men to women on any given night.[17] Our prior experiences and conversations with Satyrn patrons suggested that a large portion of the club's female patrons were lesbian. We also focused on another gay club, "Matricks," which advertised a "Ladies' Night" one night per week that drew a large lesbian clientele.

Our choice of sites for observing interactions in straight bars proved more difficult, since there were a number of straight bars downtown. We eventually chose three bars—"Prism," "Steppin' Out," and "Surf Club"— to focus on because of their consistent crowd size and because of their clientele's demographic comparability on several dimensions, including age (mostly twenties and thirties), gender ratio (a 3:2 male to female ratio), ethnicity (largely Anglo with a minority of Hispanic patrons), and social class (more difficult to assess, but the types of cars in the parking lots and patrons' attire suggested mostly middle-income people).

In our follow-up research during 1996, we attempted to focus on the same clubs but found some of them were no longer in business. Club Satyrn closed its doors in 1995 to be replaced by "BD's" as the "hot spot" in town for gays and lesbians. A lesbian bar (which we dubbed "Sappho's") opened in 1995 and immediately drew a large following. We subsequently dropped Matricks because its Ladies' Night lost much of its clientele to Sappho's. Of the original three bars we studied in 1992, only Prism was still open in 1996, and we found it had changed little in terms of its appearance or the types of interactions we observed in the bar. To replace the two straight bars dropped from our initial fieldwork, we added "Captive" and "Down Under," both of which shared enough similarities with the bars we lost to make observations across the five straight bars comparable.

ENTERING THE BARS

Even if one did not know a priori that one was entering a lesbian, straight, or gay bar, there would be obvious cues underscoring the differences in these places that would be difficult to ignore. Outside BD's (a gay bar), for example, a long line of well-groomed men dressed in tightly fitting shirts and pants waited to enter the bar through a darkened foyer with heavy metal doors. An older man with gray hair and a moustache, wearing an official-looking security uniform, checked patrons' identification using a large, black metal flashlight (the type that police officers often carry that look like batons), which he shone down at the card he was inspecting and then into a customer's face. Although his size was not intimidating, his gruff attitude squelched most conversations between patrons as they presented their identification to him. Immediately upon entering the club, after adjusting to the pounding music, darkened lighting, and dark walls, one would discern the large dance floor packed with an undulating crowd of men (and a few women). A number of men lined up against the chest-high wall that borders the dance floor. Once one was on the dance floor, it was difficult to exit to the other areas of the bar without pushing through the thick crowd. Framed by a bright neon light, the main bar area projected an eerie blue light. Next to the main bar the DJ booth was almost hidden in a dark corner, and two other men, one dressed in a tie and jacket, kept watch over the entire room.

By contrast, the ratio of women to men standing in line at Sappho's (the lesbian club) was heavily skewed toward women, with an approximate ratio of 4:1. At the single entrance door, a woman checked patrons' identification in a well-lit, open-air foyer. The woman at the door did not look particularly big or "tough," nor did she have security paraphernalia (e.g., metal flashlight or a uniform) that distinguished her from other employees and patrons. She often made small talk with the patrons as she checked their identification. The lighting just inside Sappho's was not overly dark or bright. The main room's walls were painted pink with black and white accents and featured poster-sized sketches of women and a six-foot by six-foot florescent-lit picture of Marilyn Monroe that dominated one wall of the bar's main room. Sappho's was the only bar we visited that was carpeted and decorated with a theme not accented by beer companies' logos. The employees (who were all women except for the DJ) typically wore black pants or shorts and a teal or purple polo-type shirt. On special theme nights, employees were more formally dressed in white button-down shirts with black ties.

Off from the main area of the bar was a small, intimate conversation room. When the door to this room was closed, it was completely closed off from the main club, although the club was still visible through the smoked glass wall surrounding the door. Two floral-print sofas and a few high-back, upholstered chairs framed a polished cherry wood coffee table. On each end of the sofas were end tables on which sat two lamps that provided much of the soft lighting for the room. Gold-framed, Monet-style paintings of Victorian women and flowers adorned the walls. A phone on one of the end tables was available for local calls. The room was relatively quiet—one could hear the music from the main room, but only faintly.

By contrast, straight bars heightened one's sense of the bars' potential dangerousness because of their beefed-up security. At each straight bar, groups of three to five bouncers greeted patrons, who, because of their size and youth, looked to be either current or former football players from the local university. Whatever the straight bar, the ritual was the same. One bouncer would check IDs, often scrutinizing patrons with a stern look. Once he verified to his satisfaction that the ID matched the patron and that the ID was not a fake, he would pass the patron on to a second bouncer, who would motion the customer into the bar. Other bouncers merely stood by, although most kept their eyes on customers as they passed by.

The physical arrangements of the straight, lesbian, and gay clubs were somewhat similar, as all were dominated by at least one large dance floor. Like Sappho's, most of the straight clubs had separate, smaller rooms, which typically contained separate bars and smaller dance floors. None contained a living-room setup like Sappho's. Moreover, none of the straight bars contained rooms with different themes, although two had restaurants. At all of the straight clubs, DJ's constantly announced drink specials and other promotions (e.g., dance contests or "wet T-shirt" contests) and urged those assembled to "party" and "get it on." In addition, two of our study sites (Prism and Captive) were dimly lit, which gave them a more sinister feel since it was more difficult to see people. The better lit bars (Steppin' Out, Surf Club, and Down Under) also had slightly larger dance areas and main rooms. All of the bars had installed video systems that showed music videos and other recorded material.

Across all of our study sites, people claimed territories of the self in a variety of ways. They elbowed or bumped someone to carve out space on the dance floor. They smiled at one person and then quickly turned away to closely interact with another person, thus closing off interaction with the first person. They might claim particular tables by always keeping one or two people from their "group" at the table to signal to others that the space was "taken." Individuals also engaged in a variety of tactics to repel invasions of their personal preserves, including gently tapping someone on the shoulder or arm and motioning him or her, generally with a head nod, to "move on"; turning away from the intruder; exiting a particular physical locale and moving their preserve elsewhere; or simply ignoring a territorial violation, especially if it involved the gaze (e.g., long staring). Some of the more physical mechanisms for claiming space (e.g., bumping, elbowing, pushing) occurred under cover of dancing or while trying to move from one part of the bar to another (e.g., to buy a drink or visit the restroom). The loud music in all the clubs (except for the "living room" at Sappho's) constrained the verbal enactment of territories of the self except under some conditions. Aside from these general patterns, the dynamics of creating and maintaining territories of the self varied a great deal across straight, gay, and lesbian bars, as well as within particular bar types with respect to gender. It is to this variation that we now turn.

Territories of the Self in Straight Bars

Consider the following scene at Steppin' Out on a typical Friday night:

It's 10:30 p.m. and the place is packed. Loud, fast rock music pervades the large main room. Cigarette smoke hangs in the air despite huge air conditioning vents arrayed across the high, black ceiling that are blowing air. Scattered about the room away from the main dance floor are small black tables at which pairs and groups of three to six people sit. The crowd is especially thick between tables as pairs and larger groups of patrons hold their positions in tight clumps. Pairs often touch one another as they stand face to face; small groups of women form elbow-to-elbow circles and face inward to each other, chatting and laughing. A few all-male groups stand close to one another, rarely touching, but look outward toward the dance floor and the audience. All stand their ground against the pushing and elbowing of others attempting to move across the room. The crowd becomes somewhat frenzied and dense as one nears the main bar, which stretches about sixty feet along one wall. A dozen bartenders work furiously as patrons push toward the front of the bar (some with ten and twenty dollar bills in their hands), shouting: "Two Coronas here!" " A vodka tonic and a rum 'n Coke!" "Jack on the rocks, please!" or "Come on, two white wines and a Lite beer—I've been waiting here for ten minutes!" Waitresses congregate at one end of the bar to load trays full of drinks and then make their way into the crowd to serve patrons sitting at tables. Close to our vantage point are several small tables informally segregated by gender. The four men at one table rarely turn their gaze inward toward those they are sitting with, instead staring in the direction of the dance floor or women in other parts of the main room. At a nearby table, four women glance periodically toward the dance floor and the rest of the main room but also turn their attention toward the other women at the table with whom they are chatting and drinking. What appears to be a couple (they are holding hands and sitting so close that their bodies are touching) at another table turns their attention almost exclusively to each other. At a mixed-gender table nearby, men and women alternate their attention to their colleagues and to the dance floor. Standing near these tables are two men, who do not appear to know one another, leaning up against a wall staring out at the dance floor. A woman in a tight-fitting skirt and low-cut top briskly walks by one of the men. One of the men looks her up and down as she approaches and turns his head so that he can watch her as she walks past him down a corridor that leads to a restroom. A man approaches a woman seated with two other women at a table near the dance floor and begins talking with her. She smiles, he smiles. He motions toward the dance floor. After a few minutes, he escorts the woman to the dance floor, where they dance to the rest of a song and then return to the table. He sits down with her and then gets up to make his way to the bar. A few minutes later, he returns with a glass of wine and a beer. He sits down and they begin to talk.

As we noted previously, and as this excerpt illustrates, all bar patrons claim some form of territory of the self for themselves or contribute to group preserves. Such space is organized around bodily positioning and tie signs of various sorts and is facilitated by tables. Beyond this somewhat banal observation, perhaps the most intriguing aspect of this excerpt concerns how violations of territories of the self in straight bars vary by gender and relational ties. As underscored by the example of the all-male table in the excerpt, men in pairs or larger groups often stare at the dance floor and the main bar areas with fixed gazes (that they rarely interrupt except to buy a drink or visit the restroom). The two men leaning up against the wall staring at the dance floor also illustrate a common pattern, as does the man who, with his eyes, blatantly followed ("scoped") the woman who walked by him on her way to the restroom. By contrast, we rarely observed women in straight bars standing alone or in small groups staring fixedly at the dance floor or obviously scoping men with their eyes. The informal conversations we were able to have with patrons suggested that those women who did scope did so more subtly, with quick glances, rather than with unmistakable stares. The exception to this pattern for men occurred in the context of obvious romantic pairings in which men turned most of their attention to their "partner" (although some men sneaked peeks to check out provocatively dressed women as they walked by—sometimes to the visible consternation of the woman they were with).

In addition to eye-based violations, touch-based violations occurred as people moved from one part of the main room to another. Most physical violations were accompanied by various forms of "remedial interchanges"— interaction intended to lessen or ameliorate the violation.[18] In straight bars, remedial interchanges occurred quickly and under some conditions could almost be missed by those to whom they were directed. Some of these behaviors included a raising of the eyes as if to say, "Pardon me," a hand wave in the direction of those whose space had been compromised, or a quick "Sorry about that [walking through one's space or brushing up against someone]," "Excuse me," or the less polite "Comin' through!" Occasionally, a territorial violation required more extensive response, as when a "crasher" sat at a table obviously controlled by a group or a dyad. Under these conditions, awkward conversation might occur among the crasher and territorial claimants, which, in turn, might result in the claimants vacating their territory. Women in straight bars who engaged in touch-based violations exhibited much the same behavior, although we witnessed a few more women than men making physical contact with those they brushed up against (e.g., patting them on the shoulder or back) as if to say, "no harm done." As in the excerpt above, we did not see women or men respond to violators with touch.

The end of the scene we described above illustrates what we observed on numerous occasions: men initiating conversation of some kind with women, men asking women to dance, men buying drinks for women. In nearly all these instances, it appeared, from the lack of tie signs, that the principals did not have a previous relational connection. The vast majority of women would engage in a male-initiated conversation, if only for a few minutes. Sometimes (as in the scenario above) we observed such conversations stretching on for longer periods of time, during which the man would buy the woman a drink. Occasionally, we watched the two actors leave the bar together. In most instances, women turned men down who approached them solely to request a dance. The end result of these encounters resulted in the woman further ensconcing herself in whatever territorial preserve she had established (e.g., moving her chair closer to members of a group at a table or, if alone, focusing her attention on her drink while turning away from the direction from where the man had originated) or exiting that area of the bar. As one woman put it, "You've got to be careful out there these days. I'm not going out on the dance floor [with a guy] without at least talking with him for a couple of minutes. It gives you a chance to check the guy out and to let others see him." By contrast, we rarely witnessed a woman asking a man to dance and less frequently (compared to male-initiated conversations) witnessed women initiating conversations with men with whom they did not appear to have a previous relationship. These patterns also illustrate the importance of safety in straight bars relative to territories of the self and the meaning of dancing—at least in the straight bars we studied. Some women used their personal preserve, especially if it was constituted with a group, as a safe haven to "check out" a man who initiated contact with them. For these women, the physicality of dancing placed them in a more "intimate" personal preserve with an unknown male than they were comfortable with. Other women (particularly those at a bar with only another female friend) believed that dancing was a more "arms length" territory of the self from which a woman could more easily "break away" from an offending male if she needed to.

Dancing provided another venue in which to observe territories of the self in action, as our observations on a Saturday night from Prism illustrate:

Nearly midnight. The dance floor is filled with dozens of patrons gyrating and swaying their hips, hopping, snapping their fingers, moving their arms as if running, shaking their heads, shimmying their

shoulders, marching in a circle with exaggerated knee lifts, and occasionally clapping their hands over their heads—all more or less to the
beat of the music. Nearly all the dancers are paired off, with most
dancers staying in a six- to eight-square-foot area as they dance, in
which they are never more than two to three feet from their partner.
There is a great deal of jostling as dancers run into each other, elbow
one another for space, or turn their bodies in such a way as to create a
"human wall" that protects their area of the floor. In one corner of the
dance floor and near its center, a few women dance without partners.
Those in the corner dance solo, engaged in much of the same movements as dancing pairs. Those near the floor's center are in a small group
arranged in a tight circle with all of the dancers facing inward. As they
shuffle their feet or slightly move their hips to the music, one of the
women occasionally leans forward to say something to another member
of the group. In another corner of the dance floor, a group of men and
women dance in a circle, accompanying their movements with loud
howls. Many of the men in this group hold bottles of beer, laughing and
taking occasional swigs of beer as they dance and watch the all-female
group of dancers on the opposite side of the floor.

The pattern above was quite common at our straight sites. Men danced
with women or in mixed groups, while women danced with men, with
each other, and alone. Rarely did we observe a man dancing alone in a
straight bar. This pattern also constituted differences in territories of the
self relative to gender. While dancing in straight bars, men typically
defined other men as part of their territories only if women were also
included in the territory, and they rarely defined a territory all to themselves on the dance floor. By contrast, women included other women and
men, either together or separately, in their territory when dancing. Women
frequently claimed territory all to themselves while dancing, although this
territory was frequently subject to eye-based violations by men both on
and off the dance floor.

Finally, one's "sheath" (e.g., clothing, skin)—to use Goffman's term—is
an aspect of one's territory of the self that exhibited pronounced differences among men and women in the straight bars we studied. At these
sites, men's clothes concealed their bodies more than women's did. Specifically, the male "uniform" consisted of loose-fitting jeans; a T-shirt, button-
down, or polo shirt; athletic or oxford-style shoes (occasionally boots);
and a short haircut. A small minority of men would wear tight tank
tops or tight jeans and long hair. Women in straight bars wore summery

slip-dresses, tight shirts (often revealing cleavage and/or a bare midriff), tight shorts, high heels or sandals, and long, styled hair.

Territories of the Self in Gay and Lesbian Bars

The following two scenes from BD's and Sappho's illustrate aspects of territories of the self in the gay and lesbian bars we studied:

AT BD'S: Just past midnight on a Saturday night and the place is overflowing with patrons lined up to get in the main bar/dance area. Loud, hard-pounding techno pop (a fast-paced electronic dance music with a pronounced backbeat) pervades the club. Some men crowd the main bar trying to buy drinks. The majority of the three dozen tables that dot the main area of the club are filled by all-male groups of two to four men. Mixed in with these tables are a few tables at which men and women sit and two all-female tables. The vast majority of patrons crowd into the "ring" of men (with a smattering of women), standing three deep against the wall that surrounds the dance floor. The ring has grown so crowded that it melds into the mass of dancers on the dance floor. All of the men in the ring around the dance floor intensely watch those dancing. Occasionally, one of the watchers turns his head to follow a man leaving the dance floor to walk over to another area of the main room. Some watchers crane their necks to get a better look at the dancers; some laugh and point to particular areas in the mass of dancers as they do. About half of the men who watch the dance floor from the ring hold some sort of beverage; almost no one on the dance floor does. All-male pairs dominate the floor, with half a dozen male-female pairs and three all female-pairs sprinkled in. At various spots near the edge of the floor, a few men dance solo without any discernible partner or in larger groups. A few feet off the floor, in the heart of the ring, a man spontaneously begins moving his hips and shoulders to the rhythm of the music. Two other men near him join in with him. The three use their elbows and hip movements to make a small open space for themselves. Every so often, a man "dances" through the three men, pausing for a minute to laugh and bump hips or shimmy close to one of the dancers. On the dance floor, men dance with men in tight-knit pairs or alone. Even though they dance just a few inches from their dance partners, occasionally brushing their hips or chest up against one another or running their hands along each other's hips, the men also keep turning their heads occasionally to look out into the crowd around the dance floor or to turn their heads to follow, with their eyes, other men who are dancing nearby. The solo male dancers constantly scan the dance floor and crowd as they move to the music, turning their heads to follow various men as they push and slide their way through the crowd either on or off the dance floor. A few all-female and male-female pairs dot the dance floor. These pairs also dance close to one another, rarely facing any direction other than the direction of their partners. On one side of the dance floor, a small group of four men dance together, periodically pairing off, and constantly turning their attention from each other to other dancers and members of the ring near the dance floor. Nearby, an all-male triad dances in a closed circle. A man, who was dancing alone a few feet away and staring in their direction through a several-minute stretch, moves in their direction. As he approaches the group, he catches the attention of one of the group's members, who smiles and ushers him into the group with an exaggerated hand wave.

AT SAPPHO's: Friday night at 11:00 p.m. and a short line to get into the club leads to the crowded main bar area. Standing at the main bar are twenty to twenty-five patrons, sipping and buying drinks. Pervading the main bar is loud, pounding disco music. Suddenly, the disco music gives way to fast-paced Tejano (an accordion-based mix of Mexican folk music, Texan swing, and Spanish lyrics with R&B and pop music influences). On the dance floor, the swirl of dancers (all women) who have been bumping, grinding, and brushing their bodies up against one another in close pairs to the beat of the disco music transform themselves into choreographed pairs of "two-steppers" (a swinglike dance). At the music transition, about a third of the dancers leave the floor, and the crowd—clumps of all-female groups surrounding the dance floor—swells to the point that it spills out into the main bar area. Most eyes in the crowd around the dance floor are on pairs of dancers twirling around the floor, only inches from each other's bodies, yet rarely touching each other except for their clasped hands and their hands in the small of each other's backs. Prior to the transition, the entire floor was all female, but now three male-female pairs are on the floor. There are also groups of four to six women sitting at the small tables scattered around the main room of the bar. Those seated at the tables lean over close to one another, sipping beverages, smiling, and talking. Three women who have been sitting at a table get up and amble back to the "lounge," where they drape themselves on the couch and in one of the easy chairs. They begin to chat. Another women joins them a few minutes later. Out on the dance floor, the first Tejano song melds into another. A few pairs leave the floor, edging their way through the crowd to be replaced by other pairs from the area surrounding the floor. As they move through the crowd, the pairs brush up against other women and are patted, sometimes hugged, in response. A group of four women near the edge of the dance floor are hopping up and down together to the music as they laugh. One of them motions for another woman from the surrounding crowd to join them on the dance floor, which she does by hopping over to the group.

As in straight bars, solo individuals, pairs of individuals, and larger groups in gay and lesbian bars claim territories of the self both on and off the dance floor. Across all three contexts, we find territories off the dance floor constituted by both same- and other-sex individuals. On the dance floor in both gay and lesbian bars, not surprisingly, same-sex pairs and larger groups dominate personal preserves, although on nearly every field visit we observed some mixed-sex pairs in both gay and lesbian bars. Strikingly absent in the lesbian context are solo dancers, which are quite common in both gay and straight contexts (although usually involving only women in straight bars).

The biggest difference between the straight bars and the lesbian and gay clubs concerns the focal activities that command patrons' attention. At the lesbian and gay clubs, dancing and watching dancers dominate the activities of most patrons as they crowd at or near the dance floors. In the straight bars, the predominant focus of attention is drinking, with patrons observing each other as they stand at or near bars and secondarily on the dance floor. Customers in the straight bars who appear to be "coupled" or in preexisting groups typically face inward toward their "partners" or group members, on occasion turning their heads to watch events in the bar. Indeed, the most crowded nights at the straight bars are those with evening-long drink specials. As an informal measure of the difference in alcohol consumption across the different types of bars, on any given night we counted between one-half and two-thirds of the patrons at the gay and lesbian bars engaged in behaviors we could reasonably classify as "drinking" (e.g., holding a beer bottle, glass of wine, shot glass, or, for a smaller minority of patrons, what appeared to be a mixed drink). At the straight bars, nearly everyone off the dance floor constantly held or tended some sort of drink (although some may have been holding what appeared to be a mixed drink that did not contain alcohol), and more than a few on the dance floor held drinks. Dancers at gay and lesbian bars, as the excerpts above illustrate, rarely held drinks while dancing.[19]

Patrons provided various shorthand accounts for the intense collective dance floor watching that occurs in gay and lesbian bars. Some accounts focused on simply seeing the "bodies" on the floor—different shapes, sizes, attributes, and so on. About one-third of the accounts we collected explicitly focused on who might be "available" relationally and or sexually. More patrons referred to dance floor watching as entertainment because it enabled one to tie into the bar's "fun," "wildness," or "exuberance." Gay and lesbian patrons, in contrast to the straight bars, considered drinking to be ancillary to dancing and watching the dancers. Although patrons in both gay and lesbian bars watched the dance floor and intensely watched individual dancers whom they found attractive in some fashion, we did not observe women in lesbian bars intensely and blatantly watching other women from afar in the fashion that men in straight bars "scoped" (to borrow from the vernacular) women or men in gay bars scoped other men. Women in lesbian bars typically hid their scoping by sneaking looks or engaging women in conversation, and they watched other women from a distance.

The excerpts above also underscore the differential responses to physical violations of territories of the self in gay and lesbian bars. Touch responses to territorial violations occurred frequently in gay and lesbian bars. In straight bars, the same types of behaviors, when they did occur, often were labeled as "groping" or even "copping a feel." Indeed, we were touched in nonoffensive ways in gay and lesbian bars that we would have regarded as "inappropriate" or even dangerous in straight bars. These differential reactions to violations of territories of the self suggest that personal preserves in gay and lesbian bars are less restrictive and more permeable than in straight bars.

We did not observe what appeared to be previously disconnected women or men in gay and lesbian bars approach other women or men (as in the straight bars) to ask them to dance or buy a drink. On the dance floor, such approaches primarily involved solo individuals joining groups larger than two to dance. This occurred more often in gay bars than lesbian bars. We admit that such approaches can unfold in more subtle ways in gay and lesbian bars than the obvious approaches we observed in straight bars. However, our forays into the "quiet" areas of bars (including Sappho's living room and the restrooms at Matricks and BD's) suggest that few overt approaches between previously disconnected men or women were being made on the premises.[20] Moreover, we did not observe approaches that imitated stereotypical male-initiated approaches to women in straight bars or butch/femme role playing. That is, we did not observe men approaching other men who played passive roles or women approaching other women who played passive roles.

Like women in straight bars, men in gay bars dressed to showcase their bodies. At BD's, for example, it was not uncommon to encounter men without shirts. Men who signaled a theme to their clothing—whether "queens" in formal gowns, men dressed as construction workers, or a man wearing only brief-style underwear with a leather chain harness and collar around his neck—also dressed to accentuate some aspect of their bodies. In contrast to women in straight bars and men in gay bars, women in lesbian bars wore attire that typically revealed little of their bodies. On any given night at Sappho's, for instance, most women would be dressed in loose-fitting jeans, T-shirts or button-down-collar shirts, and athletic or oxford-style shoes.

Tie Signs in Straight, Gay, and Lesbian Bars

Another noticeable difference between territorial interaction in gay and lesbian bars and the interaction occurring in straight bars related to the tie signs we observed in each context. Consider these examples from straight bars:

- A man slowly guides a woman through a crowd at Prism by walking behind her with his hands tightly cupped on each of her shoulders. They stop, and he takes his hands from her shoulders and stands only a couple of inches from her. They begin to move again and he places his hands on her shoulders to guide her through the crowd.

- A woman and a man sit at a table in Captive with their chairs touching, leaning forward toward one another so that their faces are a couple of inches apart. After a few minutes, the man pulls his chair back and sips his beer and the woman sips her drink. A few minutes later he pulls his chair back so that it is touching the woman's and puts his arms on the back of her chair and on the table so that her torso is between his arms.

- A woman walks into the main area at Down Under and throws her arms around another woman, lightly kissing her on the cheek, as the other woman hugs her. After the embrace, they back away from each other, holding each other's hands as they face each other, and talk in animated fashion for several minutes

- A man walks into the main bar area at Steppin' Out and shakes the hand of another man, simultaneously slapping him on the back. They begin conversing facing each other only inches apart. They do not touch again.

As illustrated by the first two of these representative interactions, ties signs among male-female pairs in straight bars varied by gender. Men typically extended their arms to touch a women (often without moving their torsos together) or put their arms on a physical prop (such as a chair, a table, or the bar itself) to signal the boundary between common space and their and the woman's territory. In response to this, women moved their torsos or chairs close to men. Some bar patrons called this modal tie sign the process of a man "reeling in" a woman. Another feature of male-female tie signs in straight bars, illustrated by the second excerpt above, was their episodic character. That is, they would begin, desist, and then be reinitiated (more often than not by men rather than women). Tie signs among all-female groups (either pairs or groups) were limited to short hugs and handholding that would typically last for a few seconds to two or three minutes. Men in straight bars limited their tie signs to shaking hands, sitting with one another, or standing close to one another (although never touching).

Now consider these tie signs among pairs in gay and lesbian bars:

· Two men sit at a table in BD's hugging each other tightly for several minutes, their chairs and torsos touching. Occasionally, they kiss each other on the mouth, never breaking their hug.

· A group of three men stand near the dance floor at BD's with their arms and torsos commingled tightly such that when one shifts his weight they all must readjust themselves.

· Two men greet each other at BD's with a hug that lasts a full minute. The continue to embrace and talk for several minutes before parting ways.

· Two women walk through the crowd at Sappho's with their arms tightly around each other. They pause for a moment and kiss each other for a few seconds and then continue on to the dance floor.

· Two women greet a third woman near the dance floor at Sappho's, hugging each other simultaneously and exchanging long kisses. After this encounter, the solo woman and the pair go in separate directions.

These excerpts underscore the greater intensity, uninterrupted character, and mutuality of tie signs in gay and lesbian bars. Indeed, the panoramic view of the main bar areas on any given night in the gay and lesbian bars captured a crowd that was constantly and physically intertwined with one another in various tie signs. Such tie signs involved various kinds of sustained touching between people's torsos, chairs, arms, and heads. Indeed, the modal tie sign, particularly in Sappho's, was the full hug that involved both parties touching their torsos as they embraced for extended periods.

CONCLUSION AND IMPLICATIONS: INCLUSION, INTRUSION,
POWER, AND PERSONAL RELATIONSHIPS

Our research underscores the distinctive differences in the enactment of gender and sexual identities across quasi-public contexts associated with particular patterns of sexuality. One way to analytically summarize these differences and to provide a point of departure for discussing the theoretical implications raised by our research is to conceptualize these patterns as falling along two continua: "inclusion" and "intrusion." *Inclusion* refers to the incorporation of others into territories of the self. A territory can be more or less inclusive based on the different types of people (e.g., same or different sex) typically allowed into particular territories, as well as the openness of territories to visual (e.g., wearing revealing clothes or dancing alone) and/or physical (e.g., touch, walking through a territory) encroachment or violations. Less inclusive territories constrain others from physically or visually entering into or encroaching upon personal preserves. *Intrusion* refers to the initiation of territorial violations. The more intrusive a context, the more people actively violate or attempt to violate, either physically or visually, territories of the self maintained by others.

Figure 7.1 presents in stylized form the overall patterns of inclusion and intrusion in the three contexts studied, based on our comparative observations.[21] A quick glance at Figure 7.1 suggests an important pattern with respect to gender: men in gay and straight contexts tend to be more intrusive than women in either straight or lesbian contexts.[22] In gay and straight bars, men are more likely to scope, touch, and encroach upon others who are not within the boundaries of their territories of the self. In gay bars such intrusion is primarily directed at other men, whereas in straight bars male intrusion is almost exclusively directed toward women.

Beyond these overall differences, the enactment of gender intersects with sexual identity to produce distinctive patterns with respect to inclusion and intrusion. Men in gay bar contexts are simultaneously the most intrusive and inclusive, which means that territories of the self in gay bars are at once permeable and encroached upon more often than in any of the

FIGURE 7.1
Stylized Depiction of Intrusive and Inclusive Dynamics by Gender
and Predominate Sexual Identities in Bars

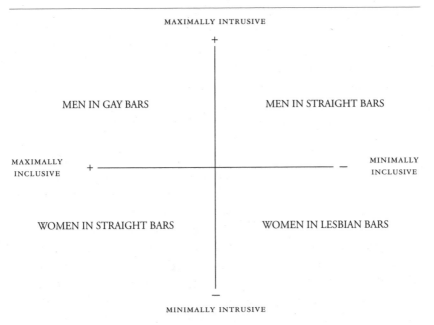

MAXIMALLY INTRUSIVE

+

MEN IN GAY BARS | MEN IN STRAIGHT BARS

MAXIMALLY   +   —   MINIMALLY
INCLUSIVE   INCLUSIVE

WOMEN IN STRAIGHT BARS | WOMEN IN LESBIAN BARS

—

MINIMALLY INTRUSIVE

Note: The placement of groups in the quadrants is based on interpretive inferences drawn from the analysis of our field data.

other bar contexts. Indeed, normative male behavior in the gay bar we studied required that men engage in the constant physical and visual commingling of personal preserves. At the opposite extreme were the modal behaviors exhibited by women in lesbian bars, who simultaneously were the least intrusive and, except for men in straight bars, the least inclusive. Women in lesbian bars engaged in highly durable and intense tie signs to signal the boundaries of their territorial preserves, engaged in limited forms of individual gaze (although they did engage in collective forms of gaze at dancers on the dance floor), and wore relatively unrevealing clothing that reduced the invitation to gaze at them. Men in straight contexts patrolled the least porous territorial boundaries by not dancing alone, by limiting the types of people permitted in their territories of self on the dance floor to women, and by not wearing clothes that explicitly revealed their bodies. At the same time, they were quite intrusive in terms of scoping women individually and collectively. Finally, women in straight bars tended to be inclusive visually (e.g., wearing clothing that revealed their bodies), less so physically (in terms of inviting touch and other physical encroachments), but were not particularly intrusive either physically or visually. Aside from providing a way to conceptualize normative patterns in three contexts we studied, our observations and inferences regarding inclusion and intrusion also carry implications for the interrelated nature of gender, sexual identity, personal relationships, and social power in public contexts.

The differences in inclusion and intrusion between women and men in straight bars also underscore the normative conceptions (informal "codes" in Goffman's terms) to which people orient themselves as they enact and recognize behaviors associated with particular gender and sexual identities. In straight bars, the enactment of behavior oriented to such codes approximates what Goffman describes as the "courtship complex" in which women "[make themselves] available for review in public" by men, who exercise power by either bestowing or withdrawing interest "at any point."[23] Although the onus of approaching a potential partner and maintaining the personal territory around an existing partner rests primarily with men at straight bars, this is accompanied by the power to decide whom one will approach, who will be included in one's preserve, and how one will maintain one's own personal preserve. As a result, men in straight bars are less likely to be the object of another person's desire. Additionally, women's territorial inclusiveness in straight bars can put them at a disadvantage relative to men with whom they are interacting. Similarly, males in straight bars are advantaged by their lesser inclusiveness and their tendency to invade others' space.

In gay and lesbian bars, the social power implications of personal preserves are not as easily discernible. For one thing, applying the courtship complex frame to interactions in gay and lesbian bars is problematic because stereotypical gender interactions are less prevalent. This is especially so in gay bars, in which the simultaneous preservation of one's territories and violation of others' territories are common. We suspect that the "negotiated order" of interpersonal power in such contexts is quite complex and perhaps based on issues other than territoriality.[24] At the same time, the ability to manage these two dynamics may itself demarcate status or confer some degree of social power on particular actors. For example, we witnessed some men in the gay bars who appeared to derive immediate notoriety from being especially inclusive *and* intrusive in their interactions and displays. By contrast, at lesbian bars, we witnessed far fewer violations of another's personal space, which suggests that interpersonal power in lesbian bars has less to do with simultaneously managing intrusion and inclusion than it does with managing exclusion.

Our focus has been on the linkages between gender and sexuality in particular locales—gay, lesbian, and straight bars. But our research also carries implications, albeit somewhat speculative, for broader issues relevant to the interpersonal dynamics of gender and sexuality in public places, and personal relationships more generally. Sociologists often note that women are "situationally disadvantaged" in public places because of pervasive normative assumptions about a woman's "limited" competence in such settings compared to men. Traditionally, women were discouraged from going out in public unaccompanied by a man, and in more recent rhetoric women are advised to prevent being criminally preyed upon by wearing "drab" or "unremarkable" clothing.[25] Our findings suggest that territories of the self both build on these assumptions and contribute to their reproduction. Territories of the self in straight contexts build not only on the courtship complex identified by Goffman but also on normative assumptions of what it means to be a woman in public. That is, the personal territories of which women are members remain open for intrusion *and* exclusion (control) by men. Lesbian and gay contexts—undergirded as they are by different normative assumptions about gender—do not display these tendencies. We do not argue that social power and predation are absent from these latter contexts but rather that social power does not turn on conventional conceptions of masculinity and femininity.

In conclusion, our research raises several questions about gender, sexuality, territories of the self, social power, and public places. The first of these concerns the relationship between gender and sexual identities as they are enacted in public places and their dynamics in private settings. What constraints and opportunities do private and public places offer for the departure from heterosexual normative conceptions regarding gender and sexual identity? How much does being on the public stage compel individuals to be mindful of stereotypical heterosexual enactments of gender and sexual identity? How do the interpersonal advantages in straight public places that men enjoy relative to women regarding territories of the self influence relational dynamics in private places? A second area for future research could focus on the broader contextuality of gender and sexual identities. How do conceptions and enactments of gender, sexual identity, and personal space differ across cultural and historical contexts? Finally, we need more research that links personal space and social relationships with larger spatial formations associated with particular gender and sexual identities. For these larger spaces (i.e., bars, neighborhoods, personal communities) in part regulate personal relationships by legitimating and instantiating normative conceptions and practices relevant to gender, sexual identity, and personal relationships. Studies of this sort would further our understanding of how the meanings associated with public places influence the "nexus"[26] between personal relationships, gender, and sexual identities.

METHODOLOGICAL PROCEDURES AND REFLECTIONS

The Team

Our team consisted of three people with different gender and sexual identities and different experiences in bars. All of us self-identified as Anglo. One researcher is active in the lesbian/gay community and had attended several gay and lesbian bars both locally and in other cities prior to beginning the study. The other two researchers had attended many straight bars both locally and in other communities. Our differences in prior experience in the bar community afforded the team different vantage points as "insiders" and "outsiders"[27] that we could enact simultaneously in the bars we studied. This stance meant, especially at the outset of research, that some of us were already participants in the bars we studied and had achieved "complete membership" roles, whereas other members of the team adopted more "peripheral" roles.[28]

These multiple vantage points afforded us the ability to approach each site with both a fresh and an experienced eye; to collect data simultaneously as naive visitors and experienced insiders. This also created interesting debates on the team as we discussed the significance of our findings, and it provided opportunities for reexamining assumptions about settings well known to parts of the team. For example, those with experience in straight bars took for granted the patterns of inclusion and intrusion observed among men and women there. To those with more experience in gay and lesbian settings, however, the patterns carried a mechanical and rigid feel that eventually led to insights regarding their power implications.

Our prior experiences also created concerns about our abilities to fit in at the different research sites. Early on, we used the collective resources on the team to overcome this anxiety by initially visiting the bars in pairs that included at least one person with substantial prior experience with that particular place. This strategy allowed us to "blend" into each place even at the outset. On the same night, for example, Karlin and Reid went to both Sappho's and Prism. At Sappho's, a female employee was selling tickets for a comedy show the next Friday. Trying to get us to buy tickets, she said, "Come on, you can make an evening of it. You can go on a date together, go out to dinner, then come to the show. It will be a great time." Later at Prism, we were approached by two men who asked us to dance. Both incidents suggest that others assumed that we were perceived by patrons as "belonging" at the bars we studied.

Another issue surfaced regarding our closeness/distance with the field relevant to the interval between our first and second periods of data collection. On the one hand, the time between the two fieldwork periods enabled us to approach coding all our data sets in a fresh way. Some of this development resulted from adding a new team member, Karlin, who brought a slightly different take on gender and social interaction than that shared by Reid and Bonham-Crecilius. Also during the interval, Reid discussed the chapter's direction with Calvin Morrill and David Snow. Nonetheless, we also feared that our time away from the field might diminish the subtleties we were able to infer from our fieldwork. Fortunately, we were able to establish continuity because we concretely linked our field notes from the first to the second fieldwork period and because two of the three researchers had participated in the first period of data collection.

Fieldwork

At the start of the project, the first (Reid) and third (Bonham-Crecilius) authors engaged in fieldwork, with the second author (Karlin) joining the team during the second data collection period. Reid and Bonham-Crecilius initially spent time together at every one of our original sites and then split up to work each site on different nights. Each fieldworker visited his or her sites an average of two nights per week, with each site visit lasting a minimum of three hours between 9:00 p.m. and 1:00 a.m. On some occasions we visited more than two of our study sites during a single night for "spot" comparisons. We also met at a late-night restaurant to compare notes and debrief after fieldwork nights. Reid and Bonham-Crecilius initially varied the days of week for their fieldwork but ultimately concentrated most of their time on weekends because the clubs drew larger crowds then. Because Reid and Bonham-Crecilius worked each of the five sites, their efforts provided us with some basis for assessing the consistency of our data across sites and researchers. In 1996 Reid and Karlin continued with the fieldwork, most often working together in the field twice per week in three- to four-hour blocks. They again concentrated on weekends and other high-volume clientele nights (e.g., promotional nights).

Whether working in pairs or alone, we carefully positioned ourselves in each bar to maximize the viewing angles we had of dance floors, as well as the tables and chairs surrounding them. On a periodic basis each night, we also engaged in "tours" around the clubs to get a feel for what was happening away from the floors or where drinks were being served. We took field jottings down in notebooks at our table and during visits to the restroom, where we also overheard conversations between men and women about situations out in the club. The loudness of the music at the clubs precluded eavesdropping, although we did manage conversational interviews with clientele in order to better understand aspects of their strategies (e.g., tie signs) for carving out and maintaining territories of the self.

Coding

During our initial data collection, we became particularly sensitive to personal space issues as we noticed the attention bar patrons devoted to carving out physical and social niches for themselves in the bars. This initial observation led us to Goffman's work on personal space and, ultimately, its relationship to gender and sexuality. We began coding our field notes by asking very basic questions about specific pieces of data to ascertain what we "thought" people were doing and/or trying to accomplish (e.g., "get a drink," "talk to a woman," "ask someone to dance") as they engaged in particular kinds of social interaction in the bars.[29] These questions led us to break our notes down into initial, broad categories within and across the research sites and to seek out patrons for conversational interviews to gain more insight into their activities in the bars. As our coding became more focused and we began to write short analytic memos about our initial findings, we concentrated on the way territories of the self are maintained and violated by men and women within and across our three sites, and we developed a grounded sense for how places can be associated with sexual and gender identities. The analytic utility of team research was underscored by our joint coding activities as much as by our fieldwork.

EIGHT

Breaking Up and Starting Over

Emotional Expression in Postdivorce Support Groups

AMY S. EBESU HUBBARD AND CINDY H. WHITE

DEMOGRAPHERS PREDICT THAT IF CURRENT trends continue, more than one-half of Americans getting married today will ultimately divorce, and approximately two-thirds of American children under the age of ten will find themselves living in a single-parent household at some point in their lives.[1] These trends and the recent concern about the stability of long-term, intimate relationships have sparked increasing interest in the social causes and psychological impacts of divorce.[2] Far less research considers how adults actually experience and negotiate the aftermath of divorce. These dynamics can be especially difficult in that they often involve continuing relationships with ex-spouses (particularly if dependent children are involved).[3] Although such dynamics often play out in the most private of places (e.g., households and lawyers' and counselors' offices), they also unfold in a variety of public places, including courtrooms, sidewalks, and parks. One context where these dynamics increasingly occur is in the postdivorce support group. Postdivorce support groups operate as a group-based therapy that attempts to help divorced individuals come to grips with the social and psychological consequences of divorce. Such groups are "quasi-public" in that they are not purely private *or* public. They have constraints on membership (being open only to divorced individuals) and dedicated functions (being focused on discourse about divorce) that purely public places typically do not have. At the same time, during group meetings the private experience of divorce—particularly the expression of intense emotions—is shared among other members who are almost always nonintimates and whose relationships, once constituted, often do not exist beyond the group. As we will argue below, the anchored nature of relationships in the group facilitates the disclosure of intimate details and emotions of divorce as individuals attempt to construct their own personal identities, understand their emotions, and manage whatever ties they have with their ex-spouses.

In the next section, we briefly discuss the therapeutic ideologies that inform postdivorce support groups, their quasi-public nature, the typical social relationships found in them, and the dynamics of emotional expressions among group members. We then discuss our field site and the field methods we used. The following section turns to aspects of emotional expression in the groups we studied. We conclude the chapter with implications of our research for the study of divorce and personal relationships in a variety of contexts.

POSTDIVORCE SUPPORT GROUPS, TRANSITORY SOCIALITY, AND EMOTIONAL EXPRESSION

Many of the psychotherapies that emerged in the United States during the 1960s emphasized the "unique, creative, and spontaneous aspects of individual experience"[4] in group contexts that provided an immediate "moment" where members could explore, in unfettered ways, their "authentic" selves and emotions.[5] Relationship support groups emerged as one such therapy that embodied this hybrid ideology.[6] These groups operate from the premise that individuals need to "get in touch" with their feelings about relationship loss in order find their "true selves" (or to construct new personal identities) that fit with their current life situations. Although some relationship loss programs are modeled after twelve-step programs for recovery such as Alcoholics Anonymous,[7] the postdivorce groups we studied focus on divorce as a life transition. To achieve self-discovery, group members typically receive instruction (by a group facilitator) using a variant of a "stage" model that enables individuals to work through their feelings and orientations toward their divorce and ex-spouse. Postdivorce support groups thus "provide sufferers and those around them with a means to grasp the nature of their distress."[8] Although postdivorce support groups share some things with contemporary step programs, postdivorce groups do not create a communal-like social setting (outside group meetings) that envelops participants.[9] Postdivorce group members typically enter the group without prior ties to other participants, but from the outset they are urged to publicly share intimate details of their experiences with the group. It is this seeming social mismatch—the sharing of personal experiences in a group of nonintimates—that gives postdivorce support groups much of their quasi-public character. This mismatch also compels individuals to be "freer" in the sense that their interactions with other members are largely unconstrained by prior relational obligations or interaction routines. Participants can live in the moment and eliminate layers of normative constraints that have repressed their own needs. Over time, group members usually develop relationships with one another that are firmly situated in the group itself but do not typically endure beyond the group.[10] In this sense, relationships among group members are anchored in the group, but they are ultimately transitory because they cease to exist once the group ends (over the several-week period that it meets).

Postdivorce support groups hold as especially significant the individual expression of intense emotions, especially anger. From an interactionist perspective, emotional expressions, no matter how idiosyncratic or individualistic they seem on the surface, are themselves embedded in ongoing processes of social interaction. As Jack Katz argues, emotional expressions occur through a person's intertwined "readings and responses" of others regarding the meaning that a line of action carries for a single moment and beyond.[11] Emotional expressions thus occur in dialectic processes both as something people subjectively enact and as "embodied" forces that appear to take over and compel people to act in particular ways. To express emotions, individuals "creatively mine," in subtle and complex ways, whatever resources (e.g., bodily, material, cultural) are available to convey their feelings.[12] Nonverbal gestures, facial configurations, social identities, and broad cultural narratives about how feelings "should" be expressed are all drawn upon to portray emotion. At the same time, emotions often reside beyond the horizons of people's consciousness as something invisible, either simmering beneath the surface (in Freudian images of the subconscious) or as a seeming physiological response that occurs apart from self-reflective cognition.

In postdivorce groups, emotional expressions play out amid flows of stories by group members that both respond to what the group is about (trying to help people come to grips with the aftermath of divorce, especially its emotional aspects) and are explicitly oriented toward broader contexts, including biographical details about former marriages, ongoing connections with ex-spouses, personal identities, or even culturally prescribed definitions of what "marriage" is about. In this way, emotional expressions are both "situationally responsive" and "biographically transcendent" in that they anticipate and respond to people in immediate situations but also reach to representations of contexts and identities that exist beyond the here and now. As people tell about their divorces in postdivorce groups, for example, they respond to the norms of the group to "tell their story" but also focus on what it means to be in a personal relationship more generally.

Finally, postdivorce groups are partly in the business of teaching *how* to express emotions—especially behavior that corresponds with particular definitions of "healthy" emotional expression. The teaching function of postdivorce groups is especially apparent with respect to family groups that include the children of divorced parents. Such groups often feature explicit exercises that involve teaching both discursive and embodied emotional expression.

What is unclear from this brief discussion is how postdivorce group members accomplish emotional expressions in the quasi-public context of the group and the anchored (albeit temporary) relationships among members. In the following sections we explore this issue, drawing from observations we made while participating in two postdivorce groups. But first we discuss the setting where we conducted our study—an organization that we will call "Divorce Assistance."

DIVORCE ASSISTANCE

Divorce Assistance is a nonprofit organization in Southwest City that organizes support groups for adults and families who are divorcing. Divorce Assistance groups are free to the public, although a donation is requested after each meeting. People generally come to meetings by personal referrals or through other support organizations. The advertised goal of the adult groups is to allow group members to discuss their experiences and to provide information about the divorce process. The family groups have similar goals, but parents and children participate in separate subgroups. The Divorce Assistance program is oriented around a "model of divorce" that incorporates three stages: "endings" (in which a marriage is legally dissolved), "the neutral zone" (in which one "gets one's bearings"), and "new beginnings" (in which one is open and "ready" to begin at least entertaining the possibility of meeting new people). This model is presented to group members as a practical tool designed to show the types of emotions and events people will experience in each stage, which in turn will enable them to explore their own feelings and orientations toward divorce. Each group meets for ten weeks, approximately ninety minutes per week. The first two meetings are considered "open" enrollment, after which new members are not added. New groups start every three weeks. Trained volunteers, who are often former Divorce Assistance group members, facilitate each group.[13]

We spent over sixty hours in the adult and children groups over a four-month period. In addition, we conducted informal interviews totaling seventeen hours with four adult participants, an adult group leader, a children's group leader, and a parents' group leader. White gained access to an adult support group, also run by Divorce Assistance, through a contact at the local university. Members of the group agreed to allow the researcher to participate in the group and gather information for the research project. There were twenty-two members on the adult group roster (eight men, fourteen women). Average attendance at each weekly session was fourteen. Aside from some obvious cues (e.g., people volunteering that they were originally from Mexico), it was difficult to discern the social class backgrounds and ethnicities of group members. Some members spoke eloquently, suggesting a college or postgraduate level of education, while others were inarticulate, whether from nerves or as a function of educational background. Each group in which we participated also contained two facilitators (a man and a woman) who had at least a college education and some postgraduate training in counseling. Although our differences in participation meant that each researcher experienced a somewhat different perspective during her fieldwork, these differences proved advantageous because they raised questions about inferences drawn by each researcher during the course of the fieldwork. Ebesu Hubbard gained access to a family-child support group by working as a volunteer. She assisted in the five- to six-year-olds' group by helping a trained group facilitator with the preparation and implementation of lesson plans. There were nine children in the group studied (five boys, four girls). Average attendance at each weekly meeting was six.

EMOTIONAL EXPRESSION AT DIVORCE ASSISTANCE

At the outset of each adult group meeting, a facilitator would invite participants to "check in," during which members would tell the group "how it was going," "what their week was like," or "how they felt" about a significant event relevant to their divorce. Comments by the facilitator and other members would sometimes occur either during or in response to these stories. The facilitator also controlled the pace of interaction among group members, stopping to enable the group to reflect on a point he or she believed was particularly salient or moving the group along when the conversation lagged. The facilitator also formally led the group through a discussion of the simple stage model (endings, neutral zone, and new beginnings). Throughout the ten-week session, group members would sometimes refer to the stage they were in with statements such as "I guess I'm still stuck in neutral" or "I think I'm entering a place where I can begin a new relationship." In this way, the stage model standardized some of the proceedings by providing a common touchstone for participants in their emotional expressions. At the same time, much of the discourse and interaction in the groups did not explicitly refer to the stage model, instead focusing on the sharing of emotionally charged stories and observations about interactions with ex-spouses.

Adults Checking In: Establishing Common Ground

Aside from learning fragmented aspects of each person's recent experiences, most group members knew few, if any, biographical details, about other participants at the outset of a session—save that each member was divorced. Nonetheless, in a matter of a few minutes, group participants would share aspects of their relational lives with one another that are typically not shared with anyone outside a close circle of friends or family, or are not shared at all. Consider this scene recounted from our field notes that occurred one night during check-in. In it, Sue, who had recently divorced her spouse after a thirty-year marriage, began discussing a situation with her now ex-spouse:

> As members were going around the circle "checking in" with each other, Sue revealed that on Wednesday she had driven by her ex's house—just to check on him—and noticed that his car was not in the driveway. Thinking her ex had not arrived home yet, Sue decided to check back later. On this second pass his car was still not in the driveway, and Sue became convinced that he was out on a date, which made her mad. She continued to stew about this until later that night, when she wrote her ex a letter telling him just how she felt about him and how he had treated her during their marriage. Letter in hand, she drove over to his house—for the third time that evening—and dropped the letter in his mailbox, noticing that his car still was not in the driveway! A few days

later, she received an angry letter from her ex. Sue told the group that she had been feeling guilty about this because she found out the next day, from her son, that her ex's car had broken down and he had been home all evening. As Sue talked, others in the group looked intently at Sue, some nodding their heads at various points in her story. After Sue finished her story, group members chimed in with statements about how they "understood" what she was going through and offered short excerpts describing similar situations in which they had structured an opportunity to "run into" their exes and had been foiled in the attempt.

This scene was typical of the way in which a "check-in" story unfolded. Each individual would generally speak for a few minutes, often sharing an emotionally wrenching situation about his or her divorce or an interaction with an ex-spouse. Occasionally, a group member would take a lot of time for his or her check-in and would be gently interrupted by the facilitator so that the group "could move on" to another participant. This example also illustrates the normative ground rules of the group that approximate those found among nonintimates in public places, where overt evaluations and judgments of others are often suspended.[14] With regard to Sue, group members did not criticize her for being upset that her ex might be out on a date. Nor did they question Sue's detective work with regard to her husband's whereabouts that night or contradict her interpretation of the events. Through these processes—all of which occurred within a compressed few minutes—the group constituted the common ground necessary for individuals to engage in emotional expression.

Aspects of Adult Emotional Expressions: Transcendence, Artful Embodiment, and Identity

Interlaced with the check-in are several aspects of emotional expressions. Consider this story by Rick, an Anglo male in his mid-thirties:

Rick reported to the group that his wife had continued to call him even though he had asked her not to call. On their wedding anniversary, she telephoned again. Rick had made plans to do something that evening to keep busy (and presumably to avoid contact), but when his plans fell through he felt alone, so he returned his ex-wife's phone call. The conversation got out of hand, and they fought. Rick said he had been thinking constantly about this since it happened and was upset about allowing her to make him angry and to draw him in. As Rick finished his story (about seven minutes), group members offered assessments of the situation that legitimized his anger at his spouse (but not his current sadness or shame about fighting). One member, Ted, told Rick that "things happen for a reason, so this conflict probably *needed* to occur [emphasis by the informant]." And another group member, Steve, said that he thought it was "okay to fight because Rick was being honest with his ex about how he felt at the time."

In response to this story, the facilitator pointed out that expressing anger was one of the most important and difficult aspects of divorce—a point that she had made several times in previous group meetings. Rick's recounting and the responses by those in the group were thus both situationally responsive and situationally transcendent on multiple levels. On the one hand, Rick responded to the immediate situation of the group and its requirement of emotion talk. That is, the group required that individuals talk about their feelings with respect to divorce and their ex-spouses. At the same time, Rick's story, and the responses to it, transcended the moment by helping to shape his understanding of what it meant to express anger with an ex-spouse and perhaps in close personal relationships more generally. Consistent with the overall theme of "authentic" emotional expression, group members overtly valued the content of Rick's story as a positive occurrence, as something that was "healthy" and "had to occur" if he was to become a healthy individual. The process of valuing and validating emotional experience is important because rather than encouraging a sense of responsibility for emotion, it naturalizes the emotional experience, making it an understandable part of the divorce experience. Finally, Rick's emotional expressions moved away from the proximate context to shape his understanding of what it meant to conduct personal relationships in quasi-public contexts.

Consider another story, this time told by Tina, an Hispanic woman in her early forties, about an incident that had recently occurred when she had gone out to her van to go to church the previous Sunday:

One day, she saw oil under the van and, upon checking, found a visibly apparent hole in the van's oil pan. When she found the oil problem, she was sure that the hole in the oil pan had been made "intentionally," and she "just knew" that her husband or his family (whom she had reported earlier were driving by and bothering her) were responsible. She was angry and went to confront her husband about the situation where he lived; he denied involvement and they fought "ferociously" on the doorstep of his place. Tina's ex-husband's neighbor called the police as the fight escalated to shouting and name calling. Upon their arrival, the police separated Tina and her ex, and Tina quickly departed the scene without incident. As Tina recounted her story, her body slightly shook and she raised her voice to a high pitch. Members of the group shook their heads from side to side and grimaced. At the conclusion of the story, some commented that they "supported" and could understand her response to the situation and had experienced similar situations but were sorry the police had become involved.

Like Rick, Tina acted in accordance with the group-based situational norms that required her to disclose her feelings freely. And like Rick, her story and the responses to it transcended the situation by speaking to the general way she "handled herself" and to situations in their own lives that paralleled what Tina had experienced rather than inquiring about the details of the situation or her role in creating the situation.

But there was more to her emotional expression than responding in lockstep fashion to the individualistic, therapeutically informed norms of the group. For Tina artfully drew from various kinds of dramatic conventions and "embodied practices"[15] to tell her story. Her narrative exhibited all the markings of a made-for-television legal melodrama in which a dramatic tension emerges during mundane activities (the discovery of oil and the hole in the oil pan), which in turn leads to a hypothesis of responsibility (her ex-husband's family) and a confrontation between the victim and alleged offender, followed by a quick resolution. As her story unfolded, we also noticed how her body and voice were used to convey the intensity of the experience. Is the point that she constructed, in some consciously reflective way, the emotions she had experienced at the time and was, in part, reexperiencing in the group? She certainly constructed the emotion in the sense that her narrative, bodily movements, and tonal qualities of her voice wove together a performance of sorts. But her expression also depended on group members' responses to define the situation and sustain the performance. However, like a lot of stories told in the group, a member's performance was embodied in that the emotion was also expressed through Tina's bodily movements rather than solely through her discourse. Her nonverbal gestures and the tone of her voice carried, with respect to emotion, what her words could not. Moreover, her embodied practices guided the collective attention of group members toward her emotional responses to both the situation she recounted and the situation at hand in the group. In this way, her emotional expression was, in part, beyond her conscious reflection. It is interesting that in a group that was designed to allow people to reflect on their experience, the "demands" of the group and the experience of narrating personal experiences created an environment where emotional experience seemed beyond conscious reflection.

A final feature of the interactive dynamics of emotion expressions concerns personal identities. Personal identities—those aspects of self that signal an individual's uniqueness—involve the processes through which people classify each other in "systematically related categories,"[16] which, in turn, enable meaningful social interaction to occur. Such identities emerge in powerful ways during emotional expressions in that one's sense of self is dependent upon the lines of action that are joined in with others. Stan, a forty-something white male, underscores this observation during the following story in the group:

> After check-in was over, Stan told a story during which he indicated that he had been "caught" in a lot of contact with his ex-wife. She tried to commit suicide and was subsequently hospitalized. He said that things had been "fairly smooth" for him and then this had happened. He visited his ex-wife several times in the hospital. He said he had feelings of love for her but found it hard to deal with this because he now "had his own life." He also mentioned that during his visits he made a point of putting on his wedding ring. At one point, he told the group in a low voice, "I guess that's kind of phony." Group members responded with words that indicated that they "understood" Stan's situation. Some even volunteered a short story that tried to draw an analogy between what Stan experienced and their own lives.

In this story, we see Stan wrestling with the interplay between an identity he no longer believed it was legitimate to project—being a husband to and caring for an ill wife—and the sense that his "self" was being compelled by (emotional) forces that were beyond his control. This story reveals a dualism of identity with respect to emotion that was often evident within the group. Individuals often viewed themselves as both subject (in the active sense that they were doing something) and object (in the sense of being acted upon) within the emotional dynamics they were producing and experiencing.[17] Moreover, Stan seemed almost mystified by what he had revealed about his "phoniness" at putting on his wedding ring to visit his wife in the hospital.

Emotional Expression in the Children's Group

Unlike the adult group, which had a free-flowing character, the children's group exhibited a structure closer to the kinds of lesson plans one might encounter in the early grades of primary school. Much of the initial sessions focused on teaching children how to think about themselves and represent their emotions in the aftermath of their parents' divorce. In the first meeting of the ten-week session, for example, the group facilitators told children that they were attending the meetings because each of them was "a child of divorce." They then provided the children with a set of terms designed to help them understand how to cope with divorce and express themselves. Included in these terms were various modifications on the stage model (in simplified language) taught to adults. The facilitators also worked with children to say the word *divorce* during their participation in group exercises. The following interaction between the facilitator and a six-year-old in the group illustrates this pattern:

FACILITATOR
(TO THE GROUP): Why are we here?

CHILD: We are here to talk about IT [emphasis by the informant].

FACILITATOR
(RAISING HER VOICE A BIT): What are we here to talk about?

CHILD: We are here to talk about divorce.

This exchange prompted a round of applause initiated by the facilitator because, according to her, this was a "breakthrough" in that it was "the first time in the group this particular child had uttered what many of the children call the 'D' word."

In another early meeting during the ten-week session, children of all ages were brought together and asked to create a list of emotions, which the facilitator wrote on a big sheet of white butcher paper on one side of the group. The group created a list of twenty words to represent various emotions. Then the facilitators divided the larger group into subgroups (by age) in order to discuss the list. Both older and younger children repeated the terms they had just listed, but in distant, almost rote fashions that left a distinct impression that the meanings of these words and the emotions they represented were unclear to the children. Much of the discussion of the lists, regardless of the ages of the children in each subgroup, was left to the facilitators, who led the children through the exercise but were often unable to pry opinions from the children about the emotions they were discussing. In subsequent sessions, the facilitator asked children of different ages to recall their collective emotion list, at which point the children only generated five of the previously listed emotions: "worried," "lonely," "sad," "scared," and "mad." Indeed, these emotions, especially "mad" (as in the adult group) often occupied center stage in exercises and discussions among the children. In an effort to expand the list to encompass "positive" emotions, the facilitator prompted the children to add some of the terms they had previously listed, including "love" and "surprise." Although the children agreed to add these words to their list, the facilitator was unable to generate any meaningful discussion, and it was unclear that the children could relate to these terms in any significant way.

Other exercises in the group with regard to emotion were designed to encourage the children to put their sadness or anger "behind them." From the perspective of the facilitator, such exercises were an attempt to "push" the children beyond the stages of ending or neutral toward new beginnings. Consider this excerpted observation that occurred during one of the last group meetings in the ten-week session. During this meeting, the children completed an exercise that required them to draw a picture to represent being "sad":

> The facilitator began drawing her picture of sadness and the children followed suit. Stick figures with tears, suns covered with clouds, and other images filled the pages upon which the children drew. When everyone had completed his or her picture, the facilitator led a short discussion of what the images drawn by the children had meant to each of them. Most of the children simply described what they had drawn without much connection to the emotion of "sadness." (Interestingly, not a single child cried during this exercise.) As the discussion wound down, the facilitator stated in a matter-of-fact tone that she was no longer sad, ceremoniously crumpling up her picture into a wad, and throwing it decisively into a trash can that stood on one side of the group. All of the children, except one little boy, followed suit by crumpling their papers and throwing them away. When asked why he had kept his picture, the little boy said that he was not "over his sadness yet."

In this exercise we see the teaching of both the aesthetic (the representation of emotion in a drawing) and the corporeal (the act of throwing away one's sadness by throwing away a drawing that represents it) aspects of emotion, albeit without much discussion of either among the group.

Whether children simply followed the teacher's example in rote fashion, thus creating a cascading effect among themselves as they imitated each other, or enjoyed the playfulness of the exercise (e.g., getting to throw something away) is unclear. Perhaps most interesting is the little boy who would not throw his paper away because he clearly connected on a fairly deep level with the exercise.

Many exercises in the children's group incorporated explicit corporeal expressions of emotion, especially anger. Much of the time these exercises took the form of asking children to think of different, "constructive" ways of expressing their anger. The children offered many ways of expressing their anger, including yelling at their parents or siblings, hitting their fists against the wall, or simply screaming. Among these emotional expressions, the facilitator underscored a few as "good," including "hitting a pillow on a bed," "hitting a pillow on a wall," or "yelling into a pillow." The facilitator added "scrunching up a newspaper" and "riding a bicycle" to this list. What was most interesting about these examples is that they all involved expressing emotion via embodied actions rather than language. Like an acting coach, the facilitator of the children's group also provided examples of good "props" (e.g., pillows, bicycles, newspapers) that could be used during the expression of emotion and appropriate ways to stage an emotion (e.g., be alone so as not to hurt or disturb anyone). The corporeal and solo character of modeled children's emotional expressions offered a contrast to those legitimated for adults, who were often encouraged to express their anger via language (rather than physically) to ex-spouses as a necessary part of the postdivorce process.

All of these examples and our commentary point to the idea, sustained within the discussions and exercises in both the adult and children's groups, that emotion, especially anger, was foundational to the divorcing experience. In both groups, adults and children were pushed to "get things out," to become aware of their emotions. In everyday interactions, by contrast, emotion typically occurs without such cognitive and discursive self-awareness. That is, most people, acting in the moment, do not perceive a source of irritation and then "construct" their anger via a conscious process. Rather, they read and respond to a situation in a sensual way, as a "living poetry."[18] The groups attempt to teach both adults and children to be more self-aware of their emotions in order to control their expressions. Thus the "insight" that adults and children gain about emotional expressions from the groups is diametrically opposed to typical experience and enactment of emotion outside the group.

Throughout this chapter, we have sought to understand how people express emotions regarding their postdivorce experiences in the context of a support group. In the adult group, such expressions centered on stories told by participants about their continuing relational connections with ex-spouses. Many of these narratives involved anger and ventured into guilt or shame. Through these stories, we explored the artfulness, situational responsiveness, transcendence, and personal identity aspects of emotional expressions. In the children's group, we observed how group facilitators structured exercises in an attempt to "teach" children "appropriate" ways to express emotion, yet often failed to meaningfully engage children in discussion about emotion. Children responded in more active ways when emotional expression turned on aspects of embodied practice rather than language. Aside from these patterns, our findings point to two implications regarding the complexity of the concept of "public" as it relates to emotional expression and a final ironic speculation about what postdivorce groups may "really" teach their participants.

As we noted at the outset of this chapter, we regard postdivorce support groups as quasi-public. At first glance, such a pairing—postdivorce support group and public—may seem odd or even mistaken. Postdivorce support groups contain discussions of some of the most intimate and gut-wrenching details about people's lives. Moreover, the groups do not exhibit the usual accessibility and visibility associated with most public places, such as streets, plazas, parks, bars, or bus stops. Postdivorce support groups are not accessible to everyone (one must be divorced or, in the case of the children's group, the child of a divorced parent), and their inner dynamics are not visible to broader social audiences. Our initial argument regarding the publicness of the groups hinged on two social dimensions rather than geographical or regulatory characteristics. First, the groups predominately contained nonintimate relationships in that participants were unacquainted with one another prior to each ten-week session and developed anchored ties within the group. These ties were ultimately transitory because most did not survive outside the group. Second, aspects of each member's intimate lives became publicly available for inspection by other members of the group.

These characteristics underscore the complexity of the boundaries between private and public contexts and point toward the social side of public contexts—what Lyn Lofland calls "social realms."[19] Social realms are constituted by the predominance of particular relational forms rather than aspects of place. "Public realms" are dominated by stranger-stranger relations and fleeting relationships that are compressed temporally but nonetheless may carry some emotional currency. In contrast, close, durable relationships predominate in the "private realm." Between these realms is the "parochial realm"—a social territory of acquaintances, workmates, and neighborhood co-residents. Postdivorce groups, and perhaps all similarly conducted support groups, do not fit easily into any one of these categories because they typically contain strangers (characteristic of the public realm) who develop limited relationships that approximate those found in parochial realm gatherings in which people share information that one would expect in the private realm. More precisely, one could argue that postdivorce groups constitute a social border that operates in multidimensional social space at the interstices between the public, parochial, and private realms. It is in these border regions that the norms of multiple realms are mixed. In urban settings, such border or transitional regions can create confusion, even conflict, as people navigate through them.[20] In the postdivorce group, this seemingly contradictory and multivalenced normative order, because it exists in a safe haven with regulated boundaries and limited visibility, compels and facilitates individuals to share their feelings. We should point out, however, that this interpretation is paradoxical with respect to one of the ostensible purposes of the group that purports to help members come to grips with their divorces by providing them a standardized lens (the stage model) through which to understand their experiences. Group participants do, from time to time, refer to the stage model, but they mainly tell their stories in their own ways, spurred on by the facilitator to share and be authentic in their emotional expressions. Our contention is that the therapeutic goals of the group are facilitated by operation in a social region where people are freed from the relational conventions that they might experience in either the private or parochial realms but where they have more relational opportunities than in purely public realms.

A second, albeit speculative, implication that our work points to is the irony of what participants learn in the groups. Although it is unclear what children learn, and certainly some adults come away with insights into their own emotions that enable them to start fresh intimate relationships, our sense is that adults also come away from postdivorce support groups with a very different set of relational skills (about intimate relationships) than what the group purports to teach them. The quasi-public character of the group means that group members, in order to consistently and successfully participate in discussions in the group, must become adept at accomplishing relational practices with strangers that are usually reserved for the private realm. In the public realm, interactional norms and practices stress social distance and a kind of minimalist orientation to social interaction with strangers. In the group, by contrast, these norms and practices are turned upside down: group members reveal the most intimate details of their lives with people they do not know. At the same time, group members engage in interaction norms that are more typical of public contexts, such as following norms of interaction that discourage being openly critical of other members or holding others accountable for their actions.[21] Group members, then, become more adept at explicitly blurring the differences between relational intimacy and nonintimacy. Thus one of the unintended skills learned by individuals in postdivorce groups is the ability to kindle, in relatively compressed periods, a sense of social intimacy with strangers. Rather than developing the insight and skills needed to begin new intimate relationships that lead to long-term commitments, group participants may develop the ability to flexibly adapt to nonintimate social relationships in contemporary urban life, especially in public places and realms.

In sum, we used the overlapping contexts of divorce and postdivorce support groups to study emotional expression. We contend that this study continues the expansion of relationship research by investigating aspects of relationships and their dissolution heretofore overlooked by previous studies. The contextual aspects of personal relationships, especially those that occur on the borders between different social realms and in the complex interstices of intimacy and nonintimacy, are areas worthy of additional inquiry.

METHODOLOGICAL PROCEDURES AND REFLECTIONS

Perhaps the most challenging aspect of our fieldwork involved collecting information during the group sessions. The groups did not allow us to tape-record conversations, which meant that we had to rely upon jotted field notes. Fortunately, some members also took notes during the groups, which provided us cover. Ebesu's role as a volunteer also enabled her to hold a clipboard on which she jotted field notes.

As our fieldwork proceeded, we regularly read our field notes in chronological order, incorporating the newest sets as we produced them. We also began to "open-code" our field notes to obtain a sense of the range and depth of information available in them.[22] As we came to regard our notes as a data set rather than a set of jottings, we attempted to identify and label the types of talk that occurred in the groups.[23] Two questions guided our initial analyses: What are the activities accomplished in the group? and What are the recurring themes discussed in the groups? These questions ultimately yielded a "mixed typology"[24] drawn from our own labels for the themes and activities of the group and categories that the group members used. This typology also fed into our data collection as we focused our observations around it. Our data collection and analysis thus unfolded in constant interplay with one another throughout the research. For the purposes of this chapter, we focused on a subset of our observations that dealt with how group members engaged in emotional expressions.

Niele is the Hawaiian word for inquisitiveness or curiosity, but it is often used in the pejorative sense to mean a busybody who asks things that should not concern him or her. Our experience as ethnographic researchers in support groups involved constant consideration of how to handle intellectual inquiry in situations where individuals are truly hurting and concerned about their privacy. We believe that working as a team on this project helped us manage this complex issue and better understand the nature of the groups we studied. Gaining access to the groups and finding an appropriate role within the groups were important challenges in this research project.

Our original intent was to study personal relationships in transition, which led us to the idea of contacting groups that help people through this process. These efforts met with the typical access problems fieldworkers face as they attempt entree into many contemporary settings, including several weeks of telephone "tag," missed appointments, brush-offs, alternative leads, and then, finally, a minor breakthrough when we achieved direct contact with the Divorce Assistance program manager. This program seemed an intriguing place to understand how people experience a relationship transition. As we discussed earlier in the chapter, we quickly realized the central importance of emotional expression in the groups and the fact that the recounting of intimacy and pain we observed was occurring under watchful gaze of fellow members in the group—all strangers. Our discussions with the director suggested that our best bet for access would be to get involved with groups as they were starting their sessions. We began by contacting Divorce Assistance volunteers who would be leading groups in the near future.

Negotiating Access to the Adult Group: Cindy's Experience

I called the leader of an adult support group, Karen, on a Tuesday evening. Karen is a professional counselor who works as a volunteer for Divorce Assistance. Early discussion of my research interests seemed to go well, but when the discussion turned to consideration of my actual participation in the group, the tone of the conversation shifted. Karen was very reluctant to allow a researcher into the group. She told me that she knew that the group would be really "out of it" and that some of them would be "basket cases." Attempts to convince her that the intrusiveness could be minimized didn't work; in fact, as the conversation progressed, Karen become quite anxious and suggested I was "just using people." This was not an auspicious start! Afraid that I had "blown" this contact, I worked to keep Karen on the phone long enough to reestablish a sense of rapport. I acknowledged her concerns about the intrusion and reassured her that our interests in the group were tied to a desire to understand the process of relational dissolution and to do a better job of assisting people through it. Karen then suggested that perhaps it would be best if I "went undercover" and simply told members of the group I was divorced. I wasn't comfortable with this, it flew in the face of several institutional research ethics, and I believed it could ultimately limit my ability to interact with group members. We agreed to talk through these issues with the co-leader of the group, Ron, who had previously participated in a Divorce Assistance group. After some discussion, Karen and Ron suggested that I function as an "assistant" group facilitator and present some information about the research project at the second meeting of the group.

During the second meeting, I spoke to the group for about ten minutes explaining my interests in the project and sharing a bit about my own marriage and my experience with my parents' divorce (this proved to be a useful credential in convincing the adult group to allow me to participate). I was a little nervous about making the proposal. Before the meeting began, one new member protested to Karen about having to put her name and address on a sign-in sheet. She asked, "You can't even be anonymous in a help group?" It was clear to me that at least one group member was concerned about the privacy of the group. After my talk, I answered two questions from members. The first question was whether members would be able to see what I was writing. I explained that the notes would be made available and that I planned to provide a copy of the paper produced from the project to members of the group who were interested. I was also asked if this was a dissertation project; I explained that it was a class project.

As this point, the leader suggested that I leave the group so that they could discuss this at the end of the meeting. However, one member of the group interjected by saying, "Well, first off, I think the problem in divorce is lack of communication, not communication, but I think we ought to let her stay. I don't know if I should be the spokesperson for the group because I may not be here the whole time, but I think we ought to vote and see about letting her stay." He explained that he had participated in groups like this before and thought that I would miss a lot of good information if I left. A second man (who I later learned used to be a university professor) seconded the motion and suggested they vote on this. There was some awkward silence at this point. Two women, the one who protested about putting her name on the list and the woman next to her, appeared to dislike the proposal. They oriented themselves away from me, crossed their arms, and would not make eye contact with me. I then suggested that I would leave the room for a bit while the group conferred. About ten minutes later, the co-leader of the group came out to tell me that I could stay but the group members wanted the option to ask me to leave if anyone felt uncomfortable with what I was doing. I readily agreed. My role in the group did not become one of "assistant" leader, as Karen and Ron had suggested. Instead, I became a participant observer who was reflecting on my childhood experiences of divorce and the nature of marriage. These experiences allowed me to participate in the discussion, although I did so less than most other group members. I was treated as a member of the group, although group members did ask periodically how my research project was progressing. My role did not seem to change the dynamics of the group significantly, which I believe speaks to the ability of researchers to study personal relationships up close without disrupting the interaction process.

Gaining Access to the Children's Group: Amy's Experience

My entrance into the children's group proved less eventful than Cindy's experiences. Whereas the members of Cindy's group were initially aware of Cindy as an outsider who would be studying them, I, more than the group I studied, was very aware of being an outsider and worried about the group asking me questions. How do you study a group when you feel like you are an outsider, a stranger? How do you try to blend into a group that you are studying and try to be as unobtrusive as possible when you look and feel different from the other people there and those people are naturally curious about where you are from and what you are doing there? This is how I felt. I was even more apprehensive because I had been away from home

(Hawaii) for only a year and I had driven across town to ask a group of strangers to let me into their support group. I am of Japanese ancestry, and the people in the Divorce Assistance groups were primarily Hispanic and Anglo. I was different in another way. I was not divorced, not even married, and my parents were high school sweethearts who were still married after forty years.

When I arrived at the first Monday night meeting, I walked into the group meeting room and there were several people standing around, talking, and signing in. One person greeted me at the door and put her arm around me because she said I looked a "little lost." I asked her if she was the person in charge, but she wasn't. She pointed out the group leaders, and I went up to them to ask if it would be all right for me to observe the group. I explained that I was a graduate student working on a class project. The leader abruptly said, "Okay, let's take a vote right now." Of the three people standing there, two said "yes," but the third person voted "no." The group decided that the split vote meant that I could stay. The leader who had voted "no" patted me on the back, letting me know that things would work out. I was in!

However, my role in the group had not yet been decided. The adults believed that introducing me as an observer could make the children in the group nervous and uncomfortable. They suggested that they introduce me as a volunteer assistant so that I could help out among the children. This role is indeed the one I adopted in the children's group for the balance of the fieldwork. Throughout this period, the adults seemed to forget my dual role as a researcher, and the children seemed unconcerned as to who I was. From their perspective, I was just another adult running the group—akin to the student teaching assistants they routinely experienced in their classrooms at their schools.

In the end both of us adopted very different roles in the groups we studied that approximated the typical member with our social characteristics: Cindy used her experiences as a daughter of divorced parents and a married person in the adult group to blend with the group, and I became an adult instructor in the children's group, constantly and awkwardly trying to access the children's experiences in much the same way as the other adult facilitators. From these two vantage points we came to understand how the two groups converged and diverged with respect to emotional expression and relational understanding.

PART THREE

Maintaining the Interaction Order

NINE

Civility and Order

Adult Social Control of Children in Public Places

CHRISTINE HORNE, MARY KRIS MCILWAINE,
AND KRISTIE A. TAYLOR

IN LATE 1997, Richard and Karen Thorne flew to Russia to meet and bring home their two four-year-old adoptive daughters. Before and during the long plane ride home, both girls constantly screamed, fought with each other, and indiscriminately kicked strangers. The Thornes responded with increasingly aggressive verbal and physical actions to suppress the children. On May 28, shortly after arriving in New York City, the Thornes were arrested, accused of beating and verbally abusing the two girls during their plane flight back from Russia. The Thornes testified in court that "they had each hit the girls once, but not on the face, and that although they were angry, embarrassed, and exhausted, they had not crossed the line to abuse."[1] Although this is a somewhat unusual case of public parental control of children because it involved adopted children from another country, it does illustrate the pressure many parents experience during such incidents. Would the Thornes have felt the same pressure in a different setting—for example, on an excursion to a local public park? In a different setting, would they have used different strategies to quiet their children? Would different behavior by the children have drawn different responses from the Thornes? Would the boundary between discipline and abuse have been different had they been in another public place other than a trans-Atlantic plane flight with high visibility and no hope of easy exit?

At a more general level, these questions address how social context influences the social control of children. The relationship between context and control has been a staple in social science analysis at least since Emile Durkheim's classic writings on mechanical and organic solidarity.[2] At the level of social interaction, Erving Goffman catalogued the ways individuals manage normative breaches of "civility" in public places. Implicit in both macro and micro analyses of social control is that social contexts require various "ritual competencies"[3] for routine social interaction. Most adults can express such competencies as part of a "religion of civility."[4] Young children, however, are more likely to behave in non-normative ways during routine social interaction because they have yet to fully learn how to deploy these competencies, especially in contextually appropriate ways.[5]

In this chapter, we focus on parental approaches to controlling children interpersonally in public places. Specifically, we identify ways in which they react to deviant actions by children for whom they are parents and examine how place influences these strategies. Our observations suggest that parents respond differently depending on the context of the interaction. The same child behaviors that receive severe sanctions in one public place can be treated very differently in another. Place—the physical attributes and accompanying behavioral expectations of a setting—appears to affect the ways in which parents react to transgressions by children.

CHILDREN AND RELATIONAL ORDER IN PUBLIC

Our analytic perspective on children and relational order situates parent-child social control in public places—those settings that have high social accessibility and visibility relative to private places, such as households or formal organizations with zealously guarded boundaries. Drawing from an interactional perspective, we specifically focus on how parents in public maintain relational "order" with children for whom they are or feel responsible. Although the concept of order can mean many things depending upon one's perspective and can certainly vary from situation to situation, our use of the term is closest to Goffman's concept of the "orderliness"[6] of social interaction. From this perspective, a great deal of interpersonal interaction in social relationships is predictable and displays a working level of coordination in conversation and nonverbal interaction.

What most adults take for granted about relational orders in public can seem impossibly complex from a child's perspective. To begin with, "in public . . . large numbers of persons, alone or in small groups, are encountering large numbers of other persons, also alone or in small groups."[7] Under these conditions, people confront a plethora of working "ground rules" for individual and coordinated action, including rules for such varied activities as choosing a seat on a bus[8] and assisting a stranger in trouble.[9] Such rules often are submerged just below the surface of explicit consciousness, emerging only through routine interaction or becoming highlighted through breaches of etiquette.[10] Moreover, normative expectations that apply in one sort of place may not apply in another.[11] Thus individuals must be sensitive to which rules apply to the setting they are in and the situations under which they have efficacy, lest they "lose face" due to behavior that is inappropriate for the situation.[12]

Young children are more likely than adults to be unfamiliar with these context-specific, emergent rules. Children may stare inappropriately, ask embarrassing questions, violate the invisible barrier of another's personal space or make disturbingly loud noises, thus breaching the normative order that adults come to expect.[13] These behaviors not only can offend the stranger who is a victim of the "assault"[14] but can be a source of embarrassment for the parent who accompanies the child. As the incident with which we opened this chapter underscores, adults often feel compelled to control the immediate problem and, by doing so, uphold the normative order of both their personal relationship with the youthful "offender" and the public place in which such transgressions occur.

Just as social contexts contain various normative repertoires for social interaction, they carry normative repertoires of social control behaviors. As people learn the subtle ground rules for interaction in various public contexts, they also learn the norms that govern appropriate social control behaviors and how far they can stretch the normative repertoire before they cross the boundary to inappropriate behavior.[15] In adult-child interactions, the relationship between context and control is particularly complex, for it involves important components missing from most research on interpersonal social control. The first of these components consists of the considerable age differences between most parents and young children. This means that social interaction and social control typically match relational players of very different experiences and skill levels. Further complicating an interactional understanding of adult-child control in public is the possibility that normative repertoires to which parents and children respond are imported from private to public contexts, especially the household. Viewed from this perspective, then, parents and children in public must navigate relational interaction that often involves multiple sets of ground rules, which in turn can create ambiguities for parents and explicit confusion for children.

We cannot hope to sort out all the issues raised above given the space permitted in this chapter. We can, however, explore two basic questions about parent-child social control in public that must be answered prior to more subtle analyses: What is the range of public actions that parents use to exercise social control over children for whom they are responsible? How can we analyze the influence of public places on parent-child social control? This last question, in particular, explicitly addresses the situational character of parent-child social control.

PUBLIC PLACES AND ADULT-CHILD TROUBLE

To answer the research questions above, we conducted fieldwork in twenty-four public places in Southwest City over the course of seven months in 1996 and 1997.[16] Our goal was to observe how parents manage young (aged approximately three to ten years) children they defined as misbehaving.[17] The places where we conducted fieldwork included retail stores and malls, restaurants, public parks, playgrounds, a zoo, churches (open to the public), an airport, a public library and the open mall surrounding it, bus stops, city buses, a Greyhound bus station, a city convention center, a public assistance agency, and plaza areas outside apartment complexes. We organized our observations around "trouble cases," which are "incidents of hitch, dispute, grievance, trouble . . . and what was done about it."[18] The following incident is typical of the information contained in many of the 142 cases from our observations:[19]

Hugging Santa

It is early October, but Christmas Towne, a shop that sells Christmas decorations and artificial Christmas trees, already is stocked full. One midweek afternoon, an older white woman (a senior citizen) and two young girls (probably under ten years of age) move through the shop admiring artificial trees. "Lookit, Grandma!" the smaller girl says, as she points out something on a tree. "Yes, that's nice," the woman replies. The older girl looks a little uncomfortable in response to the younger girl's words. The two girls hover closely around the tree, looking at it intently. Grandma moves to the next tree. "Look at this," she says. The three of them keep moving from tree to tree. Grandma seems to be gently herding the children in the direction of the exit; she is the one who always moves to the next tree first. As Grandma takes a long look at a shiny ornament on a tree decorated with animals, the younger girl gleefully shouts, "Grandma, it's Santa!" Grandma whirls around to see the younger girl with her arms around a figure of Santa Claus that stands as tall as the girl. Grandma scurries over and quietly says, "No, Ginger, let go now. Ginger, let go. It's to look at." Grandma puts her hand on Ginger's shoulder and tries to pull her from Santa while the older girl stands by and silently watches the commotion. Ginger grasps Santa tighter and starts rhythmically repeating in a loud cheerful voice, "I'm hugging Santa! I'm hugging Santa! I'm hugging Santa!" Finally, Grandma lightly spanks Ginger's behind, provoking wide-eyed surprised look from her. "I said let go," Grandma says in slow, even tones. Ginger's arms drop by her sides and her eyes fill with tears. "I was hugging Santa," she sobs. Grandma takes her hand, looks at the older girl, and leads Ginger out of Christmas Towne. The older girl follows.

This case also illustrates the differential restrictiveness of the places where we observed children.[20] In each public place, the amount of noise, bodily movement by adults and children, and physical enclosure came together in various ways to communicate to a greater or lesser degree "Be quiet!" "Stay still!" and/or "Show a little respect. You're indoors!" Highly restrictive places, for example, would typically be very quiet, with constrained bodily movements by all participants and with physical enclosures that restricted movement. In moderately restrictive places there would be a modicum of noise, movement, and more open space. Permissive places were quite open with respect to physical space, encouraged movement, and tolerated variable levels of noise.

ADULT STRATEGIES FOR CONTROLLING CHILDREN IN PUBLIC

On the basis of our observations, we identified several strategies that adults utilize in trying to control children in public: confrontation, explanation, keying, and avoidance.

Confrontation

Confrontation accounted for 54 percent ($n = 113$) of the total number of strategies in our sample. It also composed over 50 percent of the strategies we identified in each type of public place—permissive, moderate, and restrictive—that we studied (see Table 9.1). Confrontation involves an adult's direct expression of disagreement with a child's statement or action,

TABLE 9.1
Public Places by Adult Control Strategy

Adult Strategy	Permissive Places	Moderate Places	Restrictive Places	Totals
	%	%	%	%
	(N)	(N)	(N)	(N)
Confrontation	57.7	52.8	63.3	54.6
	(30)	(66)	(19)	(113)
Explanation	23.1	30.4	6.7	25.1
	(12)	(38)	(2)	(52)
Keying	19.2	16.8	30.7	20.3
	(10)	(21)	(9)	(42)
Total	100.0	100.0	100.0	100.0
	(52)	(125)	(30)	(207)

Note: Frequencies appear in parentheses; chi-square = 10.47, $p < .05$.

typically with some form of outward aggression. As such, it trades on the currency of coercion and an adult's positional authority relative to a child (i.e., the child is expected to comply with the adult's directives because of "who" the adult is). Confrontation "without qualification put(s) pressure on the child to change his [sic] . . . behavior immediately."[21] Actions that constitute confrontation include coercive bargaining (e.g., "Behave, or I'll take away your karate lessons"), commanding (e.g., "Stop that!"), nonverbal displeasure (e.g., sighing, glaring), physically restraining a child (e.g., grabbing a child before he or she hits another child), physically punishing a child (e.g., spanking, slapping), stonewalling in response to a child's repeated requests for something (e.g., "No!"), verbal displeasure (e.g., "You're more trouble than you're worth"), and corrective assertions in the face of repeated assertions by the child as to the character of something or someone (e.g., "That gum is sugarless" or "Yes, you know him. He plays on your team").[22]

To illustrate how confrontation unfolds in public, consider the following representative trouble incident that involved a woman and a girl in city bus one weekday afternoon:

The Button Incident

A woman and a girl (about seven years of age) sit closely together on a crowded city bus during rush hour. The girl wears a white dress that has round, imitation pearl buttons going down the front. Her hand clutches the top button as she sits on the bus bench. She lazily fiddles with the button, buttoning and unbuttoning it. The woman with her is talking and laughing with a man seated across the aisle when, suddenly, the woman turns to the girl and says firmly, "Hey, stop playin' with that. Just wear your clothes." She reaches over and aggressively buttons the top button on the girl's dress. Then she looks back at the man with slightly embarrassed smile. The girl goes back to playing with the button by rubbing it between her fingers without unbuttoning it. Only now she accompanies herself with song and begins to squirm in her seat. For a several minutes, the woman continues her conversation with the man across from her while the girl keeps on playing with her top button and singing. Again and without warning, the woman looks back at the girl and slaps her hand gently while firmly saying, "Don't play with your clothes." Immediately, she returns to her casual conversation with the man. At the next bus stop, the woman and girl exit the bus.

In this incident, the woman delivered two verbal commands for the girl to stop playing with her button and clothes. She also slapped the girl after she did not obey the first command. One aspect of this and similar interactions that we found interesting was the adult's ability to monitor child's behavior without seemingly being distracted for very long from other (typically adult-adult) social interaction. We came to understand this phenomenon as a "sixth sense" in that adults could anticipate when a child in their charge was misbehaving without directly observing him or her. It is important to note that the place in which this incident occurred we labeled as restrictive because dyadic talking would be noticed by others and because the bus constrained movement and was enclosed. We observed more manifestations of this sixth sense in restrictive places than in more permissive ones. In effect, adult surveillance of children became more focal as the physical arrangements and behavioral expectations of place became more restrictive. This incident also illustrates the ease with which adults switch roles, instantaneously slipping back and forth between authoritative roles with children and friendly, social roles with other adults. Role switching occurred more dramatically in incidents involving confrontation than explanation or keying, which we present in subsequent sections.

Explanation

Explanation accounted for 25 percent ($n = 52$) of all the strategies in the total sample and appeared more prominently in permissive (23.1 percent;

n = 12) and moderate (30.4 percent; n = 38) than in restrictive places (6.7 percent; n = 2). It involves the use of reasoning to manage or alter a child's behavior "in which [adults] give explanations or reasons for requiring children to change their behavior." Such reasons include the promise of a reward (e.g., "Behave, and we'll go to the zoo"), discussion of the negative consequences of deviant behavior for the child (e.g., "If you pet the bird, it'll bite you"), or a form of tutelage in which the adult offers the child guidance (e.g., "The best way to play with blocks is by building a tower" instead of throwing blocks). The following incident includes a common type of explanation—the explanation of negative consequences. It occurred at a grocery store, which we coded as a moderately restrictive place (i.e., "a walk and look place"):

You Don't Like Kix

A boy (about seven) standing in an aisle with few other shoppers in it reaches as far as he can stretch and pulls a box of Kix cereal off a shelf. His eyes scan the box up and down as he tightly clutches it in his hands. A woman standing near him notices what he has done and says, "Don't pick that one. You don't like Kix." He continues to peer closely at the box. She adds in a knowing tone, "Trust me, you don't like that one. It doesn't have hardly any sugar in it. It doesn't taste like sugar." The boy moves a bit to his left, still with the Kix box in his hands, and looks at other cereal boxes nearby on the same shelf. The woman grimaces at the boy, pursing her lips. She says, "Just pick one. We gotta go."

One immediately notices how the explanation in this incident relies upon the adult's understanding of the child's tastes (literally) and preferences. Without such knowledge, the adult could not construct a plausible rationale for why the child should "want" to pursue another course of action. Unlike confrontational strategies, many of the incidents we observed that contained explanation included some reference, either implicitly or explicitly, to the child's perspective. Again, the point is that explanation, unlike confrontation, often requires greater cognitive effort. At the same time, adults in our sample did not engage in long dissertations with children. As in the incident above, explanation strategies typically were short and to the point even though the adult might provide the same rationale several times during an incident. Finally, the incident ended with an implicit reference to the collective interests (as represented by the adult) of the child and adult, thus making the adult control strategy potentially more compelling (and final) to the child (e.g., "we" have to go versus "I" want us to go).

We draw on another trouble incident that highlights explanation from observations at a bus stop set back from a busy intersection near a public library plaza. We coded the stop as permissive because it was rather noisy (with cars whooshing by and people talking at all decibel levels), did not constrain movement (it was placed on a wide sidewalk without a bench), and was unenclosed. In this incident, explanation rests, not on the interests of the child or the adult-child dyad, but on normative grounds:

Jeez a Weez

A girl (about four) and her mother are waiting for the bus with a few other people. The girl is restless, skipping around the bench at the bus stop and chanting to herself, "Oh God, Oh God" over and over again. The mother looks at the girl and says softly to her, "Please don't say that word like that." The girl continues to chant the phrase a few more times and then asks, "Momma, why can't I say it?" Her mother responds, "It's bad to use God's name too easy." "Everyone says it," the girl says. The mother replies, "We don't say it." "What can I say instead?" the girl asks. "Say Jeez Louise," the mother responds in a supportive tone. The girl starts chanting "Jeez a Weez" in a singsong fashion as she skips around the bus stop.

These two trouble incidents and our aggregate findings provide some basis for understanding the prominence of explanation in relatively permissive places. Permissive places in general require less normative monitoring by adults of children. As we noted earlier, restrictive places heighten an adult's normative sixth sense regarding children. In permissive settings, by contrast, children and adults are not on as tight a normative leash. As a result, adults can take the time to engage in the interaction required for explanation strategies. One could imagine, for example, how unlikely the scenario in "Jeez a Weez" would be in a more restrictive setting such as a fancy restaurant. Engaging in explanation would take too long by the normative standards of the place and could draw even more attention to a child's normative breach, itself potentially creating a disturbance.

Keying

Perhaps the most creative of all adult-child social control strategies is keying, which accounted for 20.3 percent ($n = 42$) of our total sample and appeared most prominently in restrictive places (30.7 percent; $n = 9$) than moderate (16.8 percent; $n = 21$) or permissive places (19.2 percent; $n = 10$). Goffman, drawing on a musical metaphor, argued that keying involves transposing the original meaning of a situation (its original key) into a new meaning (a new key).[23] In our trouble incidents, keying occurs when an adult changes the focus of a child's attention, thus redefining the meaning of the situation. Keying includes delaying a decision with a child (e.g., "We'll go home and think about buying that toy"), distracting a child on an unrelated subject (e.g., pointing out something the child has not yet noticed or handing the child an object with which to play), verbally praising or acknowledging a child's activity in the face of behavior defined as deviant (e.g., "Wow, you did that all by yourself"), and recalibrating the timing of an activity to move a child away from non-normative behavior ("We'll go home, then we'll go eat, then we'll come back"). All of these actions shift the focus and meaning of a situation away from a child's breach and its disruptiveness. The following interaction, occurring in a restrictive setting, a relatively empty city bus, includes some examples of keying:

How'd It Break?

A woman and a young girl (about four) are sitting across the aisle from a large window on the bus. The girl turns to the woman and says, "Mom, I wanna sit by the window," as she points across the aisle. The mother replies in an even tone, "I want to be close to you. Why don't you stay with me." The girl acknowledges the statement but remains very active, squirming in her mother's lap. A few minutes pass. The girl complains about "not sitting by the window" and attempts to move off her mother's lap. Her mother sweetly replies that she enjoys it when the girl sits on her lap. "I wanna sit by the window," the girl says again, not responding to the mother's comment as she looks mother in the face. The mother takes something out of her pocket and holds it out to the girl. "Here, look at this watch," she says. "It's broken. Can you figure out why for me?" "I wanna sit by the window," the girl says again. The watch suddenly catches the girl's attention. In a puzzled tone, the girl asks, "How'd it break?" The girl takes the watch in her hands and inspects it carefully, turning it over. She holds it against her ear and says, "Did you drop it?" The mother replies, "No, I didn't." "Oh," the girl says, "'cuz if you dropped it might be broke." For the next several minutes the girl continues to question her mother about what might have happened to the watch. She does not mention sitting by the window again.

In this incident, the mother engaged in two kinds of keying, the first less successful than the second. In her first attempt at keying, she told the girl that she liked it when the girl sat on her lap, thus shifting attention from the child's desire to sit by the window to the mother's enjoyment of the girl. The girl did not respond to this strategy and continued to express a desire to sit next to the window. Her second attempt involved both verbal distraction ("Here, look at this watch. It's broken. Can you figure out why for me?") and handing her an object.

Keying strategies attempt to alter a child's behavior, at the same time minimizing the amount of attention drawn to the interaction. In restrictive settings, children's behaviors are likely to be more disruptive and subject to disapproval by surrounding social audiences. For example, on one occasion in church (a very restrictive setting), we observed children talking among themselves and generally being restless during a sermon. We observed several adults look in the direction of the children and even whisper after looking to the person sitting next to them. At one point, it appeared that most of the congregation in this small church had some knowledge of the children talking near where we sat. An adult sitting on the pew in front of them left his seat in the middle of the service and hurriedly walked to a pew on the other side of the room. Although it is difficult to be certain of the meaning of his actions, we coded this as an instance of avoidance, presumably in response to the children's actions in back of him. While children's behavior is more obvious in restrictive settings, everything an attending adult does in attempting to control a child is readily apparent to others. In these settings, therefore, adults are more likely to be concerned with quickly changing the child's behavior through either confrontation or a more unobtrusive measure, such as keying. We also observed keying used as a preventive measure in highly restrictive settings. In church, for example, adults sitting with small children (under eight years of age) frequently brought items such as books, quiet toys, and plastic bags full of Cheerios to distract children for whom they were responsible when they became restless.

Avoidance

Avoidance proved to be the most subtle of all adult social control strategies exercised in public against children. It occurs when an adult curtails his or her interaction with a child by physically distancing him- or herself from the child—for example, by walking away or, more subtly, by turning away from the child while still remaining in his or her presence. The following incident illustrates avoidance by walking away. It took place one weekend afternoon on a path by the rhinoceros pen at a local zoo:

Rhinoceros!

A young boy (about eight) is standing on the path by the rhinoceros pen screaming excitedly, "There's a rhinoceros!" A woman who walked up to the pen while interacting with the boy now takes a position behind the boy but within arm's reach of him. She first glances at his back but then turns her face away from him, as do the other adults and children in the vicinity. The boy yells in a loud, high-pitched voice, "I want to get in there" and starts climbing over the wooden log railing of the pen. The woman continues to look away. Nobody else in the immediate vicinity pays attention to the boy. After a few attempts to get up and over the railing, the boy stops climbing and walks to another part of the viewing area near the pen, next to where the woman has moved.

In this incident, the woman who appeared to be with the boy curtailed her interaction first by looking away from the boy and then by moving a slight distance away but without manifesting any outward sign of displeasure. Interestingly, the boy did not react dramatically (as some children do when separated even by a short distance from an adult or guardian). Moreover, the lack of dramatic reaction by the boy to his guardian's actions (and the density of people near the pen) enabled the latter's actions to blend into the crowd: that is, no one else noticed what took place (except us). Finally, the boy did not climb over the railing and create a crisis (as sometimes happens when children climb into zoo animal pens). His actions constrained anyone noting her actions as an act of social control.

This incident also underscores several of the difficulties we faced in trying to observe and understand avoidance. First, outward signs of displeasure with a child's actions by an adult appear unevenly in interactions preceding avoidance. In the incident above, we were left to infer from the context that avoidance had occurred given the triggering event of the boy attempting to climb over the railing. What could appear to be avoidance to us could be an adult moving to a better vantage point at the rhino pen. Second, unlike other strategies, avoidance was accompanied by very little if any verbal accounting before, during, or after its occurrence. The lack of accounting sometimes created ambiguities regarding inferences we could draw about the normative intent of the behavior. It was difficult, for example, to discern the normative intent of a behavior, particularly whether it was intended to alter a child's behavior, uphold the public order by not a "making a fuss," or some combination of these intents.[24] Third, we observed most of our incidents in a stream of other incidents and therefore found it difficult to ask informants to clarify or illuminate what we believed were instances of avoidance (without seeming threatening).[25]

DISCUSSION AND IMPLICATIONS

Adult social control of children involves a wide range of strategies, from confrontational physical punishment to verbal explanations, clever keyings, and subtle avoidance. Although we cannot draw firm conclusions about the distribution of avoidance in our findings, our observations indicate that adults do use different child control strategies in different public places. Confrontation is the modal form of control across all places, whereas explanation appears more prominently in permissive places and keying in restrictive places, respectively. Adults are indeed sensitive to the normative "rules of thumb" found in different types of public places and fashion their responses to children's breaches on the basis, in part, of where a breach is taking place. Indeed, adults negotiate appropriate responses to trouble with their children with the place itself in mind. Along these lines, we suggested earlier that permissive places appear to enable adults the luxury of explanatory strategies, which can take more time to formulate and implement than either confrontation or keying. Keying, on the other hand, if executed properly, can quickly and unobtrusively alter a child's behavior in a normatively restrictive setting. But we are still left with two puzzling questions. Why should confrontation occur so frequently across all public places we studied? What is it about adult-child relational orders that resonates with confrontation?

We can offer several possible explanations. First, confrontation is a relatively simple strategy, requiring the least skill on the part of the adult. It therefore requires less cognitive energy or time. Because confrontation is the lowest common denominator strategy, so to speak, it is the most likely to be used, regardless of the setting. However, one could argue that avoidance is also relatively easy to execute. One can simply exit from the setting (with the child) or ignore the child. Thus the cognitive demand argument may not by itself sufficiently explain the predominance of confrontation.[26]

Perhaps more important for explaining the preponderance of confrontation is the anger closely associated with it that can quickly escalate in the face of demands for public order or a child's resistance to a adult. In such instances, emotional responses occur beyond the purview of rational reflection and the limits of adult self-control. Social control, to borrow from Jack Katz's work on emotions, becomes more "corporeal" than "discursive."[27] That is, adults respond to their children through bodily movements enacted at the moment. Such actions may be more likely to the degree that adults find themselves in a restrictive place that limits their ability to discursively explore alternatives for controlling their children. This explanation in part fits with the experiences of the Thorne family discussed at the outset of this chapter and underscores the contextualized enactment of emotion as a key factor in the adult control of children.

Finally, the social structure of adult-child relations offers another clue to the widespread use of confrontation. At the most basic level, adults can physically restrain children by pulling them away from a store display, picking them up and carrying them out of church, or putting their hand over the child's mouth. At a social level, confrontation, as we have observed it in the context of this research, is, as Donald Black would argue, a "downward" control strategy from an adult to a child. Thus it is "isomorphic" with routine, nonsocial control interaction between most adults and children.[28] Confrontation, as we have used it, could even be said to mirror the differences in power that exist between most adults and young children, regardless of the context. We would therefore expect that confrontation would diminish in prominence when power differences between children and adults are reduced.

In addition to explaining our results, our research carries several implications for future research on the maintenance and dynamics of adult-child relational orders in public places. First, it raises questions about the association between social control and aspects of primary socialization. In general, we hypothesize that children's socialization into normative repertoires of relational interaction will often highlight the vertical aspects of personal relationships because of the power differences between adults and children. At the same time, place can influence adult control strategies and could become associated in a child's mind with particular normative repertoires of relational interaction. For example, children could come to associate reasoned relational interaction with more permissive public places because of the prevalence of adult explanation. Conversely, children could associate subtle manipulation with personal relationships conducted in restricted places because of the prevalence of adult keying. Research on moral development supports these contentions. As Hoffman summarizes, "[A] moral orientation characterized by independence of external sanctions and by high guilt is associated with the use of explanations. . . . [A] moral orientation based on fear of external detection and punishment . . . is associated with the frequent use of power-assertive discipline."[29]

Second, our study suggests a number of questions for future research. Our research did not focus on public social control and resistance by young children aimed in "upward" directions toward adults.[30] What types of resistance strategies by children are triggered by place or by particular types of adult control strategies? How do adult control strategies and child responses play out beyond dyadic interaction to collective situations where multiple children are involved? Do children ever "trigger" adult social control strategies as a way to resist adult control (e.g., a child attempting to involve an adult in an explanation strategy in order to distract the adult from the child's behavior)? We also know little about the linkage between private and public repertoires of adult-child social control. Our research focused on variation in the public eye but did not examine, as we alluded to earlier, the often ambiguous normative repertoires of relational interaction and social control that can pass back and forth between private and public places. What is the relationship between private and public adult-child social control? How are tensions and contradictions between private and public adult-child social control managed? Finally, returning to the infamous case with which we began this chapter, there is little systematic knowledge about how place affects the moral boundaries between appropriate and abusive adult-child social control. We suspect this moral boundary relates strongly to the normative restrictiveness of a setting, such that the greater the restrictiveness of a setting, the narrower the repertoire of behaviors that will be considered appropriate as informal social control strategies.[31] In the case with which we began this chapter, the fact that it occurred inside a plane (which we would code as a restrictive public place) meant that the Thornes' use of confrontation and their adoptive daughters' actions were egregious breaches of the normative order from the perspective of actors in the plane. Only future research can sort out these questions. We view our work as part of the foundation on which to empirically investigate their answers.

METHODOLOGICAL PROCEDURES AND REFLECTIONS

Sampling: Trouble Cases and Public Places

We initially followed a "maximum variation" sampling logic by visiting as many different public places as we could.[32] As we gained a deeper understanding of our field settings, we engaged in purposive sampling using an analytic scheme we discuss below. Field visits involved both solo and team field research. In some instances, we visited places as a team and situated ourselves in different locations to make multiple observations of the same incidents. In other instances, we visited the same sites one by one at different times in order to maximize our exposure to the field.

We also followed a maximum variation sampling logic within field settings by attempting to observe as many adult-child interactions as possible, paying particular attention to interactions where there appeared to be "trouble." In this way, we adopted a behavioral orientation toward our observations, although we also listened for accounts that adults and children gave each other as they interacted. We found these accounts useful for identifying the relationship between the adults and children, especially whether the adult was a parent or another type of guardian.[33] As we spent time in the field, we came to define adult-child trouble as having occurred any time the adult spoke or behaved in a way that was in opposition with what the child was saying or doing. This definition has the virtue of focusing on the adult's behavior rather than the child's. Since adults are likely to be more sensitive to interaction rituals, we assumed that they, rather than children, would better signal non-normative behavior.

The incidents in our research are essentially abbreviated trouble cases, lasting from a few seconds to several minutes of sustained interaction between adults and children. That is, they enable a processual analyses of relational trouble but do not capture longer-range social interactions that flow across public and private places in which such incidents are embedded. We determined the boundaries of each trouble incident using practical considerations. A trouble incident began when one of us first observed an opposition between an adult and child. Most opposition manifested itself linguistically, although a minority of incidents were purely nonverbal. Trouble incidents ended in a variety of ways, bounded by events, settings, and participants. If the opposition ended (e.g., one or both parties did not pursue the opposition), then the incident was over from our analytic perspective. A clear resolution, however, occurred in only a few incidents. More typically, the opposition persisted well beyond our ability to pursue it (e.g., the parties moved on to a place that was difficult for us to access).[34] Despite these limitations, each trouble incident contains rich information about adult control strategies and the reactions of children in public.

With respect to our coding of public places, we coded each place along three parameters, which together were intended to capture the restrictiveness and permissiveness of each place: (1) degree of "noise," (2) degree of "movement," and (3) degree of architectural "enclosure."[35] For each parameter, we developed an ordinal scale to assess each place's characteristics (from the observer's standpoint).[36] For noise, we coded a place "2" if dyadic talking would be noticed by others in the immediate vicinity (such as in Christmas Towne in the trouble incident above). We coded a place "1" if one needed to raise one's voice to speak with another person. We coded a place "0" if one would have to shout to speak to another person in one's immediate vicinity. Our second parameter, movement, refers to the amount of human activity enabled by the physical characteristics of a place. A place that contains structures for children to play on or in (e.g., swing sets, tunnels, sandboxes), that contains spaces that enable fluid interaction, or that enables interaction with the place itself (i.e., actively touching or using aspects of place, such as swinging on the swings or crawling through tunnels) metaphorically allows for more movement than does one primarily containing rows of seats (e.g., an auditorium) or seats and tables (e.g., a restaurant). In the former, the architecture says, "move" and "use," whereas in the latter the architecture says, "sit." Places at these two extremes were coded "0" and "2," respectively. We also encountered physical arrangements that enabled mixtures of movement and stationary, distanced behavior, which we coded as "1." These "walk and look" places, as we came to refer to them, were typically retail establishments (illustrated by Christmas Towne). The third parameter, enclosure, referred to whether a place was "indoors" or "outdoors" (i.e., architecturally "enclosed" or not). Christmas Towne, for example, would receive a "1," whereas a park would receive a "0." Places receiving a score between 0 and 2 we labeled as "permissive" (e.g., public parks, a McDonald's playground). Places receiving a score of 3 to 4 we labeled as "moderately" restrictive (e.g., retail stores). Places receiving a score of 5 or greater we labeled as "restrictive" (e.g., a library).[37] Thus the higher a place's score, the more restrictive the normative expectations for behavior.

All three authors worked together to code the adult strategies contained in the trouble incidents. We first "open"-coded the incidents to look for meaningful constructs and patterns. Our first coding attempts eventually fed into a detailed two-dozen category typology of adult social control strategies. As we collected more trouble incidents and talked with adults, children, and other scholars about our research, we developed the fourfold typology that we believed meaningfully and usefully made sense of our data. The four strategies we discussed in this chapter thus constitute our units of analysis, and multiple such units can appear in the same incident.

To illustrate, we can identify in "Hugging Santa" two of the categories in our typology. From an analytic perspective, "Hugging Santa" contains two different strategies. There is confrontation when Grandma told Ginger to stop hugging Santa, pulled her away, and led her out of the store. There is also a type of explanation when Grandma told Ginger that the things in Christmas Towne are "to look at," not touch. Because many trouble cases contained more than one strategy, the 142 cases yielded 225 strategies.

Difficulties in the Field

The data-gathering phase of a sociological study is always filled with stumbling blocks. Research can be delayed because of materials missing from libraries, rerouted because of directives from editors, or slowed down because of endless computer malfunctions. On one level, our data gathering involved nothing more than what many people innocently do during the routine course of their days—"people watch." But our people watching involved children. In contemporary U.S. society, fear of adult predation on children has created a culture of suspicion about adults who watch or interact with children unknown to them, particularly in public places. As a result, we experienced many anxiety-ridden moments in the field, with our experience in data gathering being profoundly shaped by our need to keep what we were doing a secret. We spied on people to get our data.

What we were after seems innocent enough—knowledge about how adults manage the disruptive or otherwise inappropriate behaviors of their children while in public. But to really grasp this process in all its richness, we needed to stick close by when unsuspecting subjects were in conflict and be unobtrusive while doing so. We needed to remain close to our subjects so that we could hear their words and watch their faces. We needed to stare at our subjects to guess their demographic traits, such as age and race. And on top of all this observing, we needed to take notes so that we could later make permanent records of exactly what was said, shouted, gestured, or otherwise communicated.

Many times during the study, we collectively and individually thanked our lucky stars that we are women. In our culture, men are more suspect as potential kidnappers or child molesters. It thus benefited us that we were likely to be perceived by our subjects as "harmless" women. Men who lurk and hover in public places can be perceived as threatening, whereas women doing the exact same thing are less likely to be noticed.

Be that as it may, we nonetheless employed a number of techniques to blend in and seem as nonthreatening as possible. In some cases we adopted "fieldwork faces" meant to convince subjects and bystanders there was no reason to take note of us. Each of us used naive, optimistic expressions while moving about in retail settings, hoping to portray slightly "ditzy shopaholics," nonthreatening people who enjoyed shopping too much to judge what adults and children were doing. We affected jaded and bored expressions when particularly interesting adult-child interactions took place. We intended this expression to convince adult subjects in the observation area that nothing they were doing could possibly be of interest to us. We hoped this would allow them to continue their interactions without inhibition. We used an introspective expression while taking notes, with studious efforts made not to look at the subjects. The idea was to convince subjects that we were lost in thought, taking notes on something completely unrelated to them, or checking something off on a shopping list.

Another blending-in technique involved using props appropriate to each place. For instance, while doing field observations in a grocery store, we would carry products (e.g. cans of tomatoes, boxes of crackers) with us as we roamed the store scanning for adult-child trouble. We often filled a shopping basket with these products, so that we appeared to be shopping, but then bit by bit put back unwanted products, in the process using our "shopping routine" to wander legitimately near our screaming, fighting, sulking subjects.

We always noted in our field notes whenever our subjects seemed to curtail their interactions due to suspiciousness about our presence. Occasionally, these occurrences turned into what we called "bystander spooking" (as when a horse is spooked). For example, our observations of trouble between a woman and two young children at a public zoo provoked the woman to glance at us with a concerned, uncomfortable look. After a few minutes of her piercing glances and our use of every field-blending technique we knew, she seemed a bit spooked, grabbed the children by the arms, and left that area of the zoo.[38]

In addition to the special challenges brought on by our need to blend in while in the field, we faced challenges that revolved around simply sticking with the data gathering. It is emotionally arduous work tracking and recording the conflictual interactions of others. We all knew that the problems of others—however momentary—provided the grist for our data mill. All three of us possess an instinct to run the other way when we see trouble in public. This study demanded that we not only seek out such loaded interactions but attend to them, dwell on them, and process them. The fact that each of us knew that the other two team members dreaded hovering near trouble provided us some compensation for feelings. We supported each other and encouraged one another at our frequent meetings.

On multiple occasions, the three of us entered the field as a team, taking notes on the same focal interactions and later comparing our different perspectives on the events that unfolded before us. "What do you think that woman said when she talked quietly right in that boy's face? Could you hear?" An early outing to a pizza place that specialized as a "kids'" restaurant became a bonding experience, after which we felt closer to each other for having endured the flashing lights of the restaurant's video games, blaring P.A. system, obnoxious animatronic singing animals on the "stage," and all the hubbub of seven or so children's birthday parties progressing simultaneously at tables surrounding ours. The pizza was quite bad, too.

Knowing one's teammates were counting on good data inspired each of us to be bold, to do things we otherwise wouldn't have done in the course of making observations. "If I can just play dumb enough for a few seconds longer here at this checkout counter, I'll get to hear the rest of this interaction. Why is the cashier looking at me? Do I look like I'm trying to grab cash from the register drawer or something?" This and similar adrenaline-pumped moments made us sometimes feel like young adolescents who had just been "dared" to do something outlandish.

All in all, we faced our challenges of blending in and sticking to it with zest and a sense of satisfaction. There were a few empty field outings where we spent hours hanging around in likely settings only to see no trouble among adults and children. Overall, however, our time in the field was exciting and stimulated our sociological imaginations.

TEN

Order on the Edge

Remedial Work in a Right-Wing Political Discussion Group

JASON CLARK-MILLER AND JENNIFER MURDOCK

THIS CHAPTER WORKS AT THE intersection of two sets of observations regarding public life: the first concerns the commitment of citizens to developing and maintaining a "working consensus" with respect to the encounter or situation in which they are involved as interactants; the second concerns the decline of public political conversation among ordinary Americans. The first set of observations is associated most closely with Erving Goffman, who stressed in various works that the "interaction order" is predicated in part on interactants' obligation to develop a kind of "working consensus" that involves, among other things, agreement about "avoiding an open conflict."[1] The second set of observations has been articulated most clearly by Nina Eliasoph, who laments and analyzes the absence of animated political discussion among citizens, due partly to the conscious avoidance of interactionally disruptive conflict.[2] Such interactional obligations and impulses notwithstanding, citizens sometimes find themselves involved in situations or groups in which the prospect of conflict is almost continuously present and, as a consequence, have to be continuously vigilant about maintaining a working consensus so as to keep the embers of conflict from flaring up into a raging fire that devours the group.

Such was the dilemma confronting a right-wing political discussion group we studied ethnographically over the course of a year. Several features of this group make it an especially interesting case for assessing the maintenance of interaction orders within public and quasi-public contexts when the potential for group-disintegrating conflict is always on the horizon. The first is that it is a quasi-public group (it is open to anyone) that meets in a quasi-public setting (a restaurant), thereby providing an opportunity to examine the extent to which some of the normative protocols generally associated with public places are also applicable to quasi-public places. Second, it is a political discussion group that allows for conflicting points of view to surface but not to escalate or combust in a group-disintegrating fashion. Additionally, this group is interesting in that it provides a counterpoint to the stereotypic public conception of right-wing groups and movements as ideologically homogeneous. While one might think that members of such groups would not only toe a party line but actually buy into that line, such was not the case with all members of the group we studied. To the contrary, we found that there were considerable bases for ideological conflict and schism within the group. Thus an intriguing question arises: How do political discussion groups in which conflict over issues is a characteristic feature of their discussion cohere and persist? Or, stated more clearly in relation to the maintenance of an interaction order, how do group members go about achieving a "working consensus" that allows for the expression of divergent views while simultaneously dousing the flames of disintegrating conflict?

We examine this general question with data drawn from a year of ethnographic research on a right-wing, antistatist group in Southwest City. We begin with discussion of this group and the research context. We then turn to an elaboration of the problem we seek to address and illuminate: the maintenance of group coherence in the face of competing or conflicting beliefs or ideological stands. Next we discuss our procedures for assessing this question. We then identify and elaborate several sets of factors that contribute to group persistence and coherence by facilitating a working consensus. Last, we spell out the implications of our findings and analysis for understanding more fully the kinds of factors that contribute to the maintenance of an interaction order in quasi-public groups.

CONTEXT AND ANALYTIC PROBLEM

The empirical referent for our analysis was a highly conservative right-wing group, referred to as the "Constitutional Forum" (a pseudonym), that had been meeting continuously in a variety of locales in Southwest City since its founding in 1983. In its limited advertising efforts, the group described itself as a "meeting place" for those who wished to educate themselves on the reality of the U.S. Constitution and how it was being misinterpreted by public and private interests. The Forum met every Saturday morning at 8:00 a.m., attracting a crowd of forty to fifty people, consisting mainly of members and approximately ten or so guests (newcomers, friends of regular members, etc.). A local cafeteria opened early to provide physical space for the meeting in return for members buying breakfast, as most did. Regular members generally sat at the same tables (composed of six to eight people), eating breakfast with the same friends and acquaintances in the organization from week to week. Members also arrayed themselves by age, with younger members sitting predominately on one side of the room and older members on the other side.

Upon arriving, most members engaged in friendly conversation for a half hour as they ate their breakfast at their "usual tables." By 8:30 a.m., the Forum's director stepped to the podium to formally begin the meeting. In his opening remarks he welcomed the members, made a few announcements including the name of the guest speaker, and called a "prominent member" to come up to the podium and lead a prayer on behalf of the group. The prayers consistently thanked "the Lord" for providing the wisdom for distinguishing "truth from falsehoods" and "good from evil."

The speeches that followed this prayer typically lasted about forty-five minutes. These speeches were in turn followed by an "open forum" that included questions from group members; intragroup discussion between members, the speaker, and the group's two leaders; smaller discussions among members at the same or adjoining tables; and a prayer before the close of the meeting. Week in and week out, the Forum followed this script, with the same roles played by the Forum's three major sets of actors: the rank-and-file members and guests, the speaker, and the two leaders—the Forum director and the group's informal leader, a conspiracy theorist.

Demographically, the group appeared to be quite homogeneous. Although we did not do a survey of the membership, it was clear from our observations that the membership was predominantly Anglo, with the exception of an Asian woman who attended regularly and an occasional Hispanic attendee. The majority of the members were also male (around two-thirds), and they appeared to range in age from thirty-five to sixty-five, with an estimated average around forty-five to fifty. While we cannot be precise about members' religious identification, we would guess that the vast majority were Christians. There were some exceptions, to be sure, such as a few Jews, a self-identified atheist, and a handful of "New Agers."

But there is little doubt—on the basis of conversations with members, the formal talks and presentations that were a regular feature of each meeting, and the opening and closing prayers—that the Constitutional Forum was a predominantly Christian group. The following opening prayer, given on the occasion of a local politician's talk, provides an illustration of the group's Christian orientation, as well as its distrust of politicians. The prayer began with a reference to Psalms 5.9 ("Not a word from their mouth can be trusted. Their heart is filled with destruction. Their throat is an open grave. With their tongue they speak deceit") and then continued by appealing for guidance and giving thanks:

> Father, we ask that you give us the power to determine which of these men are of that nature, who do lie and deceive and speak of evil words. We ask that you be with us as we make our decisions in the coming weeks, to guide and teach us how to separate those that have your words from those that have evil words. We thank you for our speaker this morning. We ask that you be with her so that she will speak nothing but truth to us. And we ask that our hearts be open to the truth. And we thank you for this food that we have this morning and we ask that you bless it. All of these things we ask in the name of your Son and our Savior, the Lord Jesus Christ. Amen.

Given the group's apparent demographic and religious homogeneity, it would seem reasonable to assume that the group was characterized by ideological consensus or homogeneity as well. Such a presumption would be strengthened even further by the group's uncontested advertisement of itself as a "Constitutional Forum"—that is, as a regular meeting place for citizens wanting to educate themselves about the Constitution and how it was being misinterpreted and abused. But our year-long ethnographic research, including participant observation and conversational interviews with regulars and guests, suggests a somewhat more complex picture, one in which demographic and religious homogeneity created a veneer that masked or glossed considerable diversity with respect to beliefs and ideology.

To illustrate this ideological diversity within the group, we consider two potentially contentious incidents: one involving beliefs and assertions about Jews and the other entailing different assessments of the Masons. Regarding the former, it is an incontestable fact that anti-Semitism has figured prominently in the ideologies of far-right political groups throughout much of history, both within the United States and throughout the

Western world.[3] It therefore is hardly surprising that anti-Semitism constitutes a salient strand of the beliefs and ideologies associated with the militia/patriot movement today. Moreover, it is the defining dimension of a segment of the movement known as Christian Identity. Identity Christians believe, among other things, that Jews control the federal government (hence their use of the acronym ZOG, which stands for Zionist Occupied Government), that northern Europeans are the true chosen people, and that Jews are offspring of either a satanic religion or a satanic race.[4] Yet neither this deep and hard-core attitude of anti-Semitism nor the less pervasive attitudes associated with such groups as Aryan Nation and Posse Comitatus were prominently featured in the group's formal speeches, pronouncements, and discussion of the Constitutional Forum. For example, reference to anti-Semitism was made in only one of the twenty-seven (3.7 percent) formal, prearranged presentations by guest speakers. Nor did the group's leadership endorse anti-Semitism directly. However, the absence of anti-Semitic pronouncements at the formal organizational level should not be read as an indicator at the individual level of either a positive disposition toward Jews or an absence of anti-Semitic sentiments. In fact, both sentiments were present among the membership, as indicated by the following exchange among three regulars during the breakfast period prior to a formal meeting:

> While Helen is eating her breakfast, Eva leans over her shoulder and picks up a copy of a newspaper called the *People's World Weekly,* which Helen has laying on the table in front of her. Eva says, "Oh, I can't believe you read anything out of that old Jew paper." Helen responds by emphasizing that "it is not a Jew paper" and that there are some good articles in it. Eva continues to disagree. Alice tells Eva that she should read the *Post,* and Helen concurs. Eva says, "Oh, the *Washington Post,* yeah that's a Jew paper. They all are." The topic then shifts to universities, and Eva states, "Well, you know everyone at the university is a Jew too."

This was not the only encounter over Jews among Eva and other members; nor was Eva the only member who expressed anti-Semitism from time to time. But this incident does suffice to suggest the existence of an ideological fault line among the membership.

Another such fault line existed in relation to the Masons and their alleged role in undermining the Constitution and supporting a "New World Order."[5] We first became aware of this fissure when the group was addressed by the above-mentioned informal leader, who was the resident conspiracy theorist and a "leading author" on the "New World Order."[6] He began his remarks by claiming to "have discovered exactly what Bill Clinton, Al Gore, Bob Dole, and Jack Kemp believe" and argued that "none of us can vote for any of these candidates" because "the truth about their beliefs is that bad." The truth he was alluding to was their knowledge about and support of a "New World Order" conspiracy to destroy the American way of life, take over the world, and subdue the entire human population. He spent a few minutes "demonstrating" Clinton's support of this "New World Order" and Gore's worship of the earth goddess, Gaia, then turned his attention to Dole and Kemp and their membership in the Freemasons. He argued that they were "33rd degree Luciferian Masons" who had taken "blood oaths of loyalty" to Masonry and who therefore were committed to the New World Order and to the destruction of Christianity. Since the meeting ended promptly after the talk, there was little time for discussion. But the following afternoon one of the attendees called the Forum director to request a chance to respond to these charges. His formal response, which was issued at the next meeting, follows:

> It's fair to say that most of us revere the Constitution and want to preserve it. We also feel that those responsible for drafting it were honest, responsible men. Some of our forefathers who framed and were influential in the conception of the Constitution were John Hancock, Thomas Jefferson, Patrick Henry, James Madison, Alexander Hamilton, Nathan Hale, John Paul Jones, Paul Revere, and George Washington. All patriots and respected Americans.
>
> And also, all were Masons. Last week, the speaker told us that Masons were worshipers of Lucifer and took oaths to destroy Christianity. [He] cited many publications for the sources of his false premises and misrepresentations. If any of his statements were accurate the Masons just named would have done us all in a long time ago, not to mention the many Masons since.
>
> To say that Bob Dole and Jack Kemp, as Masons, have taken an oath to destroy Christianity is preposterous, because there is no such oath. Whether you like them or not, or vote for them, that is preposterous. . . . I'm an American. I'm a Mason. And I'm offended by the misrepresentations that you heard last week.

This and the previous incident clearly indicate that seeds for division and schism are deeply embedded in the group. But this potential for factionalization or disintegration notwithstanding, the group was remarkably stable and coherent during the year we studied it. Moreover, coherence and persistence seemed to be characteristics of the group inasmuch as it had been in operation for twenty years. Thus we raise two analytic questions. How did this right-wing group manage to cohere and persist in the face of potentially contentious ideological strands? And what are the implications of the answer to this question for understanding more fully the significance of achieving a working consensus for maintaining the interaction order in quasi-public contexts?

To answer the above questions, we draw on observations derived from a one-year study of the Constitutional Forum.[7] During our year in the field, this group met weekly in Southwest City. The Forum constituted a useful site for exploring the above questions because of its accessibility to members of the public and its emphasis on political discussion. In addition, as we soon discovered, when compared to other right-wing groups, such as those more directly linked to the American patriot movement,[8] the Forum took a less militant stance toward social issues, thus inviting a wider range of political views and debates than we might have otherwise expected.

REMEDIAL WORK AND MAINTAINING THE INTERACTION ORDER

So how did the Constitutional Forum manage to sustain a working consensus and thereby avert or reduce the possibility of schism and disintegration? In exploring this question, we draw conceptually on Goffman's concept of "remedial interchanges" or "remedial work".[9] Remedial work encompasses various routines and rituals used to maintain the orderly flow of social interaction in the face of actual or threatened disruptive breaches or improprieties. Drawing on our research findings, we identify and elaborate various types of remedial work employed by group members in response to threatening breaches and potential disintegrating conflict encountered during Forum meetings. In addition, we note the relational contexts in which these actions occurred—whether they occurred at the collective, group level during the more formal portion of the meetings or at the interpersonal level during the more informal segment of the meetings.

Remedial Work at the Group Level

Several types of identifiable remedial work repeatedly manifested themselves during the formal part of each Constitutional Forum, consisting mainly of a guest speaker's talk and an extended discussion (question and answer) period. These various remediation efforts included ideological work via framing, bypassing of troublesome members, and the invocation of covering norms of civility.

Ideological Work via Framing   One way in which differences of view and the potential for schism are dealt with is through a set of framing practices that can be thought of as "ideological work." The term *ideological work* was coined by Bennett Berger to capture the remedial discourse rural communards engaged in so as to "maintain some semblance of consistency, coherence, and continuity" between their beliefs and actions when circumstances rendered them contradictory.[10] Berger suggests ideological work is likely to come into play when individuals' beliefs are no longer seen as effectively serving their interests, as when events in the world call into question some ritual or pattern of behavior, or when behavior and beliefs contradict each other, as when child-raising practices are inconsistent with beliefs about how it should be done. In addition, we suggest a third circumstance calling for ideological work that involves the existence of competing or conflicting beliefs within a group that threatens its coherence and increases the prospect of schism or factionalization.

Earlier we detailed two ideological fault lines within the group that could constitute the basis for dissensus and schism. One was linked to anti-Semitism, the other to the relevance of the Masons to the alleged "New World Order." These were only two of an array of beliefs harbored by members about various salient public issues. The range of these beliefs ran from more standard antigovernment themes (e.g., socialist tendencies and constitutional violations) to the more esoteric (e.g., planetary movements as shaping U.S. destiny). This range is reflected in Table 10.1, which displays the distribution of themes and issues raised by speakers and members over a six-month period.

Two observations about the table are especially pertinent to our concerns in this chapter. First, the six thematic categories (excluding the residual "other" category) are sufficiently broad to function as cover terms or domains for a number of different beliefs and points of view. Hence each category contains the seeds for debate and dissensus, as we have already seen with respect to conspiracy and Jews. The possibility for debate and conflict is also clearly evident in the case of the morality category and the attendant issues of abortion, sexuality, and family. Thus there are a number of potential fault lines that could widen in a schismatic fashion. However,

TABLE 10.1

Hierarchy of Issues/Themes Referred to by Members and Speakers

(September 1996 to February 1997)

Issues/Themes	Frequency	
	Number (253)	Percent
Antigovernment (general negative statements about federal government)	72	28.5
Constitutional/Jurisdictional (statements indicating governmental intrusion and overreach with respect to constitutional rights)	69	27.3
Conspiratorial (statements alluding to various conspiracies as root of problem)	65	25.7
Morality/Immorality (statements regarding abortion, homosexuality, family, and the like)	23	9.1
Racial/Ethnic (statements about members of particular racial and ethnic groups)	11	4.3
Jews (statements explicitly referring to Jews)	8	3.2
Other (communism, media, political parties)	9	3.5

the fact that schism has not occurred suggests the operation of ideological work and thus begs for clarification. Second, we see that the frequencies with which references are made to each category are sufficiently different to indicate that the concerns and issues of import to the membership are arrayed hierarchically, such that some are clearly more salient than others. This finding, we contend, can be taken as evidence of ideological work as well, and it raises the question of the character of this ideological work within the group.

This ideological work was conducted at the organizational level through the strategic framing activities directed by the group's two leaders. By *framing activity* we refer to the signifying, interpretive work that individuals, groups, and organizations engage in so as to render meaningful events and occurrences within their respective life spaces and the world at large. Frames are essentially interpretive schemas that simplify and condense aspects of the "world out there," and in doing so "they function to organize experience and guide action, whether individual or collective."[11]

Framing typically manifested itself through the alignment of different points of view and issues in a manner that linked or yoked them in terms of the same frame, thus sanitizing differences and minimizing the potential for conflict. On numerous occasions, for example, we observed conversation flow without interruption around highly contentious issues, from teaching the Constitution in American schools, to the president's involvement in the New World Order conspiracy, to the courts forcing fathers to pay alimony for their children, to the government confiscating land in Utah. In these situations, typically following the speaker's presentation, rank-and-file members often voiced their own contradictory viewpoints. As the rhetoric heated up, the Forum director constantly linked disparate viewpoints and statements in the "government-is-the-problem" frame, as evidenced by his constant references to the government's expanding control.[12] Framing multiple problems in terms of the need to limit governmental jurisdiction allowed the group to problematize an array of disparate issues without discussion breaking down into chaotic challenges and ripostes. An example of this strategy occurred during the following exchange when a long-standing group member attempted to organize a protest against a public official who recently had been "outed" as gay. Other members of the group called into question whether such an action infringed upon the politician's "constitutional right to privacy":

> James announced in open forum that he was organizing a protest of Senator-elect Daltrey because of his acknowledged gay identity. He suggested that everyone had a right to know the senator's HIV status. Others began shouting him down. Then the director stepped in to reiterate the importance of knowing the medical status of elected officials but *emphasized* that the problem was not the candidate's gay identity but "just another example of the way the government withholds information."

While the argument for action clearly could have been framed in terms of morality, the director chose to frame the action in terms of the group's primary antagonist—the federal government. Such attempts to align or articulate issues in terms of a common, primary frame constituted the most common means through which the group managed potential conflict, but it was clearly not the only remedial strategy that surfaced during the formal part of group meetings.

Bypassing "Troublesome" Members or Comments   Another remedial strategy was frequently triggered by some group members' expression of opinions that were regarded as highly contentious and flammable and thus threatening to the group's interaction order. Most comments and opinions regarded as highly inflammatory entailed sweeping derogatory statements or claims about categories of individuals, such as Jews, blacks, and gays. Such categorical derogations were regarded as threatening to the interaction order because not all group members shared the expressed opinions and because focusing on social categories directed attention away from the Forum's primary concern with the federal government. Since such threatening comments were commonly made by a few members, these individuals were often bypassed by the group's leaders, or whoever had the floor, during the discussion period.

This bypassing strategy, which often resulted in temporary exclusion from participation in group discussions, typically took two forms: either skipping over and ignoring certain comments or individuals or invoking the "time is up" excuse. The sidestepping tactic was often employed by the director when dealing with Virginia, a particularly controversial member who often displayed open hostility toward the Jewish community and occasionally verbally attacked guest speakers. During a conversation on municipal, state, and federal voting procedures, for example, Virginia asked for the microphone, stood up, and stated that all elections were fixed because of the absentee ballot system. This caused a row among other group members. Rather than responding to her, the director looked at her, turned to his right, and spoke to another member of the group. Since the topic of conversation shifted when the director addressed the other group member, Virginia was forced to sit down without further comment. Several minutes later, Virginia did enter into the open forum discussion with another, albeit more tempered, set of comments.

On another occasion, when Virginia had been sitting patiently with her hand up for an extremely long time without a response, the director called on several other members around her until she finally stood up and began speaking without the microphone. When the microphone was finally brought to her, she said, "I didn't think you were ever going to call on me back here; I know you saw me." The director apologized and Virginia stated her piece. This incident exemplifies that attempts to ignore troublesome group members did not always limit their involvement, but it does underscore the efforts of the group leader, and others as well by their failure to intervene, to pass over or sidestep comments and/or their purveyors regarded as "out of order" and potentially incendiary.

Another bypassing tactic we observed involved the director's calling a halt to proceedings by indicating that there was "no time" for a discussion to continue. Often time had expired, but on some occasions this was not the case. The premature claims about exhausted time typically backfired in that they were contested by the person being bypassed and/or by other rank-and-file members. For example, toward the end of one Forum meeting, Connie, a single woman in her late sixties, asked repeatedly to make a comment about the upcoming Thanksgiving holiday. The director refused to allow her to talk, stating that they had run out of time for that issue. Connie persisted, arguing that there were fifteen minutes left before the close of the meeting. This disagreement continued for approximately one minute, with Connie asking to speak five times before the director acquiesced and allowed her to have the microphone. Near the end of another meeting, Virginia was similarly bypassed. She had come up to the microphone following another group member's speech and asked for a few minutes to read a letter she had written to Senator Daltrey, but the director indicated that there wasn't enough time for her to speak. Virginia persisted, but to no avail. This exchange went on until Virginia finally asked, "Isn't this group open for discussion? What I have to say is very important!" The director paused before responding and Virginia took the opportunity to begin reading her letter anyway. This startled the director, who then interrupted Virginia to say that she could read it but would have to "make it quick."

In both of the above instances, lack of time was used as an excuse to silence potential "trouble." However, a check of watches indicated that in both circumstances the group members were correct and that, in fact, there was adequate time remaining in the meeting. Making the excuse of "no time," then, was one strategy employed to bypass either "troublesome" individuals or comments. But in each case the challenger successfully appealed to the interaction order, claiming in effect that this form of censorship was not consistent with the group's own rules, especially the "openness" of the Forum to any person's viewpoints and participation. In every case, group members supported their claims, and the director attempted to reconcile the situation by allowing the group member to speak.

Invocation of Covering Norms of Civility   The appeals of the above bypassed individuals and the support offered by fellow rank-and-file members point to another set of remedial strategies that involved the invocation of covering norms of civility. By *covering norms of civility*, we mean norms of interaction that are relevant to all members and interaction episodes and that are applied in service of maintaining the interaction order.

In addition to appealing to the director to allow members the time to speak their piece, some members would remind the Forum of the importance of being tolerant of divergent views. That is, they would acknowledge that while not all members took the same position on every issue, they should respect each other nonetheless. This was demonstrated by several references to group members' complaints about commonly discussed topics. On three separate occasions the director stated that some members felt the group was too focused on politics while others complained that they talked about medical issues too often. The director explained that not everyone was going to be happy all the time and that he made attempts to equitably balance the issues the group discussed and the speakers who were invited to present to the Forum. He went on to point out that both medicine and politics were important and that members would have to make concessions to please the majority of people in attendance. Tolerance was brought up again during a closing prayer when the member leading the prayer said:

> Heavenly Father, we come in your presence. We thank you for the things that we have heard this morning—some we agree with and some we don't. But we thank you for the men who are courageous and brave enough to stand for the Lord Jesus and his word. We thank you for those who are still fighting the battle.

In this prayer we see a group member acknowledging that while not everyone agreed on all issues, all came with the same intentions and thus had to be respected.

Until now, our examples have implied that the group-level strategies for maintaining the interaction order were enough to prevent and suppress threatening disagreements. Sometimes, however, the disagreements festered and spilled over into subsequent meetings, as was the case with the previously discussed tension over the role of the Masons in the claimed New World Order conspiracy to destroy the American way of life. Recall that the Forum's resident conspiracy theorist addressed the group one Saturday morning, claiming, among other things, that "Bill Clinton, Al Gore, Bob Dole, and Jack Kemp" and others could not be trusted because of their commitment to the Masons and support of "a New World Order." The meeting ended after the resident expert's commentary, leaving no time for discussion. But the next day a member who was a Mason called the director, requesting that he be allowed to respond to the conspiracy theorist's charges. The director consented, so the offended member articulated a strongly stated rejoinder, quoted earlier, at the next meeting. Afterwards, one of our informants indicated that the rejoinder "really stirred up" the resident expert, prompting him to appeal to the director for a chance to "defend himself from [the] attack." A few days later, the resident theorist confided to one of us:

> It really burns me that he'd call me a liar like that in front of the whole group. I found him after the meeting and showed him the books and said, "Look, just show me where I misquoted anyone." He wouldn't do it. The Masons worship the sun god in their lodges. Period. Even (he) would know that if he bothered to read their own literature.

The theorist never got his chance to respond, as the director sensed the need to move on, almost implying that "time was up" for this issue, as if there were a kind of statute of limitations on discussion topics and claims. But this did not prevent the still angered conspiracy theorist from handing out a booklet "exposing the Masons in their own words" at the next meeting.

This festering feud and the way it was handled illustrate several points suggesting that maintenance of the Forum's interaction order was generally of greater collective salience than waging indefinite verbal combat over any single issue or claim. First, we sensed that members preferred to avoid ongoing open conflict even when they felt they had a high personal stake in "preserving the truth." For example, when we asked the offended member what he thought of the theorist's initial commentary regarding the Masons, he grimaced and said:

> It really upsets me that he twisted the truth around so much; even so, *responding to his speech was still a difficult decision because I didn't want to encourage too much animosity within the group* (emphasis added).

Additionally, the Forum director seemed to have a keen ear or eye for sensing when the character of discussion or commentary had reached a threshold beyond which conflict might well escalate in a disintegrating fashion, thus prompting him to employ one or more of the above-mentioned remedial strategies.

Remedial Work at the Interpersonal Level

Each of the above-mentioned group level strategies improved the Forum's ability to maintain the "reality" of a working consensus. But this working consensus was also maintained by the interpersonal strategies employed by individual members during the informal part of each Forum meeting. The interpersonal, informal strategies we observed on a regular basis included softening or moderation of one's stance; avoidance or withdrawal from interaction; and humorous deflection.

Softening/Moderation of One's Stance   To illustrate the existence of ideological fault lines within the Forum, we noted earlier the tension among some members regarding the derogation of Jews and their presumed influence. Recall that one member (Eva) questioned another member (Helen) about why she would be reading "a Jew paper" and also claimed that "everyone" at the local university was "a Jew." But what we didn't note was that Eva moderated her stance a bit in the face of Helen's objection and another member's (Alice's) intervention and resistance to categorizing all papers as "Jew papers." As Eva exclaimed toward the end of the exchange:

> Yah, it's all right to read those kinds of papers. I read the enemy's stuff all the time.
> I read the Talmud. You learn a lot that way.

In this example, Eva attempted to garner support for her negative views of the judicial system and the Jewish community by stating a strong view. When her efforts failed, she deflected attention toward Helen by criticizing the newspaper she was reading. When this engendered a negative reaction by Helen and Alice, Eva softened her position by indicating that even she read "the enemy's stuff" to educate herself on their views. Thus, in order to preserve the interactional relationship between herself and those seated at the table, Eva moderated her stance toward Helen's choice of reading material by explaining that there was value in reading multiple sources of information.

Withdrawal or Avoidance   Another interpersonal strategy members would sometimes employ to defuse a seemingly tense and threatening interactional episode was simply to withdraw from the conversation or perhaps even the situation. Following the resolution of the above exchange, for example, Eva changed the topic to the judicial system, and Helen, not liking what she heard, simply withdrew from the encounter by orienting herself to other members at the table, thereby avoiding the prospect of another heated exchange. Similarly, we observed that sometimes members would initiate a new encounter with other members not involved in the troublesome encounter so as to avoid further confrontation, as illustrated in the following example:

> Joe walks from where he is seated to another table, where he starts talking about a newspaper article he read about the Federal Reserve Board that implicated the Board in a scandal during the 1930s. Joe claims that the article proves the U.S. Treasury has been corrupt for the better part of the twentieth century. Betty, who is seated at the table, leans over and quietly tells her friend, Ed, that she believes "none" of what Joe claims. Ed whispers, "Ya' don't believe him, call him on it." Betty smiles, shakes her head, and begins a conversation on another topic with some other Forum members at the table.

While Betty clearly disagreed with Joe, she withdrew from interaction with him as he continued to interact with other members seated at her table, thus avoiding the prospect of heated exchange.

Finally, members or guests would, on occasion, exit physically by getting up and leaving the table and even sometimes the premises. The following excerpt from our field notes illustrates the latter exit response:

> Seated at a "mixed" table with both new and established Forum members, an unidentified man held forth in a conversation on race relations and social progress. He claimed, "If it wasn't for the white man you'd still have bones in your noses and be eating each other." I heard Elise (a longtime member) say, "That's exactly right" and Virginia say something like "He's right!" The man continued, "When you mix it [race] up you're not serving God because you end up following their religion, not God's." I heard a woman whom I did not recognize say under her breath, "Oh shit, that's just too much for me." Soon after she made the comment, she and two other people whom I had never seen at the Forum got up and left. None of the other members seated at the table noticed the three people who left. The conversation continued for another several minutes, touching on affirmative action, the legality of interracial marriage, and other race- and ethnic-related topics. The three people who left never returned to the Forum during the duration of our fieldwork.

As the excerpt above illustrates, nonconfrontational exit rarely, if ever, raises much of ruckus among regular Forum members. In the foregoing situation, Virginia noted that "maybe those people had to be somewhere" rather than ascribing their behavior to discontent with the discussion.

Humorous Deflection   Humorous deflection constituted another interpersonal strategy members sometimes employed to defuse a potentially
threatening encounter. For example, early one Saturday morning, as members were arriving,

> the Forum's informal leader (the conspiracy theorist) and the Forum's
> treasurer were manning the entrance to take donations to support the
> group. The theorist was reading from a book that the treasurer recog-
> nized as one he had held up when quoting Masonic rites two weeks
> before. The theorist was pointing to a passage in the book and saying to
> the treasurer, "You see, it's right here in the book. He said it." The trea-
> surer responded that the man he was referring to had been denounced
> and kicked out of the Masons. Their conversation ranged over a variety
> of topics related to the Masons, politics, and economics as they greeted
> people coming to the meeting. After several minutes, the treasurer
> smiled and said, "Oh, you go over there [pointing to a table that was
> filling up] and read your book. There are pretty ladies waiting in line
> here that I need to get to." Looking up at two young women coming
> through the door, the informal leader said jauntily, "Helloooo, ladies!"
> and then smiled back at the treasurer and sauntered off to read his book
> at the table.

Of course, what made this strategy effective was the co-construction by
both interactants of the "humor" in the treasurer's statement. Without
both of them upholding the definition of the situation as amusing, the
intended exchange could have been interpreted as insulting, which in turn
could have allowed a minor hitch to escalate into an open confrontation.

Humor was also used interpersonally to alleviate tensions and conflicts
that had spilled over from the formal meeting, thereby reducing the potential for escalation. We return to the previously discussed conflict over the
Masons initiated by the conspiracy theorist and continued by the offended
member's public rejoinder:

> Two weeks after his rejoinder, the offended member is seated at a table
> telling those assembled that he "wasn't surprised" that the theorist
> reacted as he did. "After all, this isn't the first time we've had this
> argument." He then launches into a lengthy recounting of several verbal
> altercations with the theorist over this issue. He cites numerous facts
> from various sources to support his position and to discount the
> theorist's views. As he takes a breath before continuing his recounting,
> the treasurer, who is also seated at the table, says that maybe next week

he will put out two kinds of jars for donations for the group: "one Miracle Whip jar and one mason jar." Everyone at the table laughs, including the complaining member. After the laughter subsides, those seated at the table move on to a different topic.

Here the humorous line worked because enough people at the table knew that mason jars have nothing to do, per se, with the Masons as a group. An inventor named John Mason patented the mason jar—a wide-mouthed screw-type glass jar used for preserving foods—in the mid–nineteenth century. Most mayonnaise jars are mason jars, including the ones the treasurer used to collect donations. More importantly, the laughter deflected the offended member from his story and effected both a topic switch and a switch in who controlled the conversation at the table.

CONCLUSION AND IMPLICATIONS

Goffman alerts us to the fact that in most circumstances individuals are constantly working to maintain the interaction order via acknowledgment of a working consensus and that when either is threatened they tend to engage in various forms of remedial work to restore social order. Drawing from his analysis, we have used the concept of remedial work to describe the formal and informal mechanisms, routines, and rituals Forum participants used to manage interpersonal and intragroup conflict and to encourage the resumption of ordinary social intercourse after a disruptive event. At both the formal group level and the more informal interpersonal level, we discerned that a number of different remedial strategies were routinely pursued in the face of divisive and order-threatening comments and exchanges. At the formal group level, both members and the leader(s) pursued such remedial or restorative strategies as ideological work via framing, bypassing of troublesome members, and the invocation of covering norms of civility; at the informal interpersonal level of interaction, members and guests worked in service of the interaction order by softening or moderating their stance when confronted, avoiding or withdrawing from troublesome or objectionable encounters, and responding humorously to lessen the potential offense suggested by comments or claims.

What these findings suggest is that members and leaders were often are willing to ignore, accept, reconstruct, or forgive certain violations of the interaction order so that the appearance of a working consensus was preserved and interaction continued. According to Goffman, this working consensus is one of the few bases of "real consensus."[13] As a result, it is necessary in order for interaction to proceed.

This holds not only for face-to-face interaction in public contexts but also for political dialogue and interchange in quasi-public contexts. As Eliasoph observes, the existence of an interaction order enables participants not only to interact in general but also to engage in political discussion. The norms of civility that undergird the interaction order also undergird public-spirited conversation—even when, as in the case of the Forum, that interaction features beliefs, claims, and values that most adherents to liberal, progressive politics would find offensive.

Beyond these findings, our research is also relevant to issues relating to the study of public civility, conflict, social power in managing conflict in political contexts; and the characterization of public-spirited, political conversation itself. Recent ethnographic work on urban settings has emphasized the importance of everyday interpersonal routines in the prevention of conflict. In a number of contexts and scenes—for example, encounters on city streets, interracial merchant-customer relations, or urban beaches—sociologists and anthropologists have argued that the norms of the interaction order constrain a great deal of open conflict. On city streets, for example, Elijah Anderson argues that street "etiquette" enables countless pedestrians of very different social and cultural backgrounds to navigate past and beside each other with little trouble.[14] Jennifer Lee, as well, describes how the norms of civility in routine interactions between merchants and customers of different ethnic backgrounds enables them to keep the peace in all but a few transactions.[15] The social order of most urban beaches, so Robert Edgerton claims, rests on a different set of interactional norms than these first two examples in that it reduces the likelihood of stranger-stranger interaction, hence reducing conflict based on misperceptions or random predation.[16] Although our study of the interaction order and threats to it occurred in a very different kind of public context than research mentioned above, we also demonstrate how the normative nature of the interaction order constrains public conflict. In particular, our analysis demonstrates how tacit codes and ritual practices work to preserve the interaction order. As such, our analysis underscores an aspect of the interaction order with respect to conflict that has been less emphasized by urban ethnographers of public contexts: how codes and assumptions associated with public interaction operate as resources that actors draw on in managing disruptions in routine face-to-face communication. In this way, norms both constrain conflict and enable the repair of ruptures in the interaction order.[17]

A final implication of our chapter concerns the nature of public-spirited, political conversation itself. We mentioned at the outset of this chapter that there has been increasing concern among scholars about the magnitude and character of such conversation among citizens, and no doubt some would question how our observations of the Forum might contribute to deeper understanding of public political conversations, especially since these interchanges were often characterized by deep bigotry, disturbing paranoia, and wild interpretations of political events and processes.[18] At the same time, Forum members would engage in meaningful exchanges (within the ideological boundaries maintained by the group) that involved the formation and sometimes the reformation of viewpoints. Most members regularly read about current events, albeit selectively, and nearly all of the members we encountered claimed to have voted in almost every public election for which they had been eligible during their adult lives. On many measures, then, Forum members could be counted among the most politically engaged members of American society. Regardless of the particular contents of the discussions we witnessed at the Forum, what our research demonstrates is that public-spirited conversation is a delicate dynamic that involves the constant achievement of civility and conversation. What is key for such conversations to persist is that individuals, regardless of where they fall on the political spectrum, conduct themselves in a fashion that honors the interaction order. Like all good conversationalists, participants in public-spirited political conversations must remain at least partially open to alternative viewpoints. Only in contexts where interaction orders facilitate meaningful interpersonal engagement can such conversations emerge and thrive.

METHODOLOGICAL PROCEDURES AND REFLECTIONS

Both authors attended the Forum's weekly meetings, logging over 130 hours in the field and yielding approximately 250 pages of field notes.[19] The first author also attended a six-month "class" on the "New World Order" taught by a Forum member and attended by several other members, which provided an additional fifty hours of observation. Since the Forum's meetings were held in a public restaurant, initial access to the group was easily achieved. In so far as ongoing access was related to rapport, however, it was cultivated continually throughout the study. Both researchers walked something of a tightrope between full-fledged covert and overt research. Neither researcher disrupted the natural flow of meetings to volunteer information on the study, but when asked, we readily explained our interests and purposes for attending meetings.[20] As alluded to earlier, the majority of the data for the study came from observing weekly meetings. However, both researchers engaged in informal interviewing of members when the opportunity for doing so arose. This interviewing took the form of direct questions as well as "interviewing by comment,"[21] or stating particular hypotheses about group dynamics to elicit responses from members. The authors benefited by being able to record the majority of meetings inconspicuously, as many members brought tape recorders on a regular basis and took notes. However, when tape recording would have drawn undue attention to the research process, such as during an informal conversation, researchers took jotted field notes. These jottings, as well as recordings of meeting events, were then expanded daily into full field notes of all observations, impressions, and analytic insights once each of us exited from the field.

In addition to these notes, we held weekly meetings to discuss ideas and new avenues for inquiry. These meetings included academics who were not as directly engaged in the fieldwork but who were interested in the study of political sociology, political discussion, and the phenomena of extreme right-wing politics more generally. Our "team" approach to fieldwork thus encompassed both authors and also extended to a broader group of academics who offered us insights from their research on progressive and right-wing politics.[22] These meetings helped combat our own personal biases and self-fulfilling prophecies by multiplying researcher perspectives both in the field and during analytic "moments" when coding field notes.[23] During these project meetings we discussed the previous week's observations and began to "make sense" of the field notes as a data set. We initially coded the data through a line-by-line "open"-coding process. We then broke these broad categories down into taxonomic subcategories that were theoretically driven by our concerns with disruptive situations and remedial strategies. As we engaged in "focused" coding, we also began writing integrative memos regarding emergent patterns and arguments relevant to remedial work, political discussion, and social relationships among Forum members.[24]

Comparing notes at the end of the day is one of the more interesting aspects of team ethnography. Since we sat in different areas of the room where the Forum met and interacted with different people, our respective experiences were filtered through the different sets of members with whom we interacted and observed. Nevertheless, our notes generally corresponded, and except for activities that occurred outside the other's purview we generally recorded the open-forum dynamics in much the same fashion. For the most part, our debriefing sessions consisted of checking the accuracy of our transcripts of speeches and sequencing of events and recounting events that occurred backstage during the discussions around us. However, debriefings also gave us a chance to share our emotional impressions of the group and its individual members. It was at this emotional level that our experiences diverged the most. Perhaps the differences were related to biography (the first author grew up in rural Texas and experienced firsthand many of the beliefs and perspective espoused by Forum members, while the second author grew up in a decidedly urban context with less exposure to such beliefs), or maybe they had something to do with the fact that we spent time with different people. Whatever the reason, we each saw different things when we looked at group members and had different emotional struggles to reconcile. Below, we deal with two classic questions related to these issues: (1) How does the ethnographer usefully and effectively manage strong emotional reactions to events in the field? and (2) How does the ethnographer exit relationships with informants that have been built up over long periods of time?

For us, one of the most difficult discoveries we made was that as time progressed we genuinely liked these people whose views on so many issues were different and in fact offensive to us. Reconciling our own feelings of responsibility to and concern for group members was particularly difficult after meetings that deeply contradicted our own value systems. In reviewing our field notes to write this section, we were reminded of an especially emotionally challenging week, which we recounted above. At that week's meeting, a group member called for a protest of a local politician who just one week before had publicly identified himself as gay. This member suggested that because the politician was gay he was most likely HIV positive and therefore a threat to society. Following this incident, another individual shared a letter she had written to the same politician in which she suggested that he and his employees were working for the Devil and should resign because of their immorality. Both of us found these views shocking and deeply offensive, the second author more so because of her work as an AIDS activist and educator. Initially, we wanted to return to the Forum to hotly contest these views (or, alternatively, to disengage from the fieldwork altogether because our research unintentionally "dignified" such "perverse" beliefs). Writing field notes of the meeting was especially challenging, and we found that only after expressions of outrage to one another (as well as to the group with whom we met to discuss our findings) could we return to the Forum to see how the objectionable call to action played out. (Such a protest was never held.) Indeed, it was through this emotional lens that we actually began to realize—even have a minor breakthrough—regarding the central analytic hook of our work. Taking a cue from anthropologist Renato Rosaldo, we drew on our emotional experiences in the field as a resource as we analyzed and wrote up our work.[25]

Over the course of our research, and afterwards while the first author was collecting network data for another project, the first author got to know quite well both the Forum's conspiracy theorist and his antagonist. This shouldn't be surprising, since they were among our "key informants" during the team phase of research and were sponsors during the second phase when the first author had trouble collecting network data from some members. While we didn't agree with most of their views, we came to appreciate the honesty with which they answered questions and to respect the sincerity of their convictions. Fortunately, we rarely had to deal with the overtly racial or ethnic prejudice common among many on the extreme political right, and some in the Forum, so at times we found listening to their accounts of global conspiracies quite interesting and often amusing. In this manner, the second author formed friendships with two people that he probably would have never come into contact with had it not been for an interest in far-right political movements.

What was surprising, however, was how difficult it was to leave the group and the people we had spent so much time with. No one "taught" us systematic procedures (maybe they don't exist) for how to disengage from "research subjects." From the vantage point of our experience, the two most difficult and demanding components of ethnographic research are getting established in a setting at the start of a project and leaving it behind at the end. Ethnographers talk and write a great deal about the first issue but only in passing about the second. So how does one disengage? We really had no idea at the time.[26] As the data collection phase of our project came to a close, we spent increasing amounts of time poring over field notes and decreasing amounts of time in the field. In the end, we simply muddled our way through as one would in dealing with a difficult transition in any personal relationship, trying to be responsible to the feelings of our informants and our own feelings. We told our informants that our project had ended and that we were moving on to other projects (and, in the case of the second author, to a different career). At some points, we still felt as if we had used, or otherwise betrayed, our "friends," especially in the case of the first author. That feeling did not dissipate for some time, as he returned periodically to the Forum, not to collect more data, and not because he particularly enjoyed the breakfasts or topics of conversation, but because he found it interesting and missed the people he used to eat breakfast with.

ELEVEN

Taking Stock

Functions, Places, and Personal Relationships

CALVIN MORRILL AND DAVID A. SNOW

There will be possibilities for the rapid development of closeness
between and among persons, a closeness which is not artificial, but is
real and deep, and which will be well suited to our increasing
mobility of living. Temporary relationships will be able to achieve the
richness and meaning which heretofore have been associated with
lifelong attachments.

CARL ROGERS,
"Interpersonal Relationships U.S.A. 2000"

THROUGHOUT THE TWENTIETH CENTURY, NUMEROUS scholars noted
that the character of social relationships in contemporary society had
changed due to rapid urbanization, social mobility, and technological
advances.[1] These trends, at least within industrialized countries, can be
found in the shrinking sizes of families and friendship networks, with
social ties among intimates flung across vast geographic, cultural, and economic expanses.[2] Among other things, these changes have meant that
much of the daily social interaction in which one engages, especially in
urban settings, is likely to involve strangers and nonintimates in public
places. Although forty years ago Jane Jacobs, in *The Death and Life of
Great American Cities,* famously pointed out the importance of public
sociality for the health and well-being of cities and their inhabitants, indicators of this type of interaction are still difficult to find in institutional
records or to study with the usual social scientific tools—the survey
instrument and the experiment. Such relationships do not have the look of
traditional primary ties or the kinds of associational relationships that

make their way into organizational records. Nonetheless, the contributors to this volume vividly demonstrate how personal relationships in public places can matter a great deal to people. To close this collection, then, we turn to what the nine studies, taken together, have taught us.

FUNCTIONS AND PLACES

In this section, we organize our discussion around two central questions that enable us to rethink, at a broader level, the contributions of the nine studies in this volume: How does public sociality matter? and How does place influence public sociality? Both of these questions incorporate themes that run through the volume and also point toward key issues regarding the study of social relationships in public. To address these questions, we draw on two core concepts: *functions* and *places*. The concept of function, for present purposes, refers to the consequences (whether intended or unintended) of particular social behaviors.[3] A function of a personal relationship signals what it does or means for those involved and the social audiences privy to it. In an age of social change in which public sociality has taken on increasing importance, understanding these functions is a crucial first step toward gaining insight into what Karen Cook calls the "complex forms of association that will emerge in the [twenty-first] century."[4] These functions, however, do not unfold in geographic or social vacuums. As we discussed in chapter 1, the concept of place denotes a specific locale, which carries a particular mixture of social, cultural, institutional, and physical attributes. The works in this volume underscore how public and quasi-public places channel, facilitate, and, under some conditions, are transformed by social interaction among people. In the sections below, we first turn to the multiple functions of public sociality, as illustrated by the nine studies. We then delve into the ways place influences public sociality.

How Public Sociality Matters: Material, Social, and Psychological Functions

The preceding chapters illuminate the *material, social,* and *psychological* functions of personal relationships conducted in public. The material functions of public sociality concern its role in shaping economic transactions involving material resources, such as money, goods, or services. The social functions of public sociality concern its role in constituting and sustaining a variety of interactionally based associations and identifications, including personal ties, social networks, communities, and identities.

Finally, the psychological functions of personal relationships capture the interplay between social interaction and actors' emotional expressions and overall outlooks. How these functions are accomplished and unfold vary considerably across the types of public sociality (fleeting and anchored personal relations) investigated in this volume. In practice, public sociality can simultaneously feed into more than one function at a time, and functions can undermine and contradict each other. Below, we discuss each function in turn for ease of analytic exposition, noting along the way the tensions sometimes experienced as multiple functions intersect.

Material Functions   The earliest field research on public sociality focused almost exclusively on the material functions of fleeting and anchored relationships. In his groundbreaking study of consumer-clerk relations in the early 1950s, Gregory Stone observed that Chicago housewives developed "personalizing ties" (friendly relations and interactions that included conversations about aspects of their personal lives) in the course of routine interactions with retail clerks despite not having any contact with the clerks away from the stores. In particular, he found that housewives were more likely to shop where they had personalizing ties to clerks, even if it meant traveling a longer distance from their residences to do so.[5] To cast Stone's work in a more contemporary light, one could argue that many daily economic transactions become "embedded" in public sociality such that fleeting and anchored social relationships create obligations and routines that channel exchange.[6] Indeed, social embeddedness can occur in a myriad of retail and service situations that require only momentary face-to-face contact between clerks and customers, including forms of commerce that occur over great geographic distances, yet are conducted via electronic means (e.g., e-mail, telephone).[7]

Public sociality does not need to be durable or to carry a sense of authenticity to function in this fashion. As Massey and Hope (chapter 4) demonstrate in their fieldwork among male customers and female dancers in a strip club, transitory sociality can embed material transactions as long as participants define it "as if" it constituted a personal tie. The momentary fictive ties between dancers and customers in a strip club during "personalized" table dances are but a special case of the many kinds of everyday rituals that people willingly engage in when, as Goffman notes, they insulate themselves by "half-truths, illusions, and rationalizations" to get on with (and facilitate) the business at hand with as little threat as possible to their sense of self.[8] In the case of the customer and stripper, the business at hand is both commercial sexuality *and* the pretense that there is more "going on" (regarding the emotional friendliness exhibited by the dancers in the interaction) than merely pay-for-view simulated sex. Indeed, dancers who are not adept at quickly inviting and creating a fictive stereotypical heterosexual romantic relationship with customers soon find themselves unable to attract paying customers for lucrative table dances. For some customers, however, the illusion of emotional connection slides toward authenticity, which can create difficulties for both the dancer and the customer as the former tries to exit from a table dance and the latter attempts to overlay his sense of a longer-term relationship on the interaction. Under these conditions, dancers exit in abrupt ways, using whatever spatial (i.e., the dancer's dressing area) or social control (e.g., calling over a bouncer) resources are at hand.

Personal relationships in public not only facilitate market-type exchanges but also supply conduits for material support that occurs outside economic contexts. Under these conditions, the material and social functions of public sociality become intertwined as individuals, in the course of creating and sustaining personal relationships, begin to exchange material resources. Munch in chapter 6, for example, notes how the anchored relations among softball fans in a public park facilitated material support of all kinds, including monetary loans, the exchange of food and blankets, the provision of baby supplies (such as bottles, formula, and diapers), and advice about job opportunities.

Social Functions   As the fans described by Munch exchange material support, they also illustrate an important *complementary* social function of personal relationships in public. Public sociality functions in complementary ways to the degree that it helps sustain aspects of preexisting primary ties. For fans with kin ties to one another, familylike personal connections at the ballpark fulfill this function. For other fans, personal relationships in public function in a *compensatory* way by providing aspects of primary ties that are missing in people's lives. Other chapters also illustrate this compensatory function. Beattie, Christopher, Okamoto, and Way in chapter 3 describe men and women who return to singles dances week after week in part because they are missing meaningful primary relationships in their private lives and find pleasure in the fleeting ties they experience with other participants. Likewise, some of the customers in the strip bars studied by Massey and Hope in chapter 4 are also missing meaningful relational partners in their lives and take solace in the momentary fleeting relationships they enjoy with dancers. Finally, the divorce group participants described by Ebesu Hubbard and White in chapter 8, while they come seeking strategies for coping with their relational losses, also find temporary compensatory relationships in the group.[9]

Aside from these functions, personal relationships in public offer vital opportunities for generating and sustaining personal, social, and collective identities. In a broad sense, identity is the way people classify others in "systematically related categories," which, in turn, enables meaningful social interaction to occur. Personal identities (such as a proper name or a singular set of traits) signal one's uniqueness, whereas social identities (e.g., being an African American woman or a regular member of a group that congregates at a bar) locate one as part of a broader social role. Collective identity involves identifying groups in terms of their attachments and attributes (for instance, a sports team's fans or a political discussion group identified as "progressive" or "right wing").[10] Social encounters and fleeting relationships, in particular, leave what might be called "traces" of identity in the sense that individuals use the cues contained in brief interactions to identify the characteristics of those whom they communicate with, including persons who may cause trouble.[11] The very act of engaging in an encounter or fleeting relationship can itself constitute an identity that triggers social expectations, routines, and rituals, which, in turn, instill an orderliness in social interaction.[12]

Along these lines, public sociality figures prominently in the enactment and experience of gender and ethnic identities. Carole Brooks Gardner, for example, argues that a wariness toward transitory public sociality, together with a constant vulnerability to harassment, stigma, and crime, especially when alone, is a constitutive aspect of being a women in many public places throughout North America.[13] Stern, Callister, and Jones in chapter 2 illuminate this pattern in their study of "face time" among undergraduates at a public university recreation center. They observed that both male and female undergraduates "piggybacked" their attempts to kindle long-term relationships with peers while they exercised, which nearly always led to the generation of encounters and fleeting relationships rather than durable ties. Like women in other studies of public sociality, women in the rec center were far more likely to fall prey to voyeurism and stalking behaviors by men than vice versa. Indeed, being a woman in a public place, in part, means knowing how to recognize and fend off such normative transgressions among strangers. At the same time, anchored patterns of public sociality can, under certain conditions, reconfigure shared, gendered expectations and images about particular public places, as illustrated by Reid, Karlin, and Bonham-Crecilius in chapter 7.

Public sociality also marks other groups who face particular challenges with regard to conducting personal relationships in public places. Harrison and Morgan in chapter 5, for example, document how teenagers engage in anchored romantic and friendship relations while they "hang out" in public places, including city streets, fast-food restaurants, and open-air bus stations. Teen public hangouts are tenuous, especially in places designed for a restricted set of activities. The very act of conducting personal relationships in public places can draw social control efforts from workers and police who attempt to disperse youth or return them to their homes.

Aside from their functions with regard to gender or youth, anchored relationships can function to produce collective identities that are linked to subcultures and/or forms of community. As Munch argues in chapter 6, floating communities of fans in an amateur softball league can, over time, develop dense cross-cutting ties and social obligations. These communities are not grounded in extended families or residential areas, as the image of traditional community suggests, but they do display many of the same dynamics as traditional communities. Munch, for example, observes that members of the floating fan community refer to one another with fictive family terms (such as *uncle, aunt,* and *cousin*) and engage in much of the social and emotional support that one would expect to find in a traditional nuclear or extended family. This floating community has existed for years, even though its members rarely, if ever, interact with each other outside the four-month softball season or away from the bleachers and often start new seasons connected to a new team with different players. Munch claims that the generalized social obligations and collective identity among spectators, in conjunction with institutional supports provided by the long-term viability of the softball league, bring fans back to the parks year after year. Chapter 7 illustrates how patterns of maintaining and violating personal space within gay and lesbian bars can impart widespread collective identification of distinctive "lesbian," "gay," or "straight" bars and other hangouts. Finally, the publicly anchored relations among teens, as studied by Harrison and Morgan in chapter 5, are key to the reproduction and diffusion of local youth culture.

Yet another social function of public sociality can be found in its facilitation of meaningful political dialogue, which many scholars argue is one of the key pillars of a democratic society.[14] Although one might consider a right-wing discussion group beyond the boundaries of reasonable political dialogue, Clark-Miller and Murdock in chapter 10 observed a modicum of discussion within the ideological parameters of the group they studied. They argued that the norms of the public interaction order that undergird the relationships among members of the group are integrally tied to the reproduction of the group and its ability to engage in internal political discussion.

Psychological Functions   The material and social functions discussed in the previous pages hint at the psychological side of public sociality, including how it influences emotional dynamics, personal outlooks on life (e.g., optimism, self-esteem), and mental health. Transitory public sociality, according to Lyn Lofland, often induces pleasure and amusement among urban dwellers, which, in turn, can lead to a sense of emotional well-being.[15] The brief encounters and fleeting relationships at singles dances represented by Okamoto et al. in chapter 3, and customers' experiences of fleeting ties with dancers in strip clubs represented by Massey and Hope in chapter 4, illustrate aspects of these benefits. In both contexts, many actors experience a fleeting sense of well-being about their brief interactions even when (or because) they know there will be little relational involvement beyond the immediate interchange. Some actors can articulate how they feel about these responses, but most experience these instances "corporeally" rather than "discursively."[16] People construct lines of emotional action in response to others, but not necessarily by thinking about it consciously. This dynamic may be especially true with regard to interactional cues and emotional responses in the context of transitory public sociality. In the case of the strip club, the sexual corporeal sensuality of the moment, coupled with the fictive closeness of the social interaction, can be especially intoxicating for some customers. At the singles dance, the brief corporeal pleasure of dancing or chatting is enough to bring participants back to the dances time and again. Indeed, transitory emotional dynamics of this sort may be all the more important in contemporary society given the tenuousness of family and romantic relationships.

If in fleeting relationships individuals use momentary cues to sensually feel and produce appropriate emotional responses that color such interactions with intimacy, it is in anchored relationships that these dynamics take on greater durability and depth. In chapter 6, Munch vividly describes the emotional well-being and warmth that individual fans express toward one another. These emotions at the individual level in part bolster the efforts to patrol the boundaries of the floating community that fans create.

Ebesu Hubbard and White in chapter 8 document perhaps the most complex set of emotional dynamics explored in the volume in their study of the anchored relations among divorce recovery group participants. As the participants discuss their relations with their ex-spouses, they draw on the corporeal experience of their breakups and discursively construct how they felt and may feel toward their ex-spouses in the future. In so doing, they can redefine their own and their former marital partner's identities. Finally, Reid and her coauthors in chapter 7 illuminate another aspect of public sociality with regard to how it can set group standards and "feeling rules"[17] for contextually "appropriate" expressions of emotion. As one moves across different bars with different collective sexual identities, the ground rules for relational interaction and emotion change dramatically.

As our recounting suggests, public sociality—whether in its short-lived or more durable forms—fulfills a broad and rich set of functions across a diverse range of settings. Our discussion, however, raises important questions about the conditions under which public sociality and these functions are likely to occur. This question necessarily leads to the issue of place, which contributors to this volume have used in various ways to understand variability in public sociality.

Public Sociality and Place

In chapter 1, we discussed the concept of place as a geographical locale imbued with particular meanings and practices regarding access, visibility, and use. Our contributors illuminated and expanded this orientation by moving beyond the traditional dichotomy of "public" versus "private" places to introduce dimensions of contrast between different types of public and quasi-public places. We draw from their work and that of others to explicitly sketch these dimensions by focusing on two interrelated characteristics that involve, first, the *framing of place,* including how a space is both officially and interactionally defined with regard to its uses, access, and visibility, and, second, the *regulation of place,* including the ground rules and social control processes found in particular places.

Framing of Place　The meaning of a place is not inherent in its "objective" or physical attributes but rather arises from interpretive processes that occur in the interplay between person-to-place and person-to-person interactions. This perspective is consistent with the interactionist stance taken throughout this volume that regards meaning as emerging from social interaction.[18] Central in these interpretive dynamics are what

Goffman called "frameworks of interpretation,"[19] or "frames," for short, that enable people to "locate, perceive, identify, and label" a situation, a broader context, or, importantly for present purposes, a place and the social interaction that occurs within it.[20] In this sense, frames enable actors to answer questions such as "What does this social interaction mean?" or "What is this place used for?" Thus frames facilitate the attribution of meaning by individuals and groups to a place as it intersects with understandings about the range of activities that unfold there.[21] The frames that people draw on to make sense of places are embedded in "historically contingent and cultural understandings of the terrain"[22] and are communicated via a variety of symbolic forms. Such frames derive from formal proclamations about a place's intended usage (e.g., official signage) and informal sources (e.g., idealized descriptions, urban tales, rituals, graffiti, and interactions that both conform to and violate the "official" uses of a place). Finally, different frames can be constructed and simultaneously used to interpret a place by different groups of people. Homeless persons, for instance, often frame city parks as legitimate places to conduct all the activities that one would typically identify with both highly accessible public settings *and* domiciles. Nearby residents, by contrast, typically frame city parks as appropriate for a narrower range of explicitly intended activities that exclude actions that would typically occur in domiciles.[23]

Over time, person-to-place and person-to-person dynamics can lead to cultural sedimentation such that a frame or set of frames attaches to a place and becomes institutionalized as part of its taken-for-granted interpretive backdrop.[24] In this way, we can speak about "place frames" that are used in interaction by actors to help define what a place is and is not. Institutionalized frames enable individuals to orient and organize their interpretations about places in particular ways. The distinctions drawn by our authors between public places and quasi-public places often rely upon the recognition of institutionalized place frames. City parks and open-air plazas, for example, are formally and informally framed in ways that display a relatively wide latitude with regard to intended uses, access, and visibility, which, in turn, invites a broad range of activities in them, including criminal activities and homeless camps. By contrast, quasi-public places (e.g., restaurants, bars, formally constituted groups) are framed by insiders and outsiders in narrower and more specific ways with regard to access, visibility, and their intended uses. In this sense, we can conceptualize place frames on a continuum from those that are relatively "closed," in the sense that they incorporate a narrower set of intended uses, access, and visibility, to those that are more "open," in that they focus on a broader range of activities and can be used to interpret a wide variety of actors and actions. Closed-place frames therefore constrain actors with respect to what they attend to as routine or appropriate in a particular place, whereas open-place frames facilitate actors' attending to a broader array of lines of action. As a result, the boundaries that mark what is "in" and "out" of an open-place frame are more permeable and elastic than those for a closed-place frame.[25]

In practice, the distinction between open- and closed-place frames can be complex, especially in quasi-public places. In these places, access is more constrained than in purely public places because it is contingent upon the performance of specified behaviors, status characteristics, or monetary payments of some sort. Yet the behaviors of people in these settings are publicly visible and therefore available to mutual monitoring by others. In some places, such as the strip clubs represented in chapter 4, the rec center studied in chapter 2, or the divorce recovery groups investigated in chapter 8, verbal and nonverbal behavior are readily observable and can be topics of discussion among participants in each setting. At the same time, behaviors in these settings can appear to be physically and/or socially intimate, as in the transactions that occur in strip clubs or the biographic narratives that unfold in divorce recovery groups. What makes a place public, therefore, is not only its levels of access and visibility to broad social constituents but the ready accessibility of its behaviors and discussions among nonintimates (e.g., strangers). Places that one would typically not consider to be public *or* private can thus be redefined to be the opposite under these conditions.

Regulation of Place   Closely related to place frames are the normative mechanisms that regulate prototypical, "generic public places,"[26] including taken-for-granted codes and ground rules that undergird face-to-face communication and interaction orders, behavioral strategies of social control, and the built environment. As we discussed in chapter 1, routine social interaction owes much of its apparent orderliness to sets of tacit principles on which actors draw. Much of public sociality among nonintimates in North American is governed by norms that require individuals to maintain appropriate distances from one another (despite being physically close), to be relatively retiring as members of surrounding audiences, to supply only limited aid to those in need, to collectively navigate past one another without threat, and to sustain some degree of civility in the face of social diversity.[27] These principles, however, are not set in stone and can vary according to the social characteristics and statuses of those involved, as well as the broader institutional and cultural contexts in which public social interaction occurs. As contributors to this volume and other scholars have documented, women, youth, and minorities often face different ground rules and additional forms of control, social disapproval, and even harassment in public. Indeed, as Wayne Brekhus argues, generic public places often appear "neutral" but are "actually stacked in favor of those who are endowed with invisible privilege . . . [such that they] . . . limit social extremes and encourage social cohesion."[28] Newcomers to the United States can run up against such privileges as they attempt to import very different senses and practices in public places than are common in most American cities. Although individual immigrants may adapt to the prevailing patterns and codes of public sociality in many settings, under some conditions (e.g., aggregation in certain places or cities and/or collective mobilization) they can transform the prevailing ground rules for interaction, thus transforming the bases for public sociality.[29] Thus woven into the very ground rules and practices of public sociality are the bases for social power in society.

It may be more accurate to refer to the principles of public sociality, and the strategies used to enforce them, as "repertoires" that individuals draw from as they navigate public places. To cast such principles as repertoires is to recognize them as sets of expectations and skilled actions that individuals can use with more or less ability and effectiveness.[30] This orientation also implies that different groups and individuals will have differential access to normative repertoires considered legitimate or illegitimate. Finally, normative repertoires can be manipulated in different ways at the interpersonal and group levels to achieve a wide variety of purposes. The constant physical movement and social distance required to accomplish transitory public sociality, for example, often cloaks voyeurs, petty criminals, and sexual predators in an aura of "normal appearances."[31] Stern, Callister, and Jones in chapter 2 were especially attuned to these dynamics of transitory sociality as they observed undergraduate men camouflage their voyeurism and stalking in workout routines, as well as the ebb and flow of brief encounters and social distance at a university recreation center. In the aggregate, violations of the ground rules of public sociality can themselves become the bases of constructing alternative codes for sociality that play key roles in the communication of personal and place-specific identities. Reid, Karlin, and Bonham-Crecilius in chapter 7 illustrate this tendency with the variety of ways that individuals police, violate, and reconstruct territories of the self associated with anchored relationships in gay, lesbian, and straight bars. Within these places, individuals possess different levels of social skill to enact and patrol territories of the self. The rules of engagement in anchored public relationships can also lead to tight moral boundaries, thus limiting insiders' abilities to deal with trouble occurring beyond those boundaries. A poignant illustration of the double-edged normative nature of anchored relationships can be found in Munch's observations in chapter 6 in which softball fans ignored and even verbally constrained their members from helping a woman screaming for help as she was physically attacked beyond the bleachers.

Taken together, these patterns underscore the idea that the character of everyday social order in public places is as much the result of "bottom-up" social control processes as "top-down" state mechanisms (i.e., formal policing).[32] These patterns also emphasize the integral connections between place frames and the regulation of place. In chapter 9, Horne, Mcilwaine, and Taylor's study of adult social control of children in public places offers a poignant illustration of these interconnections. From their perspective, "restrictive" public places are framed with relatively specific intents or tasks (i.e., a closed-place frame); are physically outfitted with architectural enclosures (walls, fixed seating, partitions, tables) that restrict access and the flow of bodily movement; and experience a low level of interactional "noise" (e.g., very little shouting or loud talking). A "permissive" place, by contrast, is framed more openly to include a variety of activities and inter-actional patterns; contains few architectural encumbrances to social motil-ity; and has a high noise level encouraged by ground rules that permit a wider latitude of interactional practices and play (especially among chil-dren). Restrictive public places also contain more readily available forms of social control, either embodied in a range of "officials" formally linked to a place (e.g., clerks, managers, bouncers, security guards) or expressed via peer social control. In their study, Horne, Mcilwaine, and Taylor found that adults take into account the framing and regulation of place as they handle trouble with their children. In restrictive places, adults use more aggressive social control strategies on their children than they do in per-missive places. Adult interventions of this kind are often conducted under the watchful gaze of an individual or group working in an official capacity and from unofficial sources through gaze, avoidance, or direct interven-tion. Thus more restrictive places exhibit a layering of constraint that emanates from multiple forms of social control.

How Place Influences Public Sociality

More than two decades ago, Goffman observed that the interaction order, especially as it is enacted in public places, supports "a great diversity of projects and intents to be realized."[33] The different types and multiple functions of public sociality documented by the nine studies in this volume attest to that observation. These studies also attest to the idea that the framing and regulation of a public place matter a great deal for the kinds and functions of personal relationships that flourish in a public setting. This observation is consistent with general arguments that social context significantly influences the emergence and dynamics of personal relationships, especially in public.[34]

The most direct influence of public places on public sociality concerns the range of relationships found in a locale. In this sense, public places can be said to have different "carrying capacities" such that they enable some relationships while constraining others. At one extreme are closed-frame public places with specific intents, access, and visibility, together with a range of social control processes. Such dynamics may also be reinforced with material forms that restrict bodily motility or suppress interaction. Under these conditions, we would expect the majority of social interactions to attend to officially intended or prescribed tasks. To the extent that personal considerations and orientations enter into social interaction, it is likely that much of it will be confined to brief encounters and fleeting relationships.[35] Stern, Callister, and Jones's study of a university recreation center in chapter 2, Beattie, Christopher, Okamoto, and Way's study of singles dances in chapter 3, and Massey and Hope's study of the strip bar in chapter 4 illustrate these tendencies.[36] In each of these locales, personal relationships were largely confined to fleeting relationships, except in rare instances or among actors working in official capacities (e.g., clerks, attendants). In all these settings, moreover, actors protected their "face"—the public sense of worth with which an individual is held—by camouflaging or moderating their personal inclinations with others amidst "officially" sanctioned activities. At the other extreme are public places associated with open frames, as well as material forms, that invite a broad range of activities and access. Under these conditions, the carrying capacity for social relationships will expand to include both fleeting and anchored public sociality. Thus the parks where Munch studied softball spectators (reported in chapter 6) simultaneously contained both anchored relations among fans and a broad range of more transitory social ties. A corollary to these insights concerns the functions of public sociality in different public places. Public sociality in closed-framed public places, in part because they constrain the range of personal relationships, is likely to exhibit a narrower range of functions. In these settings, we would expect public sociality to be less varied with respect to what it does or means to actors. In open-framed public places, by contrast, in which a greater range of public sociality is likely to flourish, so too its functions are likely to be more varied.

Another implication of these expectations pertains to the ecological distribution of places and the likelihood of public sociality. What Lyn Lofland calls "privatism" (the ideological and individual commitment toward removing social interaction from public to private places and social realms) and "privatization" (designing the built environment to constrain public sociality) have long histories in Western culture dating back to the seventeenth century. Where these twin thrusts are dominant, they have resulted in a paring back of public places, and with it a reduction of both transitory and durable public sociality in American cities.[37] Our distinction between open- and closed-framed public places, however, helps to both extend and specify this relationship. Following the logic that open-framed public places encourage a greater diversity of public sociality, we would expect that an overall reduction of open-framed public places would truncate the range of public sociality so that fleeting ties would be likely to predominate. As important as fleeting relationships and encounters can be for both public order and individuals, many of the functions played by anchored sociality in public would be lost.

These first propositions suggest yet another link between place and public sociality regarding the evolution of personal relationships. Specifically, how does place influence the likelihood that fleeting ties will become more durable? As research on intimate relationships tells us, a host of factors can affect the emergence of durable personal unions, including the social characteristics, biographies, communication competence, and psychological outlooks of those involved; the social networks in which the actors are embedded; and broader cultural and contextual factors.[38] Our question is more modest in scope, in that we consider only public sociality and narrow our focus, net of other factors, to the role of place. With these scope conditions in mind, we maintain that open-framed places are more likely to encourage the transformation of fleeting sociality to anchored relationships because they do not structure or control social interaction in the manner that closed-framed public places do. Although the ground rules of nonintimate sociality can constrain the formation of more durable relationships, as many of our chapters demonstrate, these rules also can be used by actors to achieve multiple purposes. As a result, open-framed places provide opportunities for people to interactionally explore one another and develop the interdependencies and commitments that can lead to more durable ties. Moreover, such places do not require individuals to focus their attention as acutely on particular tasks that do not or only involve cursory social interaction. This pattern is evident in Munch's observations in chapter 6 on the evolution of floating communities among fans. At the beginning of a softball season, many fans do not know each other or know each other only from a distance, owing to the fact that most players, while they may have played in the league for many years, do not play on the same teams over multiple seasons. During the first few games, fans' social interaction is confined to brief encounters and fleeting conversations during which they exchange information about their connections to the players and the league. Over time, interpersonal explorations like these can provide the basis for the development of the tight-knit anchored relations that constitute their spectator communities.

From one perspective, gay and lesbian bars that Reid, Karlin, and Bonham-Crecilius studied in chapter 7 would seem to be extremely closed in the sense that they do not offer freedom of access (one must be at least twenty-one years of age) or visibility to public audiences (the spaces are enclosed with distinct gatekeepers). Their well-known place-based identities may further inhibit those with heterosexual identities from frequenting them. At the same time, lesbian and gay bars are more openly framed with respect to their intents than singles straight bars, which tend to display more rigid gender practices and expectations regarding personal space and transitory interaction, as well as focusing on alcohol consumption. All else held constant, it is more likely that publicly anchored relationships will develop among patrons of gay and lesbian bars than among patrons of straight bars.

Harrison and Morgan in chapter 5 illustrate another aspect of this pattern by documenting how youths attempting to conduct anchored relationships in public are constantly driven from more closed-framed public places (e.g., fast-food restaurants) toward open-framed public places (e.g., streets, open bus plazas, parks). To be sure, the regulation that youths encounter in retail establishments not only is a function of place but also relates to their identification as potentially "disruptive" or "dangerous" subjects because of their status as teens.

Actors, Places, and Public Sociality

As important as place is in limiting or generating the types and functions of relationships likely to be found in a specific locale, this perspective leaves out actors, who obviously play key roles in all of these dynamics. The nine studies in this volume point to four issues with respect to actors and places: (1) social identity, status, and power; (2) the congruence between actors' avowed purposes and the framing of place; (3) the "interactional units,"[39] as Goffman called them, with which actors enter public places; and (4) the availability of other actors in a place. With regard to the first issue, we have already alluded to the multiple influences of gender and sexual identities on the way people constitute and experience public sociality. Similar observations can be made for other social identities, including youth (as alluded to above), ethnic minorities, and, under certain conditions, the elderly. Suffice to say that social identities, statuses, and social power both constrain and enable the kindling of personal relationships in public. Some identities and statuses (e.g., children, pregnant women, police officers) mark individuals as "open" persons who invite momentary social interaction but may not necessarily lead to further interaction that constitutes any form of personal relationship. Other statuses constrain social interaction and so can constrain the formation of any kind of social tie.[40]

At the same time, these ideas focus on the role of identity and place from only one perspective: how identity influences the public relational practices in which people engage. Yet place itself, specifically the framing of place, can alternately influence whether people highlight or diminish aspects of their identities, which, in turn, can influence the possibilities for them to create relationships. Reid, Karlin, and Bonham-Crecilius argue in chapter 7 that over time the density of gays, lesbians, and straights in bars, respectively, helps establish those places as "gay" or "lesbian." This finding relates to Brekhus's point that "*who* one is depends on *where* one is. Identity resides not in the individual alone but in the interaction between the individual and his or her social environment [italics in the original]."[41] Indeed, particular places can highlight or suppress particular aspects of one's identity and interactional practices, thus increasing the likelihood that one will enact the kinds of relational ties most prevalent in that setting.

This last point clearly intertwines with the avowed intents and purposes with which an actor enters into a place. Clearly, youths who go to fast-food restaurants to conduct their personal relationships or students who make no effort to work out while they engage in explicit attempts to meet other students at university rec centers can come under the intense scrutiny by other actors in the setting and can ultimately be shooed from the premises. Such actors come to have "marked" identities[42] that draw stigma and, under some conditions, become the grounds for explicit interpersonal conflict.[43] Here again, the framing and regulation of place play important roles. Incongruities between individual actors' or small groups of actors' avowed purposes and closed-frame places are more likely to lead to conflict because of the restricted leeway in interactional practices and actions in these settings. Conversely, incongruities between actors' avowed purposes and actions in open-framed places are less likely to carry the same implications. Although there is pressure to conform to the generic norms of open public places, differences can ultimately be avoided rather than confronted. The navigation of public places with ambiguous or multiple sets of frames in play (such as urban areas in transition from one ethnic and social class composition to another)[44] presents an additional level of interactional complexity that can be fraught with social tension and ambiguity. In these contexts, the interactional ground rules for multiple sets of actors can collide (e.g., men alone compared to women alone or domiciled vs. homeless individuals)[45] but can also lead to people working hard to construct interactions as ordinary and civil in the face of difference.[46]

Whether one enters into a public place in an interactional unit as a "single" or a "with" (i.e., in a dyad or larger group) can also be an important factor for public sociality and intersects with social identities and avowed purposes in various ways.[47] In public places, many withs, by definition, tend to be more exclusive in their control of personal and physical territories and so may delimit the varieties of social encounters and fleeting ties that develop. Withs, moreover, can displace and disrupt the normal flow of nonintimate public motility, as when youths set up temporary hangouts on city sidewalks or "take over" large portions of the seating in fast-food restaurants. Anchored relations kindled only in public, as in the floating communities that develop among spectators at sporting events, also tend to displace purely nonintimate public sociality and will typically be more inward than outward looking. At the same time, certain kinds of withs, especially parents with children, may be more prone to brief encounters or fleeting ties of solidarity with other parents, especially if they are handling trouble in a closed-frame public place. Although singles would seem to be more likely to engage in public sociality since they do not already come attached, this assumed propensity can be limited by several factors, including their social identity (e.g., women, if single, may be more constrained in engaging in social interaction in public than men) and their avowed intents. As Stern, Callister, and Jones note in chapter 2, there is a segment of rec center users who come by themselves only to work out and who are largely uninterested in engaging in social interaction or kindling personal relationships with anyone while they use the facility.

Finally, the availability of other actors with particular avowed interests offers another limiting factor for social interaction and the formation of social relationships. Some places (especially at particular times), for example, are known for their high volumes of available actors (certain parks, streets, bars, plazas, restaurants, etc.) and others are not. High volumes of actors can be present in city streets during rush hours, but their orientations lead them away from anything but the briefest of encounters as they move through public places. Again, the rec center study in chapter 2 is instructive. During early mornings, the gym is nearly deserted save for a few "hard core" exercising enthusiasts. Evening hours by contrast, except for weekend nights, are known as a "meat market" in which high volumes of students interested in social interaction are present.

TOWARD NEW QUESTIONS

As the preceding sections make clear, this volume has provided a window onto a social world that is rarely visited in the name of social science but that is important for individuals and society as a whole. Moreover, personal relationships in public places are amenable to the same kind of systemic analysis and conceptual treatment as are other aspects of personal relationships usually found in private settings. In this final section, we suggest several analytic questions relevant to public sociality that are grounded in the foundations laid by the nine studies and by our reflections on them. In so doing, we realize that these questions do not cover all that could or should be explored with respect to public sociality, but we believe that these questions are a good starting point for future inquiry.

The first question concerns the constitution of personal relationships across all contexts. Traditional definitions of personal relationships reside in notions of durability and the bounded, often private, nature of social intimacy. The works in this volume, together with previous research on public sociality, challenge these definitions by documenting a range of close ties that do not fit traditional definitions of personal relationships. More importantly, these studies raise questions about the dynamics of close relationships in public. A related question concerns new manifestations and functions of fleeting relationships in public, especially those of a collective nature. "Flash mobs"—aggregates of strangers, organized through Web sites and other Internet sources—congregate in public places for a variety of "spontaneous" purposes but typically do not result in any long-standing ties between participants. This trend has appeared in North America and a number of European cities. Although it is unclear why participants are drawn to these groups, given what is known about their composition, the pleasures of nonintimate, public sociality play an important role.[48]

A second question concerns the influences of place and opportunities for meaningful public sociality. As we argued earlier in this chapter, various aspects of how a public place is framed, regulated, and designed can influence the form and evolution of public sociality. What our discussion of the intersection of place and the interpersonal dynamics of public sociality has not considered is how broad social, economic, and political forces are rapidly transforming places in ways that reduce the likelihood of the kinds of personal relationships considered in this volume. If, as Manuel Castells argues,[49] meaningful urban places of all kinds are being replaced by the rise of "megacities"[50] that comprise scattered, segmented places less related to one another than to dispersed global networks of production and information, the overall carrying capacity for public sociality may be further diminishing. On the other hand, such predictions are never as neat and preordained as they might appear from some vantage points. The need for sociality does not disappear even as contextual constraints appear that seem to suppress it. Moreover, people appear to have almost infinite ingenuity in kindling social relationships of all kinds under very difficult conditions. Thus public sociality may play out in yet-to-be-determined ways in which fleeting relationships may have even more important psychological and social functions than they currently do. Future research needs to pursue these issues in explicitly comparative fashions across a broad array of contexts and regions.[51]

A third set of questions touch on issues raised explicitly in the early sections of this chapter and at various points in the nine studies: How does public sociality vary with the social characteristics of actors, especially minorities and new arrivals from different countries who are often subordinated to mainstream groups? How is public sociality repressed or interrupted for subordinated groups? These questions take us into terrain that confronts social and economic divisions created by political power and global capital as they are experienced interpersonally and institutionally. If public sociality is vital to any community but is suppressed or constrained for particular groups, how does this undermine the possibility for collective well-being for such groups? The question is most often explored in this volume with respect to gender, sexual identity, and youth. Largely unexplored in the volume are the functions and challenges of public sociality for different ethnic and religious groups. Of particular interest is public sociality in communities that are mosaics of established groups and new immigrant arrivals.[52]

A fourth question implicitly arises from the previous set of issues. It concerns how places can be built to explicitly facilitate public sociality. One of the most common such efforts can be found in planned communities, which are becoming more prevalent on the fringes of several large cities in North America (e.g., Los Angeles, Washington, D.C., Seattle) and some urban cores as well. Although the transformation (via "urban renewal") of cities and particular places has been well documented,[53] it is unclear how planned communities have influenced the types and rates of public sociality found in them. Of particular interest may be design movements, including the "new urbanism," that seek to integrate "mixed" usage places (e.g., retail and housing units) so as to encourage public sociality of various sorts.[54]

Fifth, an assumption undergirding the studies in this volume is that there are underlying premises of public sociality to which individual actors orient themselves as they interact with others. These premises ensure countless social interactions in public that are highly orderly with nary a snag. We do not assume, however, that such premises are inviolable; nor do we assume that they do not vary from place to place. At the same time, one might wonder how personal relationships in public link with conflict, especially violence. Horne, Mcilwaine, and Taylor in chapter 9, for example, suggest that restrictive (closed-frame) public places can inhibit conflict, violence, and social deviance to a point among parents and children, after which they can exacerbate violence among both parents and their children. These findings link to broader strategies of policing and governance that focus on the control and management of space.[55] Such strategies generally complement formal mechanisms of social control but are less well understood in relation to everyday public sociality. Multiple questions could be pursued, including: How does public sociality intersect with the formal policing of space to inhibit or foment violence and other kinds of conflict? Under what conditions does public sociality provide alternative control mechanisms that challenge formal mechanisms for controlling places?[56] In chapter 1, we noted how organized groups, such as street gangs, can change the norms of public order. Inquiry into how the norms of public civility vary across urban settings with different social class and ethnic compositions would also benefit research along these lines.

As we close this chapter and with it this volume, we return to the quote from Carl Rogers with which we began this chapter. Rogers was impressed with how contemporary social change had sped up all facets of society, including how people conducted their personal relationships. As he looked from his mid-twentieth-century vantage point toward the horizon of the twentieth century, he envisioned relational connections that could achieve the depth and meaning of "lifelong attachments" without the personal repression and cultural constraints that primary ties can sometimes harbor. We now live in the twenty-first century and it *is* clear that the relational landscape has been transformed to include a greater role for public sociality, accelerated social mobility, alternative family forms, and electronically mediated relationships that could not have been envisioned by previous generations. What is unclear is how this new relational landscape— especially fleeting and anchored relationships in public places—links to what are considered more durable, intimate ties. How and under what conditions does public sociality complement primary relationships? How and under what conditions does public sociality compensate for absent or lost primary relationships? What role does public sociality play in the formation of social capital—those social bonds that form the bedrock of communities? Robert Putnam has argued that the last two decades have witnessed a decline in memberships in voluntary organizations and the kinds of social ties typically formed through such organizations.[57] However, personal relationships in public may offer opportunities for creating niches of social capital that have largely been overlooked and are somewhat unexpected.[58] Some of these niches can evolve into sustainable collective forms with institutional supports, like the floating community described by Munch in chapter 6. Others may have only brief durations but nonetheless are significant to their participants and, in the aggregate, to the broader public contexts of which they are a part.

These questions will take us further toward understanding how the vast range of private and public sociality—however blurred the boundaries are between them—mutually influence each other. This line of inquiry may also hold important insights for practical concerns in urban development and design, public policies relevant to families, and a range of helping professions that deal with relational issues. At the same time, such questions could help bridge the gaps between the multiple, largely independent traditions that inform the study of personal relationships. What this volume begins to contemplate is an agenda for future inquiry into personal relationships that focuses on the entire range of personal relationships—from fleeting to durable, from public to private. By doing so, such research will shed further light not only on the dynamics on personal relationships of all kinds but also on the character of contemporary society itself.

NOTES

PREFACE

1. Putnam (2000).

2. It is worth noting that all of these studies were conducted in an American southwestern city of approximately three-quarters of a million residents. Certainly the design and ecology of cities can affect the extent of public sociality (Lofland 1998). However, the studies in this volume focus not on variation in public sociality across different cities but on the different ways that public sociality manifests itself in specific sites. Furthermore, we suspect that there is less variation in the character of public sociality across cities than in its volume (e.g., Oldenburg 1989).

3. For useful overviews of the development and character of ethnography, and some of the debates associated with it, see Emerson (2001a), Emerson, Fretz, and Shaw (1995), Weick (1985), Clifford and Marcus (1986), and Lofland and Lofland (1995 [1972]). For a discussion of the application of qualitative procedures to the study of personal relationships, see Allen and Walker (2000).

4. Lofland (1995).

5. Snow, Morrill, and Anderson (2003, 182)

6. See Snow, Morrill, and Anderson (2003).

7. Hammersley (1992, 52).

8. Hammersley (1992, 51)

9. On team ethnography, see Douglas (1976) and Erickson and Stull (1998).

10. On field relations, see Snow and Morrill (2004). On membership roles in field research, see Adler and Adler (1987) and Snow, Benford, and Anderson (1986).

11. Snow, Zurcher, and Sjoberg (1982).

12. These methodological discussions at the end of each chapter constitute a blend of what John Van Mannen (1988) termed "realist" and "confessional" tales. In other words, the authors recount how they proceeded, as well as their feelings and concerns associated with their fieldwork.

13. Becker (1971).

14. Emerson (2001b, 312).

15. Duneier (1999).

16. Emerson (2001b, 314)

17. Punch (1986).

18. Adler and Adler (2002, 42).

1. THE STUDY OF PERSONAL RELATIONSHIPS
IN PUBLIC PLACES

We thank Cindy H. White for helpful comments on an earlier draft and Carolyn Aman for research assistance.

1. Simmel (1950 [1903]), Wirth (1938), Milgram (1977, 24–41).

2. Knapp et al. (2003).

3. Putnam (2000).

4. Stone (1954), Davis (1959), Goffman (1963, 1971), Lofland (1973), Oldenburg (1989).

5. Duck (1993b), Duck and Pittman (1994), and Knapp, Miller, and Fudge (1994) underscore how rarely social scientists consider the kinds of personal relationships studied in this collection.

6. The overall approach in this volume is consistent with Michel de Certeau's (1984, xi–xii) line of inquiry, which shares a general interest in the sociology of everyday practices rather than in atomistic individuals.

7. See Snow and Morrill (2004), more generally, on the dynamics and challenges inherent in field relations between ethnographers and those they encounter during fieldwork.

8. McCall and Simmons (1982, 29), Snow, Benford, and Anderson (1986).

9. Duck (1985, 655).

10. On the importance of personal relations in economic life, for example, see Granovetter (1985) and Zelizer (2004).

11. For ease of exposition, we exclude research on personal relationships in the family.

12. For extensive reviews of the literature on personal relationships in this tradition, see Kelley (1986), Blumstein and Kollock (1988), Duck (1991), Duck and Pittman (1994), and Hendrick and Hendrick (2000).

13. Berscheid and Peplau (1983, 8–10), Duck (1993b), Wood and Duck (1995), Poole and McPhee (1994), Lofland (1998), and Knapp et al. (2003).

14. Duck's (1993b) collection of essays explores how social context influences the emergence, dynamics, and end of personal relationships.

15. On context stripping more generally, see Guba and Lincoln (1994, 106).

16. On institutionalized expectations regarding social relationships and social interaction, see Turner (1970), Bellah et al. (1985), Phillipsen (1992), and Swidler (2001). On relational logics, see Sigman (1995).

17. Parks and Eggert (1991), Allan (1993).

18. See Bochner (1994) for a critique of positivistic approaches to relationship research.

19. Rosenthal (1969) argues that an important source of such conflations is the researcher's own expectations and design strategies.

20. Poole and McPhee (1994, 51).

21. Knapp, Miller, and Fudge (1994, 9–10).

22. Fitzpatrick (1988), Duck (1991).

23. Freeman, Romney, and Freeman (1987).

24. Deutscher (1966), Deutscher, Pestello, and Pestello (1993).

25. Scott and Lyman (1968).

26. Edgerton (1967).

27. Hondagneu-Sotelo (2001), Ehrenreich and Hochschild (2003).

28. Davis (1959), Goffman (1963, 1971).

29. Lofland (1998).

30. Whyte (1993 [1943]).

31. Stone (1954).

32. Jacobs (1961).

33. Anderson (1976), Duneier (1999).

34. Blumer (1969). For reviews of this perspective, see Reynolds (1993), Fine (1993), and Snow (2001b). Our interactionist perspective is also sympathetic to Emirbayer's (1997) "relational" sociological approach, which maintains that actors must always be considered vis-à-vis their relations with each other.

35. Goffman (1983).

36. Warner (1992) argues that close relationships are largely private, inaccessible to most individuals beyond their borders, and marked by "intense" interaction among their participants. As we argue later in this section, some kinds of personal relationships in public places do share some of these attributes even though they are largely conducted in contexts that are generally accessible and visible by broad social audiences.

37. The literature suggests that the "strength" (Granovetter 1973) and interdependence (Kelley 1986) of a social relationship are closely related attributes.

38. Goffman (1961).

39. Blumstein and Kollock (1988, 468–69).

40. Kelley (1986) provides a comprehensive treatment of behavioral and psychological interdependence. See Turner (1970) for a perspective of interdependence focusing on daily interactions that define and sustain personal relationships in families. Such behaviors include the accomplishment of collective tasks and the co-construction and validation of personal identities.

41. Emerson (1981), Molm (1997).

42. Relational interdependence need not progress in a linear fashion as portrayed in early stage models of relational development by Knapp (1984), for example, and can include nonlinear and dialogical aspects, as argued by Baxter (1993).

43. Bohannan (1970), Parks and Eggert (1991).

44. Swidler (2001).

45. Gergen and Gergen (1987), Duck and Pittman (1994), Leeds-Hurwitz (1995).

46. Goffman (1971, 238–333).

47. Goffman (1959, 77–105).

48. Goffman (1963, 83–84).

49. Lofland (1998, 30), Couch (1989).

50. Goffman (1971) notes that making tacit interactional rules explicit can threaten those involved, particularly if the idealized conceptions of those rules do not square with their application in ongoing interaction.

51. Much of Goffman's *Behavior in Public Places* (1963) and *Relations in Public* (1971) could be said to be devoted to normative transgressions.

52. Katz (1999, 1–8). Prus (1996, 173–201) and Heiss and O'Brien (1993) also provide useful discussions of interactionist approaches to emotion and emotional expression, respectively.

53. Katz (1999, 309–44).

54. Swidler (2001) argues that relational partners draw on broad cultural models to express love in marriages. Partners who draw on a "romanticized adolescent" view of love, for instance, will express love very differently than those who draw on a "pragmatic" model of love. Again, the deployment of such models depends upon particular contexts and interactions.

55. Cahill and Eggleston (1994, 311).

56. Hochschild (1983).

57. Cahill and Eggleston (1994, 311).

58. Weintraub (1997, 1).

59. Lofland (1998, 64–70), Gieryn (2000, 464–65).

60. Goffman (1963, 9).

61. Anderson (1976, 229–30) refers to these types of settings as "interior" public places to convey their physical and moderate social boundedness.

62. Whyte (1980), Grannis (1998). Oldenburg (1989) refers to many of these locales as "third places" or "great good places" in that they offer opportunities for public leisure and, importantly, for the kindling of personal relationships of all kinds.

63. Snow and Mulcahy (2001).

64. Lamphere (1990).

65. Lofland (1998, 10–11) modifies these terms from Hunter (1985), who described realms as "orders" in the sense of a class of social settings, rather than physical places, each with a distinctive mix of social relationships.

66. Nippert-Eng (1995).

67. Mass Observation (1943), Stone (1954), Davis (1959), Cavan (1966), Anderson (1976), Katovitch and Reese (1987).

68. Lofland (1998, 51–76).

69. Milgram (1977, 51–53).

70. Lofland (1998) terms what we call a fleeting relationship a "quasi-primary" relationship to underscore that it presents some of the appearances of a primary relationship as accomplished in public places and the public realm. On dog owners, see Robins, Sanders, and Cahill (1991); on seatmates in buses and airplanes, see Greenblat and Gagnon (1983); on bars, see Mass Observation (1943), Gardner (1994), and Snow, Robinson, and McCall (1991).

71. Stamp, Vangelisti, and Daly (1992).

72. Wireman (1984) and Lofland (1998) use the term *intimate-secondary relationships* in lieu of *anchored relationships*. Such relationships have the paradoxical qualities of both a primary and secondary relation and are confined (anchored) to a particular public place. Goffman (1971, 189) uses *anchored relationship* to refer to any social tie that has a "deep" emotional footing and is recognized as such by those involved.

73. In this way, publicly anchored relationships exhibit what could be called "punctuated emplacement" in that participants' relationships are typically tied to particular public places and end at the boundaries between public and private settings.

74. Wireman (1984, 2–3).

75. Duneier's (1992) *Slim's Table* offers a poignant example of a group of African American men whose anchored relationships in a Chicago lunchroom in many ways supplanted their primary relationships.

76. Baumgartner (1988) and Morrill (1995).

77. Goffman (1971, 108–16).

78. Duneier and Molotch (1999).

79. Gardner (1995).

80. Anderson (1990, 210–11) notes that such street etiquette is especially likely among middle-class whites and less affluent blacks in urban public places.

81. On voice in relationships, see Hirschman (1971) and Cahn (1990); on self-help generally, see Black (1993); and on street encounters and violence, see Anderson (1999).

82. Horowitz (1983), Vigil (1988), Decker and Van Winkle (1996).

2. FACE TIME: PUBLIC SOCIALITY, SOCIAL ENCOUNTERS, AND GENDER AT A UNIVERSITY RECREATION CENTER

1. "Sunshine University" is a pseudonym for a large urban university in the southwestern United States.

2. Although a definitive survey of the social significance of university recreation centers has yet to be conducted, college guides, such as the 2004 *Fiske Guide to Colleges* and *The Best 351 Colleges* (prepared by the Princeton Review), note the increasing social role and marketing of student recreation centers on American university campuses. An Internet search in 2003 revealed that forty of the top fifty national universities ranked by *U.S. News and World Report* built new recreation centers or remodeled their old ones during the 1990s.

3. On the specific problems faced by women in public places, see Snow, Robinson, and McCall (1991), Gardner (1995), and Duneier and Molotch (1999).

4. "Student Characteristics and Trends, 1999–2001," Sunshine University.

5. Lofland (1998, 27–34).

6. Allon and Fishel (1979).

7. Rubin (1973).

8. Komarovsky (1985), Horowitz (1987), Moffatt (1989).

9. Lofland (1998).

10. Goffman (1983).

11. Gardner (1995, 16–19).

12. Duneier and Molotch (1999).

13. Snow, Robinson, and McCall (1991).

14. Leone (1995).

15. A complete description of our methods appears at the end of this chapter in the "Methodological Procedures and Reflections" section.

16. Snow, Robinson, and McCall (1991, 436).

17. There is also a lesbian/gay component in the targeted audience, which we do not discuss here for lack of space.

18. Lofland (1998, 30).

19. On the general process of "matching" of social interactional forms, see Burgoon, Stern, and Dillman (1995).

20. See Leeds-Hurwitz (1995), Allen and Walker (2000).

21. Duck (1993a, ix).

22. Allon and Fishel (1979), Katovich and Reese (1987), Snow, Robinson, and McCall (1991).

23. Anderson (1976, 230–35).

24. Anderson (1976, 229–30) suggests one working hypothesis with regard to these questions. He claims that quasi-public places ("interior public spaces") often contain a greater taken-for-granted sense of civility than do streets and other public places. Quasi-public places may thus exhibit greater variability in the learning of street wisdom.

25. Tschang and Senta (2001).

26. On "withs" versus "solos," see Goffman (1971, 19–27), and on "tie signs," see Goffman (1971, 188–217).

27. The majority of SU students come from suburban and urban households earning $50,000 or more, although just over one-third of students come from rural areas in either SU's home state or neighboring states. According to census figures provided by SU, the student body is majority European American (69 percent), with smaller proportions of Hispanic Americans (14 percent), Asian Americans (6 percent), African Americans (3 percent), Native Americans (2 percent), international students (4 percent), and students of unknown or multiple ethnicities (2 percent)."Student Characteristics and Trends, 1999–2001," Sunshine University.

28. Lincoln and Guba (1985), Strauss and Corbin (1990).

29. The concept of open coding originates in Glaser and Strauss's (1967) grounded theory approach and has been usefully elaborated by Charmaz (2001). This procedure is the first step in categorizing and analyzing one's field database drawing on field experiences, conceptual orientations, and guiding interests.

30. Our coding process parallels the procedures described in Emerson, Fretz, and Shaw (1995, 142–68).

31. On different fieldwork roles, see Snow, Benford, and Anderson (1986).

3. MOMENTARY PLEASURES: SOCIAL ENCOUNTERS AND
FLEETING RELATIONSHIPS AT A SINGLES DANCE

This chapter is a fully collaborative effort; the authors' names appear in alphabetical order. Earlier versions of this chapter were presented at the annual meetings of the Pacific Sociological Association (San Diego, California, 1997) and the National Communication Association (New York, 1998).

1. Although churches and schools provide opportunities to form social relationships, contemporary singles organizations differ from these traditional venues in that their avowed goal is to arrange long-term relationships among single people.

2. DeWitt (1992).

3. Ahuvia and Adelman (1992).

4. England and Farkas (1986).

5. Coontz (1992).

6. Bernard (1982).

7. Schwartzberg, Berliner, and Jacob (1995).

8. For previous research on premarital cohabitation, see Bumpass and Sweet (1989) and Thornton (1988). On sex ratios, see Glick (1988) and Guttentag and Secord (1983). On network ties, see Parks, Stan, and Eggert (1983).

9. Surra (1990), Adelman and Ahuvia (1991).

10. Davis (1990), Willis and Carlson (1993), Woll and Young (1989).

11. Cressey's (1969 [1932]) classic 1930s study of the "taxi dance hall" (so named because, like cabbies and their fares, women dancers would dance with men for a per-minute charge) underscored how few legitimate urban public places existed during the first three decades of the twentieth century where single women could meet single men.

12. A complete description of our methods appears at the end of this chapter in the "Methodological Procedures and Reflections" section.

13. Goffman (1961).

14. Lofland (1995, 1998).

15. Berk (1977).

16. Parks, Stan, and Eggert (1983), Baxter and Widenmann (1993).

17. Goffman (1961).

18. Goffman (1963).

19. Berk (1977), Darden and Koski (1988).

20. Lofland (1998, 14).

21. Burgoon, Buller, and Woodall (1992).

22. Edgerton (1979).

23. Collins (1975).

24. Parks and Eggert (1991), Duck (1993b).

25. Lofland (1998).

26. We did not discover any singles organizations that cater exclusively to lesbians or gays, although several nightclubs in Southwest City cater to lesbians and gays, as Reid, Karlin, and Bonham-Crecilius make clear in chapter 7.

27. Lofland and Lofland (1995 [1972], 46).

28. Emerson, Fretz, and Shaw (1995), Lofland and Lofland (1995 [1972]).

4. A PERSONAL DANCE: EMOTIONAL LABOR, FLEETING
RELATIONSHIPS, AND SOCIAL POWER IN A STRIP BAR

1. The stripping-as-deviant-occupation branch is represented by the works of D'Andre (1965), McCaghy and Skipper (1969, 1972), Skipper and McCaghy

(1970, 1971), Boles and Garbin (1974a, 1974c), and Carey, Peterson, and Sharpe (1974).

2. Ronai (1992), for example, focuses on her personal experiences and feelings as an erotic dancer and researcher. See also Boles and Garbin (1974bc), Gonos (1976), and Reed (1997).

3. On feminist critiques of stripping and female sex work more generally, see Barry (1979), Griffin (1981), and Chapkis (1997).

4. Wood (2000). See also Montemurro (2001) for an interactionist study of social power and social control in a male strip club.

5. Wood (2000, 9).

6. Prehn (1993). Clubs realize their revenues from cover fees and sales of alcoholic beverages or special promotions, such as meal specials or the appearance of adult film stars who perform as part of regional or national tours.

7. Boles and Garbin (1974b, 137).

8. Hochshild (1983) thus borrows from Goffman's (1959) concept of impression management.

9. Goffman (1983).

10. Hochschild (1983, 3–23).

11. Ronai and Ellis (1989).

12. Wood (2000, 22–23).

13. Stone (1954).

14. Ronai (1992), Wood (2000).

15. Molm (1997, 2).

16. Wood (2000, 9–15).

17. A complete description of our methods appears at the end of the chapter in the "Methodological Procedures and Reflections" section.

18. On the organizational status of strip clubs, see Trautner (2001).

19. Wood (2000, 15–19) also found the development of what she calls "fantasy actors" among strippers.

20. See Lofland (1998, 51–63) and chapter 1 of this volume.

21. Molm (1997).

22. Some of these arrangements take the form of "resistance" strategies by dancers aimed at customers and club management (Ronai and Cross 1998).

23. Molm (1997, 23). On negatively and positively connected exchange structures, see Emerson (1972).

24. Trautner (2001).

25. Strip club features listed in recent guides to North American clubs suggest that the number of lounges is increasing in middle-range clubs, such as the ones we studied. See Danko (1998) and Frenville (2000).

26. Stone (1954, 40).

27. Polanyi (1944), Granovetter (1985). For a review of the embeddedness literature in economic and organizational sociology, see Dacin, Ventresca, and Beal (1999).

28. Rubin (1974, 1994), Snow and Anderson (1993), Duneier (1999), and Bourgois (1995).

29. Haas and Stafford (1998).

30. All the clubs had drink minimums and waitresses who visited our table every few minutes to inquire whether we wanted "another round." Clubs allowed the second author to enter for free under a "ladies free" policy.

31. Wood (2000, 8). The lone exception to this pattern in our research was a dancer who told her "house mother" that either the police or news reporters were hounding her for information about what she did. Over the course of two conversations, we convinced her that we were neither the police nor from a newsroom.

32. We considered asking customers as they left the club whether they would consent to an interview, but we found this awkward because most customers, once outside of the bars, would quickly head for their cars and because of security issues in parking lots.

33. Our coding procedures resonate most closely with the procedures described in Emerson, Fretz, and Shaw (1995, 142–210).

34. Wood (2000, 8–9).

5. HANGING OUT AMONG TEENAGERS: RESISTANCE, GENDER, AND PERSONAL RELATIONSHIPS

An earlier version of this chapter was presented at the annual meetings of the National Communication Association (New York, 1998).

1. Corrigan (1976, 1979).

2. Thorne (1993). Of course, not all the developmental literature offers such portraits. Gilligan (1983) and Gilligan, Ward, and Taylor (1988), for example, have criticized this view for its overly linear and sexist orientations.

3. Horowitz (1983), Jankowski (1991), Moore (1978, 1991), Sanders (1994).

4. Willis (1977), Macleod (1995).

5. Schwartz (1987).

6. Adler and Adler (1998), Epstein (1998), Skelton and Valentine (1997).

7. Hall and Jefferson (1976), Hebdige (1979), Morrill and Bailey (1992).

8. Goffman (1967, 47–95).

9. A complete description of our methods appears at the end of this chapter in the "Methodological Procedures and Reflections" section.

10. Horne, Mcilwaine, and Taylor (chapter 9 of this volume) developed a similar typology to categorize public places with respect to young children.

11. Goffman (1961).

12. Fine (2001).

13. Douglas (1966).

14. Blumstein and Kollock (1988), Berscheid and Peplau (1983).

15. Paul and White (1990).

16. On corporeal emotional dynamics, see Katz (1999).

17. Anderson (1999).

18. On the relational physicality of adolescent boys, see Monsour (2002) and Youniss and Smollar (1985).

19. Rawlins (1992, 90) argues that during adolescence individuals begin to make decisions about the "respective roles that friendship and romance will play."

20. Cohen and Taylor (1992 [1976], 112–53).

21. Goffman (1967, 61).

22. Gilligan (1983).

23. Norman and Harris (1981), Paul and White (1990), Rutter (1979), Youniss and Smoller (1985).

24. Gilligan (1983), Tannen (1990). On gender cultures generally, see Morrill, Johnson, and Harrison (1998).

25. Crawford (1995, 94).

26. See Aries (1996, 48–49).

27. Youniss and Smoller (1985).

28. Aries (1996, 86–87), Crawford (1995).

29. Our difficulties are consistent with the observations of Lofland (1973, 80), who noted that the "costumes" of contemporary urban dwellers "provide rather *unreliable* clues to the 'identities' of their wearers" (emphasis in the original).

30. Snow, Zurcher, and Sjoberg (1982).

31. Emerson, Fretz, and Shaw (1995).

6. EVERYONE GETS TO PARTICIPATE: FLOATING COMMUNITY IN AN AMATEUR SOFTBALL LEAGUE

1. Putnam (2000, 26).

2. Nisbet (1965, 21–106).

3. Putnam (2000, 19).

4. Putnam (2000, 21).

5. Putnam (2000, 113–14)

6. "Southwest City" is a pseudonym, as are all identifying team, personal, and place names in this chapter.

7. Guttman (1986).

8. Murphy, Williams, and Dunning (1990), Perrin (2000).

9. Lofland (1998).

10. See Wann et al. (2001) on the social psychology of everyday spectating.

11. Edgerton (1979, 201).

12. On collective identity, see Snow (2001a). On the differentiating effects of moral boundaries, see Lamont (1992).

13. On the emotional aspects of community, see Fischer (1982).

14. Fine (1987, 33–34).

15. The concept of a floating community that moves among different locations is partly derived from Wellman's (2001) discussion of the floating and "fragmented" nature of contemporary urban communities.

16. A complete description of my field methods appears at the end of this chapter in the "Methodological Procedures and Reflections" section.

17. Angell (1988, 10).

18. Lofland (1998, 52–63); see also chapter 1 of this volume.

19. See chapter 1 of this volume.

20. Goffman (1963, 84).

21. Gardner (1995, 94–95); see also chapter 2 of this volume.

22. Goffman (1971, 188–237).

23. Gulliver (1979).

24. Fischer (1982), Wellman (2001).

25. Watson (1974, 29).

26. Wellman (2001), Fischer (1982).

27. Wellman (2001, 104).

28. Paxton (1999).

29. Adler and Adler (1987).

30. Adler and Adler (1987).

31. Emerson, Fretz, and Shaw (1995, 63–64).

32. Robben and Nordstrom (1995, 13–15), Rosaldo (1989).

7. INCLUSION AND INTRUSION: GENDER AND SEXUALITY
IN GAY, LESBIAN, AND STRAIGHT BARS

1. Connell (1985), Berk (1985), West and Zimmerman (1987), and Fenstermaker, West, and Zimmerman (1991).

2. West and Fenstermaker (1993, 155–56).

3. In this way, gender is socially constructed, through interaction, as an externalized, and taken-for-granted essence, as Berger and Luckmann (1966) argue more generally about all institutionalized social phenomena.

4. Gardner (1995).

5. On urban bars generally, see Cavan (1966), Kornblum (1974), LeMasters (1975), and Anderson (1976).

6. Ponse (1978), Herek (1986), Hankin (2002).

7. Goffman (1979).

8. Goffman (1971).

9. Goffman (1971, 32–49).

10. Goffman (1971, 188–237).

11. Goffman (1971, 50–52).

12. Goffman (1971, 44–45).

13. Goffman (1977).

14. Heritage (1984, 136–37) describes this process as "accountability."

15. The time between these two data collection periods resulted from beginning the project in Snow and Morrill's Qualitative Methods Seminar during the fall of 1992 as a class paper. In 1996, we were encouraged to further pursue the project for possible inclusion in an edited volume on social relations in public contexts. We produced multiple drafts of this chapter in 1998 and 2001 as we prepared the study for final appearance in the volume.

16. A complete description of our methods appears at the end of the chapter in the "Methodological Procedures and Reflections" section.

17. All bar names are pseudonyms.

18. Goffman (1971, 95–187).

19. All the bars had a two-drink minimum, but its enforcement in gay and lesbian bars was less consistent, primarily because there were fewer cocktail servers than in the straight bars. The long lines at the main serving areas and the sheer volume of drinks served in straight bars suggest that alcohol consumption differences across the three types of sites could not be explained by the enforcement of drink minimums alone.

20. Our observations regarding the sparseness of relational initiation among previously disconnected individuals in gay and lesbian bars certainly begs for more systematic and comparative research. Indeed, the historical timing of our research—a period when gays' consciousness of AIDS and other sexually transmitted diseases was particularly high due to highly publicized AIDS-related deaths and contractions during the early and mid-1990s—could help explain this pattern.

21. Of course, individuals can vary from the patterns we observed.

22. We did not observe enough men in lesbian bars or women in gay bars to compare them. Moreover, our data did not permit subtle comparisons of men who self-identified as gay or women who self-identified as lesbian in straight contexts.

23. Goffman (1977, 309).

24. We borrow the term *negotiated order* from Strauss (1978). It refers to the ways in which situated, tacit agreements about behavioral expectations emerge and change in the course of ongoing face-to-face social interaction.

25. Gardner (1995, 16–17).

26. Wood (1993).

27. Snow and Morrill (2004).

28. Adler and Adler (1987).

29. This question is inspired by Spradley's (1980, 78–91) approach to "descriptive" ethnographic questions and appears in Emerson, Fretz, and Shaw (1995, 146).

8. BREAKING UP AND STARTING OVER: EMOTIONAL EXPRESSION IN POSTDIVORCE SUPPORT GROUPS

This chapter is a fully collaborative effort, and authors' names appear in alphabetical order. An earlier version of this chapter was presented at the 1999 annual meeting of the National Communication Association in New York.

1. Cherlin (1992).

2. Riessman (1990), Wallerstein, Blakeslee, and Lewis (2000), Hetherington and Kelly (2002).

3. Kitson (1992).

4. Horwitz (1982, 176–77).

5. Included in these therapies are "self-actualization," "existential," and "Gestalt" therapies, as well as a multitude of self-help group therapies that mix aspects of these approaches.

6. Irvine (2000).

7. Irvine (2000).

8. Horwitz (1982, 182).

9. Horwitz (1982, 180) argues that Alcoholics Anonymous (AA) holds regular group meetings, has activities on weekends and holidays, and facilitates individual development amidst dense social networks composed primarily of other AA members.

10. Irvine (2000).

11. Katz (1999, 1–8).

12. Cultural resources include culturally prescribed "feeling rules" that help individuals understand appropriate emotional responses in particular contexts (Hochschild 1983). Metts and Planalp (2003) review research on communication and emotions.

13. During the year when we conducted our fieldwork, 306 people participated in the adult program; information was unavailable for the family-child groups. The average age of an adult group member was forty. Two-thirds of the adult members had been divorced for a year or more. The average length of marriage reported was thirteen years.

14. Knapp, Ellis, and Williams (1980).

15. Katz (1999, 5–6).

16. McCall and Simmons (1982, 62).

17. Katz (1999, 143).

18. Katz (1999, 34).

19. Lofland (1998, 10–12); see also chapter 1 of this volume.

20. Anderson (1990, 138, 162).

21. Lofland (1998, 27–34).

22. The concept of open coding derives from Glaser and Strauss (1967) and is elaborated by Charmaz (2001). This procedure is the first step in categorizing and analyzing one's field data on the basis of field experiences, conceptual orientations, and guiding interests.

23. Emerson, Fretz, and Shaw (1995).

24. Morrill (1995, 251–53).

9. CIVILITY AND ORDER: ADULT SOCIAL CONTROL OF CHILDREN IN PUBLIC PLACES

This chapter is a fully collaborative effort; the authors' names appear in alphabetical order.

1. Seeyle (1997, 42).

2. Black (1984).

3. Goffman (1971).

4. Cahill (1987).

5. Cahill (1990), Davis (1991), Stafford and Bayer (1993).

6. Goffman (1983).

7. Lofland (1989, 647).

8. Davis, Seibert, and Breed (1966).

9. Messer (1982).

10. Goffman (1959, 1967).

11. Baumgartner (1984).

12. Goffman (1967).

13. Goffman (1959).

14. Cahill (1987).

15. Morrill (1995).

16. A complete description of our methods appears at the end of the chapter in the "Methodological Procedures and Reflections" section.

17. We did not code incidents between parents and children younger than three years.

18. Llewellyn and Hoebel (1941, 21) originally used this method of organizing processual analyses of trouble and conflict to study disputing among tribal Native Americans. More recently, it has been used as a method for studying informal social control among suburbanites (Baumgartner 1988) and corporate executives (Morrill 1995).

19. Although each trouble incident included numerous adult strategies for managing children, we made no attempt to analyze how many strategies adults used in a given situation or in which order they used them (for analyses along these lines, see Wilson, Cameron, and Whipple 1994).

20. We conducted a reliability assessment among each of the three authors by coding each of our places separately on the three parameters and comparing the results. All three authors coded twenty-two out of twenty-four places the same on each parameter.

21. Hoffman (1960, 130).

22. We did not witness any violent confrontations similar to the Thornes' case. Although highly speculative, there is evidence that public norms can constrain the use of violence in many adult-children situations (Baumgartner 1992).

23. Goffman (1974, 44–46, 81).

24. Despite our portrayal of avoidance as subtle, nearly unnoticed action in our trouble incidents, it can become highly dramatic, as in cases when adults abandon their children.

25. On its face, the fact that we observed only sixteen instances of avoidance gave us pause for concern as well. Earlier research suggests that avoidance is among the most common approaches to informally handling interpersonal trouble (Baumgartner 1988). One could argue that our findings are due to the normative constraints on using avoidance to manage children in public because of the possible negative consequences for doing so (e.g., "losing" one's child in a crowd, being labeled abusive for abandoning one's child). All of these ambiguities and difficulties created problems for confidently coding all sixteen instances of avoidance we observed or drawing strong inferences from our data about avoidance. As a result, we omitted our observations of avoidance from the quantitative place-by-strategy analysis, thus reducing our sample of strategies to 207.

26. The cognitive demand argument fits with Sperber and Wilson's (1995) argument that humans generally seek out the most efficient ways of communicating. Sperber and Wilson also argue that the definition of communication efficiency varies from context to context.

27. Katz (1999).

28. Black (1990).

29. Hoffman (1984, 120–21).

30. Baumgartner (1984).

31. Erickson (1966), Bergesen (1984).

32. Lincoln and Guba (1985).

33. We did not collect incidents involving adult control of children when the adult did not explicitly identify him- or herself as a parent or guardian.

34. In some instances, we simply lost track of the group in a crowded places; in other situations, the group left the setting prior to resolution of the trouble.

In still other cases, the incident was interrupted by additional problems between other adults and children. When observation of one adult-child group ended and another began, we recorded the interactions in the new group as a separate trouble incident. In addition, when interactants involved in trouble changed settings (which happened in only a few instances), their interactions were recorded as the same trouble incident across multiple contexts.

35. Our parameters derive from our own interpretations of the core differences between places and from the literature on public places, especially Whyte (1980), Lofland (1998), and Jacobs (1961). See chapter 5 of this volume for a similar typology of public places.

36. Our conversations with regular participants (e.g., clerks, attendants, friends, and acquaintances with children) at each field site indicated that our assessments of each setting were consistent with most participants' assessments.

37. Places coded as permissive included two large, indoor retail shopping malls, McDonald's playgrounds, public parks, a public zoo, an apartment house parking lot, a public airport, and the outdoor mall adjacent to the main library of a large public university. Places coded as moderate included a large grocery store, a used bookstore, public bus stops, Christmas Towne, a large drugstore, and a Target store. Restrictive settings included a Greyhound bus station, "fancier" restaurants, the main library of a large public university, a social services agency, bathrooms in a public airport, and the inside of churches. Note as well that all of these places are public or quasi-public places. Even the most restrictive places retain a high degree of visibility and accessibility relative to private places, such as households or private, nonretail businesses.

38. This example and other bystander spooks raised the question of whether we should have debriefed those we observed. We decided against debriefing for two reasons. First, our observations did not differ qualitatively from innumerable aspects of the social and physical environments of public places that can spook an adult with a child. Second, we decided that debriefing those we observed could raise more questions than it answered.

10. ORDER ON THE EDGE: REMEDIAL WORK
IN A RIGHT-WING POLITICAL DISCUSSION GROUP

We thank William Bunis and David Snow, who were coauthors of an earlier paper, presented at the meetings of the Pacific Sociological Association in April 1997, from which a portion of this chapter was drawn and elaborated. We also thank the Social Movements Working Group at the University of Arizona for helpful feedback during the data collection for this project.

1. Goffman (1959, 9–10). See also Goffman (1971, 1983).
2. Eliasoph (1998).

3. Lipset and Raab (1970).

4. For a detailed discussion and analysis of Identity Christians, at least as they operate in Idaho, see Aho (1990, esp. chaps. 4 and 5).

5. Lipset and Raab (1970).

6. He has authored several books relevant to conspiracy theory and the claims of the far right.

7. A complete description of our methods appears at the end of the chapter in the "Methodological Procedures and Reflections" section.

8. The American patriot movement grew out of the survivalist movements of the 1970s and 1980s. Although the patriot movement is by no means a monolithic group, its central tenets concern (1) the right to bear arms generally and specifically against what is perceived to be repression by U.S. and international government; (2) enforcement of the "original intent" of the U.S. Constitution; and (3) and various Christian, often fundamentalist, identities. Strains of the patriot movement have been linked to the Oklahoma Federal Building bombings in the 1990s and other violent confrontations with private citizens and law enforcement officials in the U.S. Northwest and Southwest (Neiwert 1999).

9. Goffman (1971), Lofland (1998, 25–41).

10. Berger (1981, 22).

11. Snow, Rochford, et al. (1986, 464). The concept of frame is borrowed from Goffman (1974, 21), who called them "schemata of interpretation" that enable people to make sense of "concrete occurrences."

12. For a detailed analysis of this framing activity, see Snow and Clark-Miller (2003).

13. Goffman (1963, 40).

14. Anderson (1990).

15. Duneier (1999), Lee (2002).

16. Edgerton (1979).

17. This idea that norms act as both constraint and resource parallels general ideas about culture found in Swidler (1986), about social structure and agency found in Giddens (1979), and about social structure and culture found in Sewell (1992).

18. One irony that we contemplated is whether a person with representative views from the Forum would be engaged or even granted access to a similar discussion group on the left. A search of our own experiences in progressive groups suggested that such an individual would be unlikely to be taken seriously.

19. In addition to the fieldwork conducted by the chapter's authors, two other researchers, William Bunis and David A. Snow, periodically attended Forum meetings and took field notes.

20. Our membership in the group hovered somewhere between what Adler and Adler (1987) label "peripheral," in which one remains on the margins of a

context as a detached observer, and "active," in which one becomes more integral to the functioning of the group.

21. Snow, Zurcher, and Sjoberg (1982).

22. Included in the academic group with whom we regularly met were David Snow, William Bunis, and, on occasion, members of the Social Movements Working Group in the Department of Sociology at the University of Arizona.

23. See chapter 1 of this volume.

24. See Emerson, Fretz, and Shaw (1995, 142–68) on the evolution of analysis in fieldwork from open coding to focused coding.

25. Rosaldo (1989).

26. Of course, this is not entirely true. We read accounts of disengagement in Whyte (1993 [1943]), Wax (1971), Snow and Anderson (1993), and Morrill (1995). We also talked directly with Snow and Morrill, in whose seminar this project began. From these sources we gleaned interesting examples of how the authors disengaged their relationships with informants, but it was difficult to transfer their accounts to our context because of the odd situation of being repelled by many of the beliefs and values held by our informants, yet really liking them on a personal level.

11. TAKING STOCK: FUNCTIONS, PLACES,
AND PERSONAL RELATIONSHIPS

We thank Jason Owen-Smith and Cindy H. White for helpful early comments regarding this chapter.

1. Simmel (1950 [1903]), Lofland (1973), Black (1976, 135), Cook (2000).

2. Wellman (2001).

3. Our use of the concept of function does not imply that social behavior necessarily results in social equilibrium or harmony, as in traditional structural functionalist perspectives.

4. Cook (2000, 287).

5. Stone (1954).

6. Granovetter (1985).

7. Prus (1989), Paules (1991).

8. Goffman (1967, 43).

9. One could also imagine a third, *contradictory* social function of personal relationships in public that could undermine primary ties—for example, by compromising the time or other resources that participants might be able to devote to a primary relationship.

10. Snow (2001a).

11. See chapter 2 of this volume.

12. See chapter 3 of this volume.

13. Gardner (1995, 1–42, 233). Although not directly documented by the contributors to this volume, public sociality also carries particular challenges for those identified as ethnic minorities in terms of contemporary applications of "impugning stereotypes," extreme forms of interactional avoidance (e.g., crossing the street to minimize the potential for an encounter with a person identified as a member of a "dangerous" or "undesirable" ethnic group), and governmental imposition of segregated public places and social interaction.

14. As Fine and Harrington (2004) argue, small associational groups, which they dub "tiny publics," form the basis for civil society and thus meaningful political dialogue. See also Eliasoph (1998).

15. Lofland (1998, 229–46).

16. Katz (1999, 7).

17. Hochschild (1983).

18. This general point is emphasized by Blumer (1969), Goffman (1974, 39 n. 25), and, more recently, the reviews and elaborations of the interactionist perspective in Fine (1993) and Snow (2001b). Ericksen (1980) specifically applies interactionist perspective to territory and space.

19. Goffman (1974, 10). The concept of frame and its cognates *schema* and *script* have a long history in the social sciences dating back to the first third of the twentieth century.

20. Goffman (1974, 21)

21. Ericksen (1980).

22. Gieryn (2000, 473). Nippert-Eng (1995) makes a similar argument, albeit with different language, regarding the generation of meanings and distinctions between work and home.

23. Snow and Mulcahy (2001).

24. Goffman (1981, 63). See also Snow (2001b).

25. Goffman (1974, 201–46) used the terms "in" and "out" of frame to denote interaction that occurs outside of the primary "story line" of a social interaction or event.

26. Brekhus (2003, 18).

27. Lofland (1998, 27–41).

28. Brekhus (2003, 18).

29. Lamphere (1992). Fuwa (2003) offers an interesting example of how Japanese mothers import *koen debut* practices from Japan to reconstitute American public parks for anchored relationships that provide social support for them and their children.

30. This sense of *repertoire* is used by Swidler (2001, 24–25) to characterize all of culture, including norms, codes, symbols, and practices that compose it.

31. Goffman (1971, 239–41).

32. Black (1984), Baumgartner (1988), and Goffman (1983, 6). Harcourt (2001) argues that formal social control strategies directed at petty crimes committed in public places can disrupt informal social control mechanisms and, in some instances, produce more disorder than order.

33. Goffman (1982, 6).

34. Duck (1993a), Swidler (2001).

35. Although not in public places, personal relationships that develop in the "underground" of total institutions illustrate this logic (Goffman 1961).

36. Anderson (1990) calls these types of spaces "interior public places."

37. Lofland (1998, 143–229).

38. Blumstein and Kollock (1988), Duck (1993b), Duck and Pittman (1994).

39. Goffman (1971, 19).

40. Lofland (1998, 39).

41. Brekhus (2003, 17).

42. Brekhus (2003, 14).

43. Collective incongruities, if they overtly challenge the institutional bases of authority and are accompanied by mobilizing structures (organizations and networks), material resources, political opportunities, and compelling political rhetorics, can become the bases for social conflict, as McAdam, Tarrow, and Tilly (2001) argue.

44. Anderson (1990).

45. Gardner (1995), Leufgen (2004).

46. Such efforts may be especially likely when interactants are embedded in transactions with a future orientation, such as customer-merchant exchanges. For example, despite the broader social tensions created by Korean retail ownership in largely African American areas, Korean merchants and African American customers work hard at constructing and maintaining civil interaction. See Lee (2002).

47. Goffman (1971, 19–27).

48. Schmueli (2003).

49. Castells (1996, 376–428).

50. Davis (1990).

51. One ethnographic/historical strategy for such studies appears in a 2001 forum in the *American Anthropologist* devoted to the intersections of urban places, social order, and ideology. See Low and McDonogh (2001).

52. Lamphere (1990).

53. Lofland (1998, 179–227).

54. MacCannell (1999), Duany and Brain (forthcoming).

55. Merry (1981, 2001), Wilson and Kelling (1982), Harcourt (2001).

56. An issue along these lines concerns the regulation of "unruly places" containing illegal settlements and public sociality that challenges many of the assumptions built into many public places. On unruly places, see Smart (2001).

57. Putnam (2000).

58. Monti et al. (2003) generally argue that social capital and the capacity for community, however defined, are increasingly occurring in places and via social relationships that would have been unexpected by a previous generation of researchers.

REFERENCES

Adelman, Mara B., and Aaron C. Ahuvia. 1991. Mediated Channels for Mate Seeking: A Solution to Involuntary Singlehood? *Critical Studies in Mass Communication* 8 (September), pp. 273–89.

Adler, Patricia A., and Peter Adler. 1987. *Membership Roles in Field Research.* Thousand Oaks, CA: Sage.

―――. 1998. *Peer Power: Preadolescent Culture and Identity.* New Brunswick, NJ: Rutgers University Press.

―――. 2002. Do University Lawyers and Police Define Research Values? In *Walking the Tightrope: Ethical Issues for Qualitative Researchers,* edited by Will C. van den Hoonaard. Toronto, Canada: University of Toronto Press.

Aho, James A. 1990. *The Politics of Righteousness: Idaho Christian Patriotism.* Seattle: University of Washington Press.

Ahuvia, Aaron C., and Mara B. Adelman. 1992. Formal Intermediaries in the Marriage Market: A Typology and Review. *Journal of Marriage and the Family* 54 (May), pp. 452–63.

Allan, Graham. 1993. Social Structure and Relationships. In *Social Context and Relationships,* edited by Steve Duck. Newbury Park, CA: Sage.

Allen, Katherine R., and Alexis J. Walker. 2000. Qualitative Research. In *Close Relationships: A Sourcebook,* edited by Clyde Hendrick and Susan S. Hendrick. Thousand Oaks, CA: Sage.

Allon, Natalie, and Derrick Fishel. 1979. Singles Bars. In *Urban Life Styles,* edited by Natalie Allon. Dubuque, IA: William C. Brown.

Anderson, Elijah. 1976. *A Place on the Corner.* Chicago: University of Chicago Press.

———. 1990. *Streetwise: Race, Class, and Change in an Urban Community.* Chicago: University of Chicago Press.

———. 1999. *Code of the Street: Decency, Violence, and the Moral Life of the Inner City.* New York: W. W. Norton.

Angell, Roger. 1988. *Season Ticket.* Boston: Houghton Mifflin.

Aries, Elizabeth. 1996. *Men and Women in Interaction: Reconstructing the Difference.* New York: Oxford University Press.

Barry, Kathleen. 1979. *Female Sexual Slavery.* New York: Avon.

Baumgartner, M. P. 1984. Social Control in Suburbia. In *Toward a General Theory of Social Control,* vol. 2, *Selected Problems,* edited by Donald Black. Orlando, FL: Academic Press.

———. 1988. *The Moral Order of a Suburb.* New York: Oxford University Press.

———. 1992. War and Peace in Early Childhood. In *Virginia Review of Sociology,* vol. 1, *Law and Conflict Management,* edited by James Tucker. Greenwich, CT: Greenwood.

Baxter, Leslie A. 1993. Thinking Dialogically about Communication in Personal Relationships. In *Structures of Interpretation,* edited by R. L. Conville. Norwood, NY: Ablex.

Baxter, Leslie A., and Widenmann, Sally. 1993. Revealing and Not Revealing the Status of Romantic Relationships to Social Networks. *Journal of Social and Personal Relationships* 10 (September), pp. 321–37.

Becker, Howard S. 1971. Fieldwork Evidence. In *Sociological Work: Method and Substance.* New Brunswick, NJ: Rutgers University Press.

Bellah, Robert J., Richard Madsen, William M. Sullivan, Ann Swidler, and Stanley M. Tipton. 1985. *Habits of the Heart: Individualism and Commitment in American Life.* Berkeley: University of California Press.

Berger, Bennett M. 1981. *The Survival of a Counterculture: Ideological Work and Everyday Life among Rural Communards.* Berkeley: University of California Press.

Berger, Peter L., and Thomas Luckmann. 1966. *The Social Construction of Reality.* New York: Anchor Books.

Bergesen, Albert. 1984. Social Control and Corporate Organization: A Durkheimian Perspective. In *Toward a General Theory of Social Control,* vol. 2, *Selected Problems,* edited by Donald Black. Orlando, FL: Academic Press.

Berk, Bernard. 1977. Face-Saving at the Singles Dance. *Social Problems* 24 (April), pp. 530–44.

Berk, Sarah Fenstermaker. 1985. *The Gender Factory: The Apportionment of Work in American Households.* New York: Plenum.

Bernard, Jessie. 1982. *The Future of Marriage.* New Haven, CT: Yale University Press.

Berscheid, Ellen, and Letitia Anne Peplau. 1983. The Emerging Science of Relationships. In *Close Relationships,* edited by Harold H. Kelley, Ellen Berscheid, Andrew Christensen, John H. Harvey, Ted L. Huston, George Levinger, Evie McClintock, Letitia Anne Peplau, and Donald R. Peterson. New York: W. H. Freeman.

Black, Donald. 1976. *The Behavior of Law.* New York: Academic Press.

———. 1984. Social Control as a Dependent Variable. In *Toward a General Theory of Social Control,* vol. 1, *Fundamentals,* edited by Donald Black. Orlando, FL: Academic Press.

———. 1990. The Elementary Forms of Conflict Management. In *New Directions in the Study of Justice, Law, and Social Control,* prepared by the School of Justice Studies, Arizona State University. New York: Plenum.

———. 1993. *The Social Structure of Right and Wrong.* San Diego, CA: Academic Press.

Blumer, Herbert. 1969. *Symbolic Interactionism: Perspective and Method.* Englewood Cliffs, NJ: Prentice Hall.

Blumstein, Philip, and Peter Kollock. 1988. Personal Relationships. *Annual Review of Sociology* 14, pp. 467–90.

Bochner, Arthur P. 1994. Perspectives on Inquiry II: Theories and Stories. In *Handbook of Interpersonal Communication,* 2nd ed., edited by Mark L. Knapp and Gerald R. Miller. Newbury Park, CA: Sage.

Bohannan, Paul. 1970. The Six Stations of Divorce. In *Divorce and After,* edited by Paul Bohannan. New York: Doubleday.

Boles, Jacqueline, and A. P. Garbin. 1974a. The Choice of Stripping for a Living: An Empirical and Theoretical Explanation. *Sociology of Work and Occupations* 1 (February), pp. 110–23.

———. 1974b. The Strip Club and Stripper-Customer Patterns of Interaction. *Sociology and Social Research* 58 (January), pp. 136–44.

———. 1974c. Stripping for a Living: An Occupational Study of the Night Club Stripper. In *Deviant Behavior: Occupational and Organizational Bases,* edited by Clifton D. Bryant. Chicago: Rand McNally.

Bourgois, Pierre. 1995. *In Search of Respect: Selling Crack in El Barrio.* Cambridge, England: Cambridge University Press.

Brekhus, Wayne H. 2003. *Peacocks, Chameleons, Centaurs: Gay Suburbia and the Grammar of Social Identity.* Chicago: University of Chicago Press.

Bumpass, Larry L., and James A. Sweet. 1989. National Estimates of Cohabitation. *Demography* 26 (November), pp. 615–25.

Burgoon, Judee K., David B. Buller, and W. Glenn Woodall. 1992. *The Unspoken Dialogue: An Introduction to Nonverbal Communication,* 2nd ed. New York: Harper Collins.

Burgoon, Judee K., Lesa A. Stern, and Leesa Dillman. 1995. *Interpersonal Adaptation: Dyadic Interaction Patterns.* Cambridge, England: Cambridge University Press.

Cahill, Spencer E. 1987. Children and Civility: Ceremonial Deviance and the Acquisition of Ritual Competence. *Social Psychology Quarterly* 50 (December), pp. 312–21.

———. 1990. Childhood and Public Life: Reaffirming Biographical Divisions. *Social Problems* 37 (August), pp. 394–402.

Cahill, Spencer E., and Robin Eggleston. 1994. Managing Emotions in Public: The Case of Wheelchair Users. *Social Psychology Quarterly* 57 (December), pp. 300–312.

Cahn, Dudley D. 1990. Confrontation Behaviors, Perceived Understanding, and Relationship Growth. In *Intimates in Conflict: A Communication Perspective,* edited by Dudley D. Cahn. Hillsdale, NJ: Lawrence Erlbaum.

Carey, S. H., Peterson, R. A., and Sharpe, L. K. 1974. A Study of Recruitment and Socialization in Two Deviant Female Occupations. *Sociology Symposium* 11 (February), pp. 11–24.

Castells, Manuel. 1996. *The Rise of the Network Society.* Oxford, England: Blackwell.

Cavan, Sherri. 1966. *Liquor License: An Ethnography of Bar Behavior.* Chicago: Aldine.

Chapkis, Wendy. 1997. *Live Sex Acts: Women Performing Erotic Labor.* New York: Routledge.

Charmaz, Kathy J. 2001. Grounded Theory. In *Contemporary Field Research: Perspectives and Formulations,* 2nd ed., edited by Robert M. Emerson. Prospect Heights, IL: Waveland Press.

Cherlin, Andrew J. 1992. *Marriage, Divorce and Remarriage.* Cambridge, MA: Harvard University Press.

Clifford, James, and George E. Marcus. 1986. *Writing Culture: The Poetics and Politics of Ethnography.* Berkeley: University of California Press.

Cohen, Stanley, and Laurie Taylor. 1992 [1976]. *Escape Attempts: The Theory and Practice of Resistance to Everyday Life,* 2nd ed. London: Routledge and Kegan Paul.

Collins, Randall. 1975. *Conflict Sociology: Toward an Explanatory Science.* New York: Academic Press.

Connell, R. W. 1985. Theorizing Gender. *Sociology* 19 (no. 2), pp. 260–72.

Cook, Karen S. 2000. Advances in the Microfoundations of Sociology: Recent Developments and New Challenges for Social Psychology. *Contemporary Sociology* 29 (no. 5), pp. 685–92.

Coontz, Stephanie. 1992. *The Way We Never Were: American Families and the Nostalgia Trap.* New York: Basic Books.

Corrigan, Paul. 1976. Doing Nothing. In *Resistance through Ritual: Youth Subcultures in Post-War Britain,* edited by Stuart Hall and Tony Jefferson. London: Hutchinson.

———. 1979. *Schooling the Smash Street Kids.* London: Macmillan.

Couch, Carl J. 1989. *Social Processes and Relationships*. Dix Halls, NY: General Hall.

Crawford, Mary. 1995. *Talking Difference: On Gender and Language*. Thousand Oaks, CA: Sage.

Cressey, Paul G. 1969 [1932]. *The Taxi-Dance Hall: A Sociological Study in Commercialized Recreation and City Life*. Montclair, NJ: Patterson Smith.

Dacin, M. Tina, Marc J. Ventresca, and Brent D. Beal. 1999. The Embeddedness of Organizations: Dialogue and Directions. *Journal of Management* 25 (no. 3), 317–56.

D'Andre, Ann T. 1965. An Occupational Study of the Strip-Dancer Career. Paper presented at the annual meeting of the Pacific Sociological Association.

Danko, J. P. 1998. *Live Nude Girls: The Top 100 Strip Clubs in North America*. New York: Griffin.

Darden, D. K., and P. R. Koski. 1988. Using the Personal Ads: A Deviant Activity? *Deviant Behavior* 9 (no. 4), pp. 383–400.

Davis, Fred. 1959. The Cab Driver and His Fare: Facets of a Fleeting Relationship. *American Journal of Sociology* 65 (September), pp. 158–65.

Davis, M. R. Seibert, and W. Breed. 1966. Interracial Seating Patterns on New Orleans Public Transit. *Social Problems* 13 (Winter), pp. 298–306.

Davis, Phillip W. 1991. Stranger Intervention into Child Punishment in Public Places. *Social Problems* 38 (May), pp. 227–46.

Davis, Simon. 1990. Men as Success Objects and Women as Sex Objects: A Study of Personal Advertisements. *Sex Roles* 23 (nos. 1/2), pp. 43–50.

de Certeau, Michel. 1984. *The Practice of Everyday Life*. Berkeley: University of California Press.

Decker, Scott H., and Barrik Van Winkle. 1996. *Life in the Gang: Family, Friends, and Violence*. Cambridge, England: Cambridge University Press.

Deutscher, Irwin. 1966. Words and Deeds: Social Science and Social Policy. *Social Problems* 13 (Winter), pp. 235–54.

Deutscher, Irwin, Fred P. Pestello, and H. Frances G. Pestello. 1993. *Sentiments and Acts*. New York: Aldine de Gruyter.

DeWitt, Paula Mergenhagen. 1992. All the Lonely People. *American Demographics* 14 (April), pp. 44–48.

Douglas, Jack D. 1976. *Investigative Social Research: Individual and Team Field Research*. Beverly Hills, CA: Sage.

Douglas, Mary. 1966. *Purity and Danger: An Analysis of Concepts of Pollution and Taboo*. New York: Praeger.

Duany, Andrés, and David Brain. Forthcoming. Regulating as if Humans Matter: The Transect and Post-Suburban Planning. In *Regulating Place: Standards and the Shaping of Urban America*, edited by Eran Ben-Joseph and Terry S. Szold. New York: Routledge Kegan Paul.

Duck, Steve. 1985. Social and Personal Relationships. In *Handbook of Interpersonal Communication,* edited by Mark L. Knapp and Gerald R. Miller. Beverly Hills, CA: Sage.

———. 1991. *Understanding Relationships.* New York: Guilford Press.

———. 1993a. Preface to *Social Context and Relationships,* edited by Steve Duck. Thousand Oaks, CA: Sage.

———.1993b. *Social Context and Relationships.* Newbury Park, CA: Sage.

Duck, Steve, and Garth Pittman. 1994. Social and Personal Relationships. In *Handbook of Interpersonal Communication,* 2nd ed., edited by Mark L. Knapp and Gerald R. Miller. Thousand Oaks, CA: Sage.

Duneier, Mitchell. 1992. *Slim's Table: Race, Respectability, and Masculinity.* Chicago: University of Chicago Press.

———. 1999. *Sidewalk.* New York: Farrar, Straus, and Giroux.

Duneier, Mitchell, and Harvey Molotch. 1999. Talking City Trouble: Interactional Vandalism, Social Inequality, and the "Urban Interaction Problem." *American Journal of Sociology* 104 (March), pp. 1263–95.

Edgerton, Robert B. 1967. *The Cloak of Competence: Stigma in the Lives of the Mentally Retarded.* Berkeley: University of California Press.

———. 1979. *Alone Together.* Berkeley: University of California Press.

Ehrenreich, Barbara, and Arlie Russell Hochschild, eds. 2003. *Global Women: Nannies, Maids, and Sex Workers in the New Economy.* Berkeley: University of California Press.

Eliasoph, Nina. 1998. *Avoiding Politics: How Americans Produce Apathy in Everyday Life.* Cambridge, England: Cambridge University Press.

Emerson, Richard M. 1972. Exchange Theory, Part II: Exchange Relations and Networks. In *Sociological Theories in Progress,* vol. 2, edited by Joseph Berger, Morris Zelditch, Jr., and Bo Anderson. Boston: Houghton-Mifflin.

———. 1981. Social Exchange Theory. In *Social Psychology: Sociological Perspectives,* edited by Morris Rosenberg and Ralph H. Turner. New York: Basic Books.

Emerson, Robert M., ed. 2001a. *Contemporary Field Research: Perspectives and Formulations.* 2nd ed. Prospect Heights, IL: Waveland Press.

———. 2001b. Producing Ethnographies: Theory, Evidence, and Representation. In *Contemporary Field Research: Perspectives and Formulations,* 2nd ed., edited by Robert M. Emerson. Prospect Heights, IL: Waveland Press.

Emerson, Robert M., Rachel Fretz, and Linda L. Shaw. 1995. *Writing Ethnographic Fieldnotes.* Chicago: University of Chicago Press.

Emirbayer, Mustafa. 1997. Manifesto for a Relational Sociology. *American Journal of Sociology* 103 (September), pp. 281–317.

England, Paula, and George Farkas. 1986. *Households, Employment, and Gender.* New York: Aldine de Gruyter.

Epstein, Jonathan S. 1998. *Youth Culture: Identity in a Postmodern World.* Oxford, England: Blackwell.

Ericksen, E. Gordon. 1980. *The Territorial Experience: Human Ecology as Symbolic Interaction.* Austin: University of Texas Press.

Erickson, Kai T. 1966. *Wayward Puritans: A Study in the Sociology of Deviance.* New York: John Wiley.

Erickson, Ken, and Donald Stull. 1998. *Doing Team Ethnography: Warnings and Advice.* Thousand Oaks, CA: Sage.

Fenstermaker, Sarah, Candace West, and Don H. Zimmerman. 1991. Gender Inequality: New Conceptual Terrain. In *Gender, Family, Economy: The Triple Overlap,* edited by Rae Lesser Blumberg. Thousand Oaks, CA: Sage.

Fine, Gary Alan. 1987. *With the Boys: Little League Baseball and Preadolescent Culture.* Chicago: University of Chicago Press.

———. 1993. The Sad Demise, Mysterious Disappearance, and Glorious Triumph of Symbolic Interactionism. *Annual Review of Sociology* 19, pp. 61–87.

———. 2001. *Gifted Tongues: High School Debate and Adolescent Culture.* Chicago: University of Chicago Press.

Fine, Gary Alan, and Brooke Harrington. 2004. Tiny Publics: Small Groups and Civil Society. *Sociological Theory* 22 (September), pp. 341–356.

Fischer, Claude S. 1982. *To Dwell among Friends: Personal Networks in Town and City.* Chicago: University of Chicago Press.

Fitzpatrick, Mary Anne. 1988. *Between Husbands and Wives: Communication in Marriage.* Newbury Park, CA: Sage.

Freeman, Linton C., A. Kimball Romney, and S. C. Freeman. 1987. Cognitive Structure and Informant Accuracy. *American Anthropologist* 89 (June), pp. 310–25.

Frenville, J. 2000. *The Gentlemen's Club 2000 Edition.* New York: GCG Productions.

Fuwa, Makiko. 2003. Japanese Mothers in Public Parks: Migration and Reconstruction of Social Networks. Unpublished manuscript, Department of Sociology, University of California, Irvine.

Gardner, Carol Brooks. 1994. A Family among Strangers: Kinship Claims among Gay Men in Public Places. In *The Community of the Streets,* edited by Spencer Cahill and Lyn H. Lofland, Suppl. 1, *Research in Community Sociology,* edited by Dan A Chekki. Greenwich, CT: JAI Press.

———. 1995. *Passing By: Gender and Public Harassment.* Berkeley: University of California Press.

Gergen, Kenneth J., and Mary M. Gergen. 1987. Narratives of Relationships. In *Accounting for Relationships: Explanation, Representation, and Knowledge,* edited by Rosalie Burnett, Patrick McGhee, and David D. Clarke. New York: Meuthen.

Giddens, Anthony. 1979. Agency, Structure. In *Central Problems in Social Theory: Action, Structure, and Contradiction in Social Analysis.* Berkeley: University of California Press.

Gieryn, Thomas. 2000. A Space for Place in Sociology. *Annual Review of Sociology* 26, pp. 463–96.

Gilligan, Carol. 1983. *In a Different Voice; Psychological Theory and Women's Development.* Cambridge, MA: Harvard University Press.

Gilligan, Carol, Janie Victoria Ward, and Jill McLean Taylor, eds. 1988. *Mapping the Moral Domain.* Cambridge, MA: Harvard University Press.

Glaser, Barney G., and Anselm L. Strauss. 1967. *The Discovery of Grounded Theory: Strategies for Qualitative Research.* Chicago: Aldine.

Glick, Paul C. 1988. Fifty Years of Family Demography: A Record of Social Change. *Journal of Marriage and the Family* 50 (November), pp. 861–73.

Goffman, Erving. 1959. *The Presentation of Self in Everyday Life.* New York: Anchor Books.

———. 1961. *Encounters: Two Studies in the Study of Social Interaction.* Indianapolis, IA: Bobbs-Merrill.

———. 1963. *Behavior in Public Places: Notes on the Social Organization of Gatherings.* New York: Free Press.

———. 1967. *Interaction Ritual.* New York: Pantheon Books.

———. 1971. *Relations in Public: Microstudies of the Public Order.* New York: Harper and Row.

———. 1974. *Frame Analysis.* New York: Harper Colophon.

———. 1977. The Arrangement between the Sexes. *Theory and Society* 4 (Autumn), pp. 301- 31.

———. 1979. *Gender Advertisements.* New York: Harper and Row.

———. 1981. *Forms of Talk.* Philadelphia: University of Pennsylvania Press.

———. 1983. The Interaction Order. *American Sociological Review* 48 (February), pp. 1–17.

Gonos, George. 1976. Go-Go Dancing: A Comparative Frame Analysis. *Urban Life* 9 (July), pp. 189–219.

Grannis, Rick. 1998. The Importance of Trivial Streets: Residential Streets and Residential Segregation. *American Journal of Sociology* 103 (May), pp. 1530–64.

Granovetter, Mark. 1973. The Strength of Weak Ties. *American Journal of Sociology* 78 (May), pp. 1360–80.

———. 1985. Economic Action and Social Structure: The Problem of Embeddedness. *American Journal of Sociology* 91 (November), pp. 481–510.

Greenblat, Cathy Stein, and John H. Gagnon. 1983. Temporary Strangers: Travel and Tourism from a Sociological Perspective. *Sociological Perspectives* 26, pp. 89–110.

Griffin, Susan. 1981. *Pornography and Silence.* New York: Harper and Row.

Guba, Egon, and Yvonna S. Lincoln. 1994. Competing Paradigms in Qualitative Research. In *Handbook of Qualitative Research,* edited by Norman K. Denzin and Yvonna S. Lincoln. Thousand Oaks, CA: Sage.

Guttentag, Marcia, and Paul F. Secord. 1983. *Too Many Women? The Sex Ratio Question.* Beverly Hills, CA: Sage.

Guttman, Allen. 1986. *Sports Spectators.* New York: Columbia University Press.

Haas, Stephen M., and Laura Stafford. 1998. An Initial Examination of Maintenance Behaviors in Gay and Lesbian Relationships. *Journal of Social and Personal Relationships* 15 (December), pp. 846–55.

Hall, Stuart, and Tony Jefferson, eds. 1976. *Resistance through Rituals: Youth Subcultures in Post-War Britain.* New York: Holmes and Meier.

Hammersley, Martyn. 1992. *What's Wrong with Ethnography?* London: Routledge.

Hankin, Kelly. 2002. *The Girls in the Back Room: Looking at the Lesbian Bar.* Minneapolis: University of Minnesota Press.

Harcourt, Bernard E. 2001. *Illusion of Order: The False Promise of Broken Windows Policing.* Cambridge, MA: Harvard University Press.

Hebdige, Dick. 1979. *Subculture: The Meaning of Style.* London: Methuen.

Heiss, David R., and John O'Brien. 1993. Emotion Expression in Groups. In *Handbook of Emotions in Groups,* edited by Michael L. Lewis and Jeannette M. Haviland. New York: Guilford.

Hendrick, Clyde, and Susan S. Hendrick, eds. 2000. *Close Relationships: A Sourcebook.* Thousand Oaks, CA: Sage.

Herek, Gregory M. 1986. On Doing, Being, and Not Being: Prejudice and the Social Construction of Sexuality. *Journal of Homosexuality* 12 (Fall), pp. 135–51.

Heritage, John. 1984. *Garfinkel and Ethnomethodology.* Cambridge, England: Polity Press.

Hetherington, E. Mavis, and John Kelly. 2002. *For Better or for Worse: Divorce Reconsidered.* New York: W. W. Norton.

Hirschman, Albert O. 1971. *Exit, Voice, and Loyalty.* Cambridge, MA: Harvard University Press.

Hochschild, Arlie Russell. 1983. *The Managed Heart: Commercialization of Human Feeling.* Berkeley: University of California Press.

Hoffman, M. L. 1960. Power Assertion by the Parent and Its Impact on the Child. *Child Development* 31 (March–December), pp.129–43.

———. 1984. Parent Discipline, Moral Internalization, and Development of Pro-social Motivation. In *Development and Maintenance of Pro-social Behavior,* edited by E. Staub, D. Bar-Tal, J. Karylowski, and J. Reykowski. New York: Plenum.

Hondagneu-Sotelo, Pierrette. 2001. *Doméstica: Immigrant Workers Cleaning and Caring in the Shadows of Affluence.* Berkeley: University of California Press.

Horowitz, Helen Lefkowitz. 1987. *Campus Life: Undergraduate Cultures from the End of the Eighteenth Century to the Present.* New York: Knopf.

Horowitz, Ruth. 1983. *Honor and the American Dream: Culture and Social Identity in a Chicano Community.* New Brunswick, NJ: Rutgers University Press.

Horowitz, Alan V. 1982. *The Social Control of Mental Illness.* New York: Academic Press.

Hunter, Albert. 1985. Private, Parochial and Public Social Orders: The Problem of Crime and Incivility in Urban Communities. In *The Challenge of Social Control: Citizenship and Institution Building in Modern Society,* edited by Gerald D. Suttles and Mayer N. Zald. Norwood, NJ: Ablex.

Irvine, Leslie. 2000. "Even Better Than the Real Thing": Narratives of the Self in Codependency. *Qualitative Sociology* 23 (Spring), pp. 9–28.

Jacobs, Jane. 1961. *The Death and Life of Great American Cities.* New York: Random House.

Jankowski, Martin Sanchez. 1991. *Islands in the Street: Gangs and American Urban Society.* Berkeley: University of California Press.

Katovich, M.A., and W.A. Reese II. 1987. The Regular: Full-Time Identities and Memberships in an Urban Bar. *Journal of Contemporary Ethnography* 16 (October), pp. 308–43.

Katz, Jack. 1999. *How Emotions Work.* Chicago: University of Chicago Press.

Kelley, Harold H. 1986. Personal Relationships: Their Nature and Significance. In *The Emerging Field of Personal Relationships,* edited by Steve Duck and R. Gilmour. Hillsdale, NJ: Lawrence Erlbaum.

Kitson, Gay C. 1992. *Portrait of Divorce.* New York: Guilford Press.

Knapp, Mark. 1984. *Interpersonal Communication and Human Relationships.* Boston: Allyn and Bacon.

Knapp, Mark L., John A. Daly, Kelly Fudge Albada, and Gerald R. Miller. 2003. Background and Current Trends in the Study of Interpersonal Communication. In *Handbook of Interpersonal Communication,* 3rd ed., edited by Mark L. Knapp and John A. Daly. Newbury Park, CA: Sage.

Knapp, Mark L., D. Ellis, and B. Williams. 1980. Perceptions of Communication Behavior Associated with Relationship Terms. *Communication Monographs* 47 (November), pp. 262–78.

Knapp, Mark L., Gerald R. Miller, and Kelly Fudge. 1994. Background and Current Trends in the Study of Interpersonal Communication. In *Handbook of Interpersonal Communication,* 2nd ed., edited by Mark L. Knapp and Gerald R. Miller. Newbury Park, CA: Sage.

Komarovsky, Mira. 1985. *Women in College: Shaping New Feminine Identities.* New York: Basic Books.

Kornblum, William. 1974. *Blue Collar Community.* Chicago: University of Chicago Press.

Lamont, Michele. 1992. *Money, Morals, and Manners: The Culture of the French and the American Upper-Middle Class.* Chicago: University of Chicago Press.

Lamphere, Louise, ed. 1990. *Structuring Diversity: Ethnographic Perspectives on the New Immigration.* Chicago: University of Chicago Press.

Lee, Jennifer. 2002. From Civil Relations to Racial Conflict: Merchant-Customer Interactions in Urban America. *American Sociological Review* 67 (February), pp. 77–98.

Leeds-Hurwitz, Wendy. 1995. Introducing Social Approaches. In *Social Approaches to Communication,* edited by Wendy Leeds-Hurwitz. New York: Guilford Press.

LeMasters, E. E. 1975. *Blue-Collar Aristocrats: Life-Styles at a Working Class Tavern.* Madison: University of Wisconsin Press.

Leone, Bruno, ed. 1995. *Rape on Campus.* San Diego, CA: Greenhaven Press.

Leufgen, Jillianne. 2004. Homeless in the Park: Interactions in Public Space between the Homeless, Domiciled Citizens, and the Authorities. Unpublished manuscript, Department of Sociology, University of California, Irvine.

Lincoln, Yvonna S., and Egon G. Guba. 1985. *Naturalistic Inquiry.* Newbury Park, CA: Sage.

Lipset, Seymour Martin, and Earl Raab. 1970. *The Politics of Unreason: Right Wing Extremism in America, 1790–1970.* New York: Harper and Row.

Llewellyn, Karl N., and E. Adamson Hoebel. 1941. *The Cheyenne Way: Conflict and Case Law in Primitive Jurisprudence.* Norman: University of Oklahoma Press.

Lofland, John, and Lyn H. Lofland. 1995 [1972]. *Analyzing Social Settings: A Guide to Qualitative Research and Analysis,* 3rd ed. Belmont, California: Wadsworth.

Lofland, Lyn H. 1973. *A World of Strangers: Order and Action in Urban Public Space.* New York: Basic Books.

———. 1989. Social Life in the Public Realm: A Review. *Journal of Contemporary Ethnography* 17 (January), pp. 453–82.

———. 1995. Social Interaction: Continuities and Complexities in the Study of Nonintimate Sociality. In *Sociological Perspectives on Social Psychology,* edited by Karen S. Cook, Gary Alan Fine, and James S. House. Boston: Allyn and Bacon.

———. 1998. *The Public Realm: Quintessential City Life.* Albany, NY: SUNY Press.

Low, Setha M., and Gary W. McDonogh. 2001. Introduction to "Remapping in the City: Place, Order, and Ideology." *American Anthropologist* 103 (March), pp. 5–6.

MacCannell, Dean. 1999. "New Urbanism" and Its Discontents. In *Giving Ground: The Politics of Propinquity,* edited by Joan Copjec and Michael Sorkin. New York: Verso.

MacLeod, Jay. 1995. *Ain't No Makin' It: Aspirations and Attainment in a Low Income Neighborhood.* Boulder, CO: Westview Press.

Mass Observation. 1943. *The Pub and the People: A Worktown Study.* London: Victor Gollancz Ltd.

McAdam, Doug, Sydney Tarrow, and Charles Tilly. 2001. *Dynamics of Contention.* New York: Cambridge University Press.

McCaghy, Charles H., and James K. Skipper. 1969. Lesbian Behavior as an Adaptation to the Occupation of Stripping. *Social Problems* 17 (Fall), pp. 262–70.

———. 1972. Stripping: Anatomy of a Deviant Life Style. In *Life Styles: Diversity in American Society,* edited by S. D. Feldman and G. W. Thielbar. Boston: Little, Brown.

McCall, George J., and J. L. Simmons. 1982. *Social Psychology: A Sociological Approach.* New York: Free Press.

Merry, Sally Engle. 1981. *Getting Justice and Getting Even: Legal Consciousness among Working-Class Americans.* Chicago: University of Chicago Press.

———. 2001. Spatial Governmentality and the New Urban Social Order: Controlling Gender Violence through Law. *American Anthropologist* 103 (March), pp. 16–29.

Messer, J. G. 1982. Spontaneous Behavior in Emergencies. Paper presented at the annual meeting of the American Sociological Association.

Metts, Sandra, and Sally Planalp. 2003. Emotional Communication. In *Handbook of Interpersonal Communication,* edited by Mark L. Knapp and John Daly. Thousand Oaks, CA: Sage.

Milgram, Stanley. 1977. *The Individual in a Social World.* Reading, MA: Addison-Wesley.

Moffatt, Michael. 1989. *Coming of Age in New Jersey: College and American Culture.* New Brunswick, NJ: Rutgers University Press.

Molm, Linda. 1997. *Coercive Power in Social Exchange.* Cambridge, England: Cambridge University Press.

Monsour, Michael. 2002. *Women and Men as Friends: Relationships across the Life Span in the 21st Century.* Mahwah, NJ: Lawrence Erlbaum.

Montemurro, Beth. 2001. Strippers and Screamers: The Emergence of Social Control in a Noninstitutional Setting. *Journal of Contemporary Ethnography* 30 (June), pp. 275–304.

Monti, Daniel J., Jr., Colleen Butler, Alexandra Curley, Kristen Tilney, and Melissa F. Weiner. Private Lives and Public Worlds: Changes in Americans' Social Ties and Civic Attachments in the Late-20th Century. *City and Community* 2 (June), pp. 143–63.

Moore, Joan W. 1978. *Homeboys: Gangs, Drugs and Prison in the Barrio of Los Angeles.* Philadelphia: Temple University Press.

———. 1991. *Going Down to the Barrio: Homeboys and Homegirls in Change.* Philadelphia: Temple University Press.

Morrill, Calvin. 1995. *The Executive Way: Conflict Management in Corporations.* Chicago: University of Chicago Press.

Morrill, Calvin, and William Bailey. 1992. The Reciprocal Power of Group Identities and Social Styles: A Note on a Specimen Deviant Youth Group. In *Postmodern Political Communication,* edited by Andrew King. Westport, CT: Praeger.

Morrill, Calvin, Michelle Johnson, and Tyler Harrison. 1998. Voice and Context in Simulated Everyday Legal Discourse: The Influence of Sex Differences and Social Ties. *Law and Society Review* 32 (no. 3), pp. 639–65.

Murphy, Patrick, John Williams, and Eric Dunning. 1990. *Football on Trial: Spectator Violence and Development in the Football World.* New York: Routledge.

Neiwert, David A. 1999. *In God's Country: The Patriot Movement and the Pacific Northwest.* Pullman: Washington State University Press.

Nippert-Eng, Christena E. 1995. *Home and Work: Negotiating Boundaries through Everyday Life.* Chicago: University of Chicago Press.

Nisbet, Robert A. 1965. *The Sociological Tradition.* New York: Basic Books.

Norman, Jane, and Myron W. Harris. 1981. *The Private Life of the American Teenager.* New York: Rawson, Wade.

Oldenburg, Ray. 1989. *The Great Good Place: Cafés, Coffee Shops, Community Centers, Beauty Parlors, General Stores, Bars, Hangouts, and How They Get You through the Day.* New York: Paragon House.

Parks, Malcolm R., and Leona L. Eggert. 1991. The Role of Social Context in the Dynamics of Personal Relationships. *Advances in Personal Relationships* 2, pp. 1–34.

Parks, Malcolm R., Charlotte M. Stan, and Leona L. Eggert. 1983. Romantic Involvement and Social Network Involvement. *Social Psychology Quarterly* 46 (June), pp. 116–31.

Paul, E. L., and Kathleen M. White. 1990. The Development of Intimate Relationships in Late Adolescence. *Adolescence* 25 (Summer), pp. 375–400.

Paules, Greta F. 1991. *Dishing It Out: Power and Resistance among Waitresses in a New Jersey Restaurant.* Philadelphia: Temple University Press.

Paxton, Pamela. 1999. Is Social Capital Declining in the United States? *American Journal of Sociology* 105 (July), pp. 88–127.

Perrin, Dennis. 2000. *American Fan: Sports Mania and the Culture That Feeds It.* New York: Spike.

Phillipsen, Gerry. 1992. *Speaking Culturally: Explorations in Social Communication.* Albany, NY: SUNY Press.

Polanyi, Karl. 1944. *The Great Transformation.* New York: Holt, Rinehart.

Ponse, Barbara. 1978. *Identities in the Lesbian World: The Social Construction of Self.* Westport, CT: Greenwood Press.

Poole, Marshall Scott, and Robert D. McPhee. 1994. Methodology in Interpersonal Communication Research. In *Handbook of Interpersonal Communication,* 2nd ed., edited by Mark L. Knapp and Gerald R. Miller. Newbury Park, CA: Sage.

Prehn, John W. 1993. *On the Edge: Striptease in a Small-Town Setting.* Saint Peter, MN: Gustavus Adolphus College.

Prus, Robert. 1989. *Making Sales: Influences as Interpersonal Accomplishment.* Newbury Park, CA: Sage.

———. 1996. *Symbolic Interaction and Ethnographic Research: Intersubjectivity and the Study of Human Lived Experience.* Albany, NY: SUNY Press.

Punch, Maurice. 1986. *The Politics and Ethics of Fieldwork.* Thousand Oaks, CA: Sage.

Putnam, Robert D. 2000. *Bowling Alone: The Collapse and Revival of American Community.* New York: Touchstone.

Rawlins, William K. 1992. *Friendship Matters: Communication, Dialectics, and the Life Course.* New York: Walter de Gruyter.

Reed, Stacy. 1997. All Stripped Off. In *Whores and Other Feminists,* edited by Jill Nagle. New York: Routledge.

Reynolds, Larry T. 1993. *Interactionism: Exposition and Critique.* 3rd ed. Dix Hills, NY: General Hall.

Riessman, Catherine K. 1990. *Divorce Talk: Women and Men Make Sense of Their Personal Relationships.* New Brunswick, NJ: Rutgers University Press.

Robben, Antonius C. G., and Carolyn Nordstrom. 1995. The Anthropology and Ethnography of Violence and Sociopolitical Conflict. In *Fieldwork under Fire: Contemporary Studies of Violence and Survival,* edited by Carolyn Nordstrom and Antonius C. G. Robben. Berkeley: University of California Press.

Robins, Douglas M., Clinton R. Sanders, and Spencer Cahill. 1991. Dogs and Their People: Pet-Facilitated Interaction in a Public Setting. *Journal of Contemporary Ethnography* 20 (January–April), pp. 3–25.

Rogers, Carl. 1968. Interpersonal Relationships U.S.A. 2000. *Journal of Applied Behavioral Science* 4 (Spring), pp. 208–69.

Ronai, Carol Rambo. 1992. The Reflexive Self through Narrative: A Night in the Life of an Erotic Dancer/Researcher. In *Investigating Subjectivity: Research on Lived Experience,* edited by Carolyn Ellis and Michael G. Flaherty. Thousand Oaks, CA: Sage.

Ronai, Carol Rambo, and Rebecca Cross. 1998. Dancing with Identity: Narrative Resistance Strategies of Male and Female Strippers. *Deviant Behavior* 19 (no. 2), pp. 99–119.

Ronai, Carol Rambo, and Carolyn Ellis. 1989. Turn-ons for Money: Interactional Strategies of the Table Dancer. *Journal of Contemporary Ethnography* 18 (October), pp. 271–98.

Rosaldo, Renato. 1989. *Culture and Truth: The Remaking of Social Analysis.* Boston: Beacon Press.

Rosenthal, Robert. 1969. Interpersonal Expectations: Effects of the Experimenter's Hypotheses. In *Artifact in Behavioral Research,* edited by Robert Rosenthal and Ralph L. Rosnow. New York: Academic Press.

Rubin, Lillian B. 1974. *Worlds of Pain: Life in the Working-Class Family.* New York: Basic Books.

———. 1994. *Families on the Fault Line: America's Working Class Speaks about the Family, the Economy, Race, and Ethnicity.* New York: Harper Collins.

Rubin, Zick. 1973. *Liking and Loving: An Invitation to Social Psychology.* New York: Holt, Rinehart and Winston.

Rutter, Michael. 1979. *Changing Youth in a Changing Society: Patterns of Adolescent Development and Disorder.* London: Nuffield Provincial Hospitals Trust.

Sanders, William B. 1994. *Gangbangs and Drivebys: Grounded Culture and Juvenile Gang Violence.* Hawthorne, NY: Aldine de Gruyter.

Schmueli, Sandra. 2003. "Flash Mob" Craze Spreads. August 8. Retrieved October 14, 2004, from www.cnn.com/2003/TECH/internet/08/04/flash.mob/index.html.

Schwartz, Gary. 1987. *Beyond Conformity or Rebellion: Youth and Authority in America.* Chicago: University of Chicago Press.

Schwartzberg, Natalie, Kathy Berliner, and Demaris Jacob. 1995. *Single in a Married World.* New York: W. W. Norton.

Scott, Marshall B., and Stanford M. Lyman. 1968. Accounts. *American Sociological Review* 33 (February), pp. 46–62.

Seeyle, Katharine Q. 1997. Couple Accused of Beating Daughters Tell of Adoption Ordeal. *New York Times,* November 2, Metro Section, pp. 37, 42.

Sewell, William H., Jr. 1992. A Theory of Structure: Duality, Agency, and Transformation. *American Journal of Sociology* 98 (July), pp. 1–29.

Sigman, Stuart J. 1995. Order and Continuity in Human Relationships: A Social Communication Approach to Defining "Relationship." In *Social Approaches to Communication,* edited by Wendy Leeds-Hurwitz. New York: Guilford Press.

Simmel, Georg. 1950 [1903]. *The Sociology of Georg Simmel,* edited by Kurt Wolff. Glencoe, IL: Free Press.

Skelton, Tracey, and Gill Valentine. 1997. *Cool Places: Geographies of Youth Cultures.* London: Routledge.

Skipper, James K., and Charles H. McCaghy. 1970. Stripteasers: The Anatomy and Career Contingencies of a Deviant Occupation. *Social Problems* 17 (Winter), pp. 391–405.

———. 1971. Stripteasing: A Sex Oriented Occupation. In *The Sociology of Sex,* edited by James Henslin. New York: Appleton Century Crofts.

Smart, Alan. 2001. Unruly Places: Urban Governance and the Persistence of Illegality in Hong Kong's Urban Squatter Settlements. *American Anthropologist* 103 (March), pp. 30–44.

Snow, David A. 2001a. Collective Identity and Expressive Forms. In *International Encyclopedia of the Social and Behavioral Sciences,* edited by Neil J. Smelser and Paul B. Baltes. Oxford, England: Pergamon Press.

———. 2001b. Extending and Broadening Blumer's Conceptualization of Symbolic Interactionism. *Symbolic Interaction* 24 (no. 3), pp. 367–77.

Snow, David A., and Leon Anderson. 1993. *Down on Their Luck: A Study of Homeless Street People.* Berkeley: University of California Press.

Snow, David A., Robert Benford, and Leon Anderson. 1986. Fieldwork Roles and Informational Yield: A Comparison of Alternative Settings and Roles. *Urban Life* 14 (January), pp. 377–408.

Snow, David A., and Jason Clark-Miller. 2003. Frame Articulation and Elaboration in a Right-Wing Group: An Empirical Examination of Framing Processes. Unpublished manuscript, Department of Sociology, University of California, Irvine.

Snow, David A., and Calvin Morrill. 2004. Field Relations. In *Encyclopedia of Social Measurement,* edited by Kimberly Kempf-Leonard. San Diego, CA: Elsevier.

Snow, David A., Calvin Morrill, and Leon Anderson. 2003. Elaborating Analytic Ethnography: Linking Ethnography and Theoretical Development. *Ethnography* 4 (no. 2), pp. 181–200.

Snow, David A., and Mike Mulcahy. 2001. Space, Politics and the Survival Strategies of the Homeless. *American Behavioral Scientist* 45 (September), pp. 149–69.

Snow, David A., Cherylon Robinson, and Patricia L. McCall. 1991. "Cooling Out" Men in Singles Bars and Nightclubs: Observations on the Interpersonal Survival Strategies of Women in Public Places. *Journal of Contemporary Ethnography* 19 (January), pp. 423–49.

Snow, David A., E. Burke Rochford, Jr., Steven K. Worden, and Robert D. Benford. 1986. Frame Alignment Processes, Micromobilization and Movement Participation. *American Sociological Review* 51 (August), pp. 464–81.

Snow, David. A., Louis A. Zurcher, and Gideon Sjoberg. 1982. Interviewing by Comment: An Adjunct to the Direct Question. *Qualitative Sociology* 5 (Winter), pp. 385–411.

Sperber, Dan, and Deidre Wilson. 1995. *Relevance: Communication and Cognition,* 2nd ed. Oxford, England: Blackwell.

Spradley, James P. 1980. *Participant Observation.* New York: Holt, Rinehart, and Winston.

Stafford, Laura, and Cherie L. Bayer. 1993. *Interaction between Parents and Children.* Newbury Park, CA: Sage.

Stamp, Glen H., Anita Vangelisti, and John A. Daly. 1992. Creating Defensiveness in Social Interaction. *Communication Quarterly* 40 (Spring), pp. 177–90.

Stone, Gregory P. 1954. City Shoppers and Urban Identification: Observations on the Social Psychology of City Life. *American Journal of Sociology* 60 (July), pp. 36–45.

Strauss, Anselm. 1978. *Negotiations: Varieties, Contexts, Processes, and Social Order.* San Francisco: Jossey-Bass.

Strauss, Anselm, and Juliet Corbin. 1990. *Basics of Qualitative Research: Grounded Theory Procedures and Techniques.* Thousand Oaks, CA: Sage.

Surra, Catherine A. 1990. Research and Theory on Mate Selection and Premarital Relationships in the 1980s. *Journal of Marriage and the Family* 52 (November), pp. 844–65.

Swidler, Ann. 1986. Culture in Action: Symbols and Strategies. *American Sociological Review* 51 (April), pp. 273–86.

———. 2001. *Talk of Love: How Culture Matters.* Chicago: University of Chicago Press.

Tannen, Deborah. 1990. *You Just Don't Understand: Women and Men in Conversation.* New York: Ballantine Books.

Thorne, Barrie. 1993. *Gender Play.* New Brunswick, NJ: Rutgers University Press.

Thornton, Arland. 1988. Cohabitation and Marriage in the 1980s. *Demography* 25 (November), pp. 497–508.

Trautner, Mary Nell. 2001. Organizational Status and Commercial Sexuality: A Comparative Analysis of Exotic Dance Clubs. Unpublished master's thesis, Department of Sociology, University of Arizona.

Tschang, Ted F., and Tarcisio della Senta. 2001. *Access to Knowledge: New Information Technologies and the Emergence of the Virtual University.* New York: Pergamon.

Turner, Ralph H. 1970. *Family Interaction.* New York: John Wiley.

Van Maanen, John. 1988. *Tales of the Field: On Writing Ethnography.* Chicago: University of Chicago Press.

Vigil, James Diego. 1988. *Barrio Gangs: Streetlife and Identity in Southern California.* Austin: University of Texas Press.

Wallerstein, Judith S., Sandra Blakeslee, and Julia M. Lewis. 2000. *The Unexpected Legacy of Divorce: A 25 Year Landmark Study.* New York: Hyperion.

Wann, Daniel L., Merrill J. Milnick, Gordon W. Russell, and Dale G. Pease. 2001. *Sport Fans: The Psychology and Social Impact of Spectators.* New York: Routledge.

Warner, Kathleen A. 1992. Personal Relationships. In *Encyclopedia of Sociology,* vol. 3, edited by Edgar R. Borgatta and Marie L. Borgatta. New York: Macmillan.

Watson, Geoffrey G. 1974. Family Organization and Little League Baseball. *International Review of Sport Sociology* 9 (no. 2), pp. 5–32.

Wax, Rosalie H. 1971. *Doing Fieldwork: Warnings and Advice.* Chicago: University of Chicago Press.

Weick, Karl A. 1985. Systematic Observational Methods. In *The Handbook of Social Psychology,* edited by G. Lindzey and E. Aronson. New York: Random House.

Weintraub, Jeff. 1997. The Theory and Politics of the Private/Public Distinction. In *Public and Private in Thought and Practice: Perspectives on a Grand Dichotomy*, edited by Jeff Weintraub and Krishan Kumar. Chicago: University of Chicago Press.

Wellman, Barry. 1988. Structural Analysis: From Method and Metaphor to Theory and Substance. In *Social Structures: A Network Approach*, edited by Barry Wellman and S. D. Berkowitz. Cambridge, England: Cambridge University Press.

———. 2001. From Little Boxes to Loosely Bounded Networks: The Privatization and Domestication of Community. In *Sociology for the Twenty-First Century: Continuities and Cutting Edges*, edited by Janet L. Abu-Lughod. Chicago: University of Chicago Press.

West, Candace, and Sarah Fenstermaker. 1993. Power, Inequality, and the Accomplishment of Gender: An Ethnomethodological View. In *Theory on Gender/Feminism on Theory*, edited by Paula England. New York: Aldine.

West, Candace, and Don H. Zimmerman. 1987. Doing Gender. *Gender and Society* I (June), pp. 125–51.

Whyte, William Foote. 1993 [1943]. *Streetcorner Society: The Social Structure of an Italian Slum*. Chicago: University of Chicago Press.

Whyte, William H. 1980. *The Social Life of Small Urban Spaces*. Washington, DC: Conservation Foundation.

Willis, F. N., and R. A. Carlson. 1993. Singles Ads: Gender, Social Class, and Time. *Sex Roles* 29 (nos. 1/2), pp. 387–404.

Willis, Paul E. 1977. *Learning to Labor: How Working Class Kids Get Working Class Jobs*. Farnborough, England: Saxon House.

Wilson, James Q., and George L. Kelling. 1982. Broken Windows: The Police and Neighborhood Safety. *Atlantic Monthly* (March), pp. 29–38.

Wilson, Steven R., Kenzie A. Cameron, and Ellen E. Whipple. 1994. Regulative Communication Strategies within Mother-Child Interactions: Implications for the Study of Reflection-Enhancing Parental Communication. *Research on Language and Social Interaction* 30 (no. 1), pp. 73–92.

Wireman, Peggy. 1984. *Urban Neighborhoods, Networks, and Families: New Forms for Old Values*. Lexington, MA: Lexington Books.

Wirth, Louis. 1938. Urbanism as a Way of Life. *American Journal of Sociology* 44 (July), pp. 1–24.

Woll, Stanley B., and Peter Young. 1989. Looking for Mr. or Ms. Right: Self-Presentation in Videodating. *Journal of Marriage and the Family* 51 (May), pp. 483–88.

Wood, Elizabeth Anne. 2000. Working in the Fantasy Factory: The Attention Hypothesis and the Enacting of Masculine Power in Strip Clubs. *Journal of Contemporary Ethnography* 29 (February), 5–31.

Wood, Julia T. 1993. Engendered Relations: Interaction, Caring, Power, and Responsibility in Intimacy. In *Social Context and Relationships,* edited by Steve Duck. Thousand Oaks, CA: Sage.

Wood, Julia T., and Steve Duck, eds. 1995. *Under-Studied Relationships: Off the Beaten Track.* Thousand Oaks, CA: Sage.

Youniss, James, and Jacqueline Smoller. 1985. *Adolescent Relations with Mothers, Fathers, and Friends.* Chicago: University of Chicago Press.

Zelizer, Viviana A. 2004. Circuits within Capitalism. In *The Economic Sociology of Capitalism,* edited by Victor Nee and Richard Swedberg. Cambridge, England: Cambridge University Press.

CONTRIBUTORS

IRENEE R. BEATTIE is Assistant Professor of Sociology at Washington State University. Her research focuses on sociology of education, inequality, adolescence, and law. She is currently examining how institutional factors in schools relate to racial/ethnic and gender differences in unrealistic future expectations.

MICHAEL BONHAM-CRECILIUS was a graduate student at the University of Arizona in the Department of Sociology during the time in which the initial fieldwork for chapter 7 was conducted. Shortly thereafter, we lost contact with him.

MARK CALLISTER is Professor of Communication at Western Illinois University. His current research focuses on advertising and visual communication.

KAREN CHRISTOPHER is Assistant Professor with a joint appointment in Women's and Gender Studies and Sociology at the University of Louisville. She writes on gender and the welfare state, the feminization of poverty, and gender and race in labor markets. Her current research projects explore welfare reform and postsecondary education among welfare recipients.

JASON CLARK-MILLER is Assistant Professor of Sociology and Justice Studies at Montana State University, Bozeman. His current research investigates framing processes in juvenile courts and attempts to provide a new perspective for criminologists interested in the constructed nature of delinquency and crime. In addition, he is currently working with colleagues to understand the inappropriate use of force by police officers and the gendered nature of victimization.

AMY S. EBESU HUBBARD is Associate Professor of Speech at the University of Hawaii, Manoa. She has published numerous works on conflict in relationships, nonverbal communication, deceptive messages, and intercultural interactions.

TYLER R. HARRISON is Assistant Professor of Communication at Kean University. His research focuses on language, disputing systems, and organizations. He is currently engaged in research on collective action in prisons and worksite health communication campaigns. He is coauthor (with Susan Morgan and Tom Reichert) of *From Numbers to Words: Reporting Statistical Results for the Social Sciences.*

TRINA L. HOPE is Assistant Professor of Sociology at the University of Oklahoma. Her research examines criminological control theories, including applying the concepts from self-control and/or social control to gang membership; the overlap between gang and dating violence; and adolescent sexual activity, pregnancy resolution, and substance use.

CHRISTINE HORNE is Associate Professor of Sociology at Washington State University. Her work addresses fundamental questions about social norms, including their emergence, enforcement, and relation to other institutions such as the legal system.

LYNN JONES is Assistant Professor of Criminal Justice at Northern Arizona University. She studies law and social movements, with particular emphasis on how cause lawyers negotiate their professional and activist identities as they frame movement strategies. Her other research investigates responses to victims of violence and includes projects on crisis workers' emotion management and campus sexual assault services.

CAROLYN J. AMAN KARLIN earned a PhD in sociology from the University of Arizona and subsequently accepted a position as Assistant Professor of Sociology at the University of Central Arkansas. She is currently pursuing a second career in veterinary medicine at the University of Minnesota.

JOSEPH E. MASSEY is Assistant Professor of Communications at California State University–Fullerton, where he teaches courses in communication theory, research methods, and public relations. His research focuses on organizational image management, research methods, and organizational crisis.

MARY KRIS MCILWAINE lives in Tucson, Arizona, where she teaches sociology at the Pima Community College. Her primary areas of interest include macro- and classical-theoretic sociology. She is currently developing a sociology of religion course and works, more generally, in curriculum development for the college.

SUSAN E. MORGAN is Associate Professor of Communication at Rutgers University. Her research interests focus on health behavior change in multicultural populations. Currently, she is engaged in research on the structural features of organizations that affect success in worksite health promotion campaigns, especially those relevant to organ donation. She is coauthor (with Tyler Harrison and Tom Reichert) of *From Numbers to Words: Reporting Statistical Results for the Social Sciences.*

CALVIN MORRILL is Professor and Chair of Sociology at the University of California, Irvine. He has written numerous works on social conflict, organizations, law and society, and qualitative field methods. He is currently writing a book on youth conflict in a multiethnic high school and is engaged in collaborative research on collective action in corporations and legal consciousness in schools. He is author of *The Executive Way: Conflict Management in Corporations.*

ALLISON MUNCH is Adjunct Assistant Professor of Sociology at Washington State University. Her research interests include social networks, gender, and ethnicity.

JENNIFER MURDOCK is Associate Pastor at First United Methodist Church in Napa, California. Upon completing her graduate work at the University of Arizona, she completed a master's of divinity degree from the Pacific School of Religion in Berkeley, California. Along with her duties in the local congregation, she works actively within the faith and political communities to promote religious dialogue, economic justice, and violence prevention.

DINA OKAMOTO is Assistant Professor of Sociology at the University of California, Davis. Her research focuses on race and ethnicity, social psychology, and collective action. She is currently a visiting scholar at the Russell Sage Foundation in New York, where she is writing a book on panethnicity among Asian Americans.

LORI L. REID is Assistant Professor of Sociology at Florida State University. Her research examines the impact of inequality on groups, especially with regard to race, gender, sexuality, and child health. She is currently working on a series of papers that examine gender, sexuality, and the body.

DAVID A. SNOW is Professor of Sociology at the University of California, Irvine. He has written widely on social movements, framing processes, and identity and is the principal investigator of an interdisciplinary, comparative study of homelessness in four global cities (Los Angeles, Paris, Sao Páulo, and Tokyo). He is coauthor (with Leon Anderson) of *Down on Their Luck: A Study of Homeless Street People* and co-editor (with Hanspeter Kriesi and Sarah Soule) of *The Blackwell Companion to Social Movements.*

LESA A. STERN is Associate Professor of Speech Communication at Southern Illinois University Edwardsville. Her primary areas of research are conflict management, interpersonal communication, and more recently, communication assessment.

KRISTIE A. TAYLOR is Senior Research Analyst at Westat, a behavioral science and health services research firm in the Washington, D.C., area. Her work focuses on explaining and preventing the use and abuse of alcohol, tobacco, and other drugs by youth. She is currently working on an effort to evaluate a national sample of youth smoking cessation programs.

SANDRA WAY is Assistant Professor of Sociology at New Mexico State University. Her main fields of interest are sociology of education, social policy, and social stratification. She is currently conducting research on school and neighborhood effects, high school disciplinary climates, and graduate school retention.

CINDY H. WHITE is Associate Professor of Communication at the University of Colorado, Boulder. Her research focuses on interpersonal communication. She has published work on deception, relational loss, social support interactions, and health communication. She is currently conducting research that examines the effects of parent training programs on patterns of interaction between adolescent mothers and their preschool-aged children.

INDEX

Page numbers in *italics* denote figures.

bars *(continued)*

decor of, 139–141; gazing and, 141, 143, 149, 153; gender stereotypes and, 144, 149, 154, 155; methodological notes, 137–139, 156–158, 259n15; power dynamics and, 137, 154–155; previously disconnected individuals connecting in, 142, 144, 149, 259n20; security in, 140; sexual and gendered identifications of, 137; as site, 137–141; solo dancers, 145, 148; as terrain for social relationships, 135; territories of the self, 135, 136, 141, 152–156; territories of the self, intrusion/inclusion continua and, 152–155, *153*, 259nn21–22; territories of the self in gay and lesbian bars, 141, 146–150, 259n20; territories of the self in straight bars, 141–146; tie signs in, 136, 150–152, 153; violations of personal boundaries and, 136, 141, 143, 149, 154–155

bars, strip. *See* strip clubs

baseball, 114, 115. *See also* softball fans community

Baxter, Leslie A., 250n42

beach going, 59, 219

Beattie, Irenee R., 46–65, 228, 237

Becker, Howard, xii

Berger, Bennett, 208

Berger, Peter L., 258n3

bodily stigma, 55, 56

body language. *See* nonverbal communication

Bonham-Crecilius, Michael, 134–158, 229–230, 232, 235–236, 239, 240

Bowling Alone (Putnam), III

Brekhus, Wayne, 235, 240

Bunis, Wlliam, 264n19

Cahill, Spencer, 12

Callister, Mark, 25–45, 229, 235, 237, 242

carrying capacity for social relationships, 237–238, 243

Castells, Manuel, 243

Certeau, Michel de, 248n6

character stigma, 55–56

Charmaz, Kathy J., 253n29

Cheers, 18

Chicago, singles industry in, 47

children: divorce rates and, 159; post-divorce support groups for, 162; softball fan community and, 120–122, 123, 124, 125, 126

children, adult social control of, 181–200; avoidance as strategy for, 191–193, 262nn24–5; confrontation as strategy for, 185–187, *186*, 193–194, 195, 198, 262n22; explanation as strategy for, *186*, 187–189, 193, 194, 195, 198; keying as strategy for, *186*, 189–191, 193, 194; methodological notes, 184, 195–200, 261–263nn17–20, 33–38; normative repertoires for social control behaviors, 183–184, 193, 195; normative rules of sociality and, 182–183, 194, 195; order defined, 182; in restrictive vs. permissive places (*see* restrictive vs. permissive places, adult social control of children in); strategies for, 185–193, *186*, 193–195, 197–198; trouble defined, 184, 196, 261n18, 262–263n34; typical observation, 184–185; violence and, 181, 194, 262n22

chillin'. *See* youth hanging out

Christian Identity movement, 205

Christianity, right-wing groups and, 203–204, 205, 206, 213, 264n8

Christopher, Karen, 46–65, 228, 237

city parks: framing of place and, 233; regulation of place and, 235, 266n29; transformation from public to quasi-public, 15

civil inattention, II, 33, II7

civility: norms of (*see* norms of public sociality); religion of, 182

Clark-Miller, Jason, 201–224, 231

cliques, at singles dances, 51–53, 58

closed-place frames. *See* open vs closed-frame public places

clothing. *See* costumes; sheath

clubs. *See* bars; strip clubs

coding data sets. *See* open coding

collective identity: anchored relationships producing, 230; community and, 113; defined, 229; softball fan community and, 122–127, 132–133, 230 college students, as basis of research, 4, 40

Collins, Randall, 60

community: collapse of, 111–112; defined, 113; diversity of types of, 130; men as keepers of, 129; softball fans as (*see* softball fans community); women as keepers of, 129–130

compensatory social function, 228–229, 245

complementary social function, 228, 245

confidentiality of informants, xii–xiii

conflict: ambiguities of place-frame and, 241; marked identities and, 241, 267n43; open- vs. closed-frame places and, 244; singles dances and lack of, 59–60. *See also* transgressions; trouble; violence

confrontation: as adult strategy for social control of children, 185–187, *186*, 193–194, 195, 198, 262n22; face-time transgressions and, 38

consensus, real, remedial work as basis of, 218–219

consensus, working. *See* norms of public sociality

"Constitutional Forum." *See* right-wing political discussion group

context: and adult social control of children, 182–184; defined, 4, 39, 60; designed sociability, unintended consequences of, 60; economic transactions and, 84–85; erotic dancing and, 72–73; face-time interactions and, 39–40; gender and sexual identities and, 136–137, 234–235; research tradition and stripping of, 4–5, 40; tie-sign interpretation and, 136; violations of personal boundaries and, 136; youth hanging out and, 106–107. *See also* place; restrictive vs. permissive places

context glossing, 4

context stripping, 4

contradictory social function, 265n9

conversational preserves, 135–136

Cook, Karen, 226

cooling-out strategy, 28, 31, 38

co-presence with commingling, 11; singles dances, 59–60

co-presence without commingling: beach going and, 59, 219; civil inattention as basis of, 11, 33; face time and, 33

costumes: in gay and lesbian bars, 150; in straight bars, 145–146; of table-dancers, 73–74, 75, 76, 82–83; as unreliable clue to identity, 257n29; of youth hanging out, 107

courtship complex, 154, 155

Cressey, Paul G., 254n11

cross-cutting ties, 122, 127, 128–129

Davis, Fred, 6

Death and Life of Great American Cities, The (Jacobs), 225

debriefing of informants, issue of, 263n38

design. *See* urban design and architecture

designed sociability, 60

developmental literature on youth culture, 94

deviant behaviors. *See* transgressions

dissolution of relationships, 9

divorce groups. *See* postdivorce support groups

divorce rate, 47, 159

Duck, Steve, 3, 39

Duneier, Mitch, 7, 19, 251n75

Durkheim, Emile, 182

Ebesu Hubbard, Amy S., 159–178, 229, 232

Edgerton, Robert: community, 113, 114, 122–123; co-presence/social distancing nexus, 59–60, 219; mental patients' relationships, 6

Eggleston, Robin, 12

Ehrenreich, Barbara, 6

Eliasoph, Nina, 201, 219

Emerson, Robert, 131

Emirbayer, Mustafa, 249n34

emotional commitment, Little League and, 114

emotional energy, 60

emotional interdependence. *See* interdependence

emotional labor: defined, 68–69; in retail contexts, 68–69, 84; strip clubs and, 68–69, 72–78, 83 emotional responses: feeling rules, 12; models for, 12, 161, 250n54; muted display of, 12–13; postdivorce support and (*see under* postdivorce support groups); self-awareness and, 171. *See also* emotional responses, corporeal vs. discursive formation of; ethnography and emotions of researcher

emotional responses, corporeal vs. discursive formation of: and adult social control of children, 193–194; as dialectic, 161; fleeting relationships and, 231; group therapy and, 162, 167–168, 171, 232; teaching of, 162, 171; teens and gender differences in, 101–102

encounters, defined, 8

ethics of field research on private relationships, xii–xiii; confidentiality/privacy of informants, xii–xiii; effects of observation, xii; negotiation of, xiii; personal relationships in service of research and, xii; political and ideological perspectives of researchers and, xi; teenagers hanging out and, 110

ethnic identity: anchored relationship development and, 240; enclaves of, and public spatial resources, 14–15; impugning stereotypes and, 266n13; of right-wing discussion group, 203; wariness of public sociality and, 266n13. *See also* immigrants

ethnography: analytic, x; blending-in strategies, 42–43, 63–65, 89, 109–110, 130–131, 156–157, 176–178, 198–199, 200; "bystander spooking," 199, 263n38; children as subjects of, 198–199; descriptive questions, 158, 260n29; insider-outsider dilemma, 64, 156; peripheral vs. complete (active) roles, 156, 264–265n20; stigmatized research choices, 64–65; strengths of, in study of personal relationships in public places, 60–61; writing- vs. reading mode, 131. *See also* ethnography and emotions of researcher; team ethnography

ethnography and emotions of researcher, 222; anxiety about blending in, 63–65,

109–110, 156, 198; bigotry of informants and, 222–223; disengagement from informants, 223–224, 265n26; sticking with emotionally arduous work, 199–200; violence, response to, 132–133

exchange structures: defined, 69–70; as material function, 226, 227–228; social power resulting from, 70; strip clubs and, 69–70, 75, 79–82, 83, 84–85

existential therapy, 260n5

exit: in bars, 141, 144; face-time transgressions and, 37–38; by parents controlling children, 193; in right-wing discussion group, 216; at singles dances, 49–50; street wisdom and, 20; by strip-club dancers, 67, 78–79, 80, 81, 83, 228

experiment, as method, 5

explanation as strategy for adult control of children, *186*, 187–189, 193, 194, 195, 198

face time, 25–45; defined, 26, 29; norms of sociality as important to, 29, 34, 41; positioning and, 29–31, 37; strutting and, 31–33, 252n17; timing and, 33–34, 37–38; transgressions and responses, 28, 31, 34–38, 40–41, 229, 253n24; virtual universities and, 41–42. *See also* university recreation centers

familiar strangers: fleeting personal relationships distinguished from, 17; softball spectators as, 118

family: as private realm, 15; softball fan community and, 127, 128–129. *See also* fictive family

femininity. *See* gender stereotypes

feminist scholarship: critiques of sex work, 66, 82; on women alone in public, 120

fictive family, 123, 124, 126, 230

Fine, Gary Alan, 99, 114, 266n14

flash mobs, 243

fleeting personal relationships: avoidance of tensions and, 18–19; carrying capacity and, 237; defined, 17, 51, 251n70; face time as (*see* face time); identity traces and, 229; increasing importance of, 243; material functions of, 227–228; new manifestations of, 243; norms of sociality and, 17; privatism and privatization and, 238; psychological functions of, 231; research traditions into, 5–7; singles dances and, 51–52; social functions and, 228–229; social tension and, 17; softball fans and, 116, 118–119; strip clubs and, 84; "withs" vs. "single" and likelihood of, 241–242

flight attendants, emotional labor of, 69

"Forum." *See* right-wing political discussion group

frameworks of interpretation (frames): actors and, 240–242, 267nn43, 46; ambiguous place-frames and, 241, 267n46; avowed purpose and, 240–241, 267n43; identity and, 240; ideological work via, 208–210; interactional units and, 240, 241–242; meaning generation and, 233, 266n22; open vs. closed (*see* open- vs. closed-frame public places); origin of, 232–233, 264n11, 266n19; repertoires of norms in, 235–236, 266n30

framing. *See* frameworks of interpretation

framing activity, defined, 209

functions of social behaviors: complementary and compensatory, 228–229, 245; definition of term, 226, 265n3; material, 226, 227–228; of open- vs. closed-frame public spaces, 237–238; psychological, 227, 231–232; social, 226, 228–231, 265nn9, 13, 266n14; study of increasing and changing importance, 243, 267n51

Fuwa, Makiko, 266n29

gangs. *See* street gangs

Gardner, Carol Brooks, 28, 229

gay and lesbian bars. *See* bars

gay men. *See* lesbians and gays

gazing: in bars, 141, 143, 149, 153; and face time transgressions, 35–38

gender: bars and (*see* bars); defined, 134; fundamental codes communicated by territories of the self, 136–137; as institutional process, 134, 258n3

gender cultures, 105–106

gender differences: in norms of public sociality, use of, 41; in singles dance initiation of contact, 55; in teen emotional expression, 101–102, 104; and university workout room behaviors (*see* face time)

gender identity: wariness toward public sociality and, 229, 242; youth relationship development and, 101, 105–106

gender stereotypes: courtship complex, 154; emotional labor and, 68–69; gay and lesbian bars and lack of, 149, 154, 155; in straight bars, 144, 154, 155; strip clubs and, 70; in teen relational interaction, 101, 104, 105–106, 107

Gestalt therapy, 260n5

Giddens, Anthony, 264n17

Gilligan, Carol, 105

Glaser, Barney G., 253n29

Goffman, Erving: anchored relationships, 251n72; civil inattention, 11; civility, 182; courtship complex, 154; deference and demeanor, 95, 105; frameworks of interpretation, 232–233, 264n11, 266nn19, 25; insulation of self, 227; interaction order, 7, 9, 69, 182, 201, 218–219, 237, 240, 250n50; norms of interaction, 9–12, 250n50; personal space, 158; remedial work, 19, 207; stigma, 55; territories of the self, 10–11, 135–137; tie signs, 10; total institution, survival in, 98, 267n35; transgressions of norms, 11–12; transient relationships, 6

Grannis, Rick, 251n62

Granovetter, Mark, 250n37

group therapy. *See* postdivorce support groups

Guttman, Allen, 113

Hammersly, Martin, x

hanging out. *See* youth hanging out

harassment, interactional-norm violations becoming, 19, 28

Harcourt, Bernard E., 267n32

Harrington, Brooke, 266n14

Harrison, Tyler R., 93–110, 230, 239

helpfulness, restrained, 11, 30
high-fiving, 102
HIV/AIDS, 210, 222–223, 259n20
Hochschild, Arlie, 6, 12, 69
Hoebel, E. Adamson, 261n18
Hoffman, M.{hrs}L., 194–195
homeless persons, softball fan community and, 116, 123–124
Hondagneu-Sotelo, Pierette, 6
Hope, Trina L., 66–90, 227–230, 231, 237
Horne, Christine, 181–200, 236, 244
Horwitz, Alan V., 260n9
Hunter, Albert, 251n65

identity: definition of, 229; marked, 240–241, 267n43; personal, 168, 229; pyschological functions and, 232; social, 229, 240. *See also* collective identity; ethnic identity; gender identity; sexual identity
immigrants: approximation of homeland plazas and courtyards, 15; normative repertoires and, 235, 266n29; public sociality constrained for, 14, 243–244. *See also* ethnic identity
informational preserves, 135–136
inpugning stereotypes, 266n13
insider-outsider dilemma, 64, 156
institutionalized frames, 233
interactional vandalism, 19, 28
interactionist perspective on personal relationships in public, 7–8, 249n34, 249n36; child control by parents, 182–184; emotional expression, 12–13, 161; on erotic dancing, 66, 68, 82; interdependence, 8–9, 250nn37, 40, 42; norms of behavior, 9–12
interactionist stance, framing of place and, 232
interaction order: diversity of projects and intents realized in, 237; emotional labor and, 69; identity traces and, 229; maintenance of, 18–20; political discussion undergirded by, 219, 220; remedial work to maintain (*see* remedial work); threats to (*see* transgressions); youth hanging out and, 94–95, 104–105

interdependence: anchored personal relationships and, 18; fleeting personal relationships and, 17; interactionist perspective on, 8–9, 250nn37, 40, 42; softball fan community and, 119–122; youth relationships and, 100. *See also* emotional responses
International Society of Introductory Services Directory, 47
interpersonal survival strategies, 28; studied seriousness, 31, 32, 36; women's cooling-out strategy, 28, 31, 38. *See also* exit; transgressions
interviews: bars, gender and sexuality in, 158; right-wing discussion group, 221; singles dances, 61; softball fans community, 131; university recreation center, 43; youth hanging out, 108. *See also* methodology
intimacy: community and, 113; postdivorce support groups and, 160, 161, 174; softball fans community and, 118–120, 128; strip clubs and counterfeiting of, 68–69, 74–75, 76–77, 78–79, 228

Jacobs, Jane, 7, 225
Jones, Lynn, 25–45, 229, 235, 237, 242

Karlin, Carolyn J. Aman, 134–158, 229–230, 232, 235–236, 239, 240
Katz, Jack, 12, 101, 161, 194, 231
Kelley, Harold H., 250n37
keying as strategy for adult control of children, *186*, 189–191, 193, 194
kicking back. *See* youth hanging out
Knapp, Mark L., 250n42
koen debut practices, 236n29

Lee, Jennifer, 219
lesbians and gays: in bars (*see* bars); lack of singles organizations found catering to, 254n26; marginalization and relationships of, 85; right-wing discussion group and, 210
Little League baseball, 114
Llewellyn, Karl N., 261n18
Lofland, John, x, 62

nonverbal communication *(continued)*
table dancing and, 74–75, 76, 77–78,
83; teen play-fighting, 93, 101–103,
106; and territories of the self, maintenance of, 136. *See also* tie signs
normative repertoires for adult social
control of children, 183–184, 193, 195
norms of public sociality, 9–12, 182,
234–235; civil inattention, 11, 33, 117;
conflict constrained and repaired
through, 201, 207, 219, 264n17; consistency of across broad spectrum of
places, 27; evidence of existence of,
10–11; explicit acknowledgement of,
11, 250n50; fleeting personal relationships and, 17; gender differences in
use of, 41; postdivorce support groups
and, 165, 174; quasi-public spaces and
adherence to, 27–28, 219; as repertoires, 235–236, 266n30; restrained
helpfulness, 11, 30; of softball fan
community, 122–127, 132–133, 230; in
strip clubs, 81; teens hanging out and
spoiling of, 99; territories of the self,
136–137; tie signs (*see* tie signs); transformation of, 235, 244, 245, 266n29;
transgressions of (*see* transgressions);
visibility and, 10
note taking: postdivorce support groups,
174; right-wing discussion group, 221;
singles dance, 62; softball fans community, 131; strip clubs, 86–87; university recreation center, 42–43; youth
hanging out, 108–109. *See also*
methodology

Okamoto, Dina, 46–65, 228, 237
Oldenburg, Ray, 247n2, 251n62
open coding of field database, 253n29; bars,
gender and sexuality in, 157, 158; postdivorce support groups, 174–175,
261n22; right-wing discussion group,
221; university recreation center, 43.
See also methodology
open vs. closed-frame public places:
anchored relationship development
and, 238–239; avowed purposes and
actions and, 241; boundaries of, 234,

266n25; carrying capacity for social
relationships in, 237; conflict and violence and, 244; defined, 233–234;
functions of public sociality and,
237–238; permissive vs. restrictive
public places and, 26; privatism and
privatization and, 238

parochial realm, defined, 15, 173
"party man," 80–81
patriot movement, American, 207, 264n8.
See also right-wing political discussion
group
permissive public places. *See* restrictive vs.
permissive places
personal identity: defined, 229; emotional
expression and, 168
personalizing aspects of retail, 69, 84,
267n46
personal relationships: constitutive rules of,
9; at core of existence, 3; primary-
secondary divide, 16; research traditions on (*see* research traditions). *See
also* anchored personal relationships;
fleeting personal relationships; interactionist perspective on personal relationships
personal space. *See* territories of the
self
place: actors and, 240–242, 267nn43, 46;
carrying capacity for social relationships, 237–238, 243; definition of
term, 13–14, 226; design and (*see*
urban design and architecture); framing of (*see* frameworks of interpretation); influence on public sociality,
237–239, 267n35; patterns of social
interaction and labeling in sexual
terms, 137; privatism and privatization, 238; and realms, interaction of,
15–16; regulation of, 234–236,
266nn29–30, 267n32; restrictive vs.
permissive (*see* restrictive vs. permissive places). *See also* context
planned communities, 244
play-fighting among teens, 93, 101–103,
106
Polanyi, Karl, 84

remedial work, right-wing discussion group and, 207, 218; bypassing "troublesome" members or comments, 210–212; at group level, 207–214; humorous deflection, 217–218; ideological work via framing, 208–210, 264n11; at interpersonal level, 214–218; norms of civility, invocation of, 212–214; softening/moderation of stance, 215; withdrawal or avoidance, 215–216

repertoires, normative, 235–236, 266n30

research traditions, 3–7, 3, 248n11; community collapse, 111–112; on erotic dancing, 66; on singles and singles organizations, 48, 254n11; on youth culture, 94

resistance: by children in adult-control situations, 195; by teens hanging out, 94, 95, 96–100, 104, 105

restrained helpfulness, 11, 30

restrictive vs. permissive places: definition of terms, 185, 196–197, 236, 262n20, 263nn35–7; teen hangouts and, 95–100. See also restrictive vs. permissive places, adult social control of children and

restrictive vs. permissive places, adult social control of children and: child's association of control strategies and, 194–195; definition of places, 185, 196–197, 236, 262n20, 263nn35–7; moral boundaries of control and, 195, 236, 244; strategies of adults and, 186, 187, 189, 191, 236

retail and service situations: emotional labor and, 68–69, 84; material functions of, 227; personalizing aspects of, 69, 84, 267n46

riding shotgun, 101

right-wing political discussion group, 201–224; demographics of, 203–204; format of meetings, 202–203; ideological conflict and schism within, 202, 204–207, 230–231; methodological notes, 220–224, 264nn19–20, 26; religion and, 203–204, 205, 206, 213; remedial work to maintain stability

(see remedial work, right-wing discussion group and); as site, 201–204, 207; themes of discussion, 208–209, 209

ritual: in bars, 136, 140; competencies for social interaction, 182; identities triggering, 229; remedial work as, 207, 218, 219; singles dances, 50, 56, 59–60; strangers passing, 9–10; strip clubs and, 227–228; teen resistance to authority as, 97, 98–99, 105; tie signs as, 136

roaming, 35, 37

Rogers, Carl, 225, 245

Rosaldo, Renato, 223

scanning, by erotic dancers, 80

schematic of interpretation. See frameworks of interpretation

scoping (gazing) in bars, 141, 143, 149, 153

secondary-primary dichotomy of relationships, 16

self, insulation of, 227

self, territories of. See territories of the self

self-actualization, 260n5

self-reporting, as method, 5

Sewell, William H., 264

sexual identity: bars and (see bars); collective identities and, 230; defined, 134; fundamental codes communicated by territories of the self, 136–137; as institutional process, 134

sex work. See strip clubs

sheath, 135, 145–146

signage, social control and, 98

significance of relationships: anchored personal relationships and, 18; fleeting personal relationships and assymmetrical perception of, 17

Simmel, Georg, 1

singles bars, enduring relationships less likely to arise in, 39

singles dances, 46–65; encounters as interaction mode, 49–51; fleeting relationships, 51–52; long-term relationship formation inhibited, 52–53, 55, 57, 58, 60; methodological notes, 61–65, 254n26; orderliness of, 59–60; pleasure and, 57–58; sifting and sorting

strip clubs *(continued)*
    methodological notes, 85–90,
    256nn30–32; open- vs. closed-frames
    and, 234; power and, 66, 69–70,
    81–82, 83, 255n22; private dancing in,
    83–84; research tradition on, 66; as
    site, 67, 68, 71–72, 83–84, 255n25;
    stage shows as feature in, 68; stereo-
    typical gender roles and, 70, 77–78,
    82, 83; table dances as feature in, 67, 68
strutting, face time and, 31–33, 252n17
studied seriousness, 31, 32, 36
subordinated persons, traditional research
    and, 5–6
subtle realism, x
surface act, 12–13
surveys, as method, 5
Swidler, Ann, 205n54, 264n17, 266n30

table dances. *See* strip clubs
tacit rules. *See* norms of public sociality
Tannen, Deborah, 105
Tarrow, Sydney, 267n43
taxi dance halls, 254n11
Taylor, Kristie A., 181–200, 236, 244
team ethnography: advantages and disad-
    vantages of, x–xi; bias/pre-existing
    beliefs control, 44–45, 221; blending-
    in strategies, 42–43, 156–157; boldness
    inspired by, 200; closeness/distance
    with the field, 157; holistic data set,
    86–87; as insulating effect, 132–133;
    multiple perspectives of, 62–63,
    87–90, 132, 156, 178, 200, 221–222;
    productive intragroup disagreements,
    xi; as threat to community, 132; time
    in fieldwork multiplied by, 61. *See also*
    ethnography; methodology; note
    taking; open coding
teenagers. *See* youth; youth culture; youth
    hanging out
territories of the self: bars and *(see* bars);
    defined, 10, 135; emotional display
    and, 13; and fundamental codes of sex
    categories and sexual identities,
    136–137; inclusion/intrusion continua,
    152–155, 153, 259nn21–22; informational
    and conversational preserves, 135–136;

intrusions into, 136; physical territo-
    ries of, 135; public maintenance of,
    10–11, 135–136; sheath, 135, 145–146
therapy. *See* postdivorce support groups;
    psychotherapy
Thorne, Richard and Karen, 181, 194, 195,
    262n22
tie signs: bars and, 136, 150–152, 153;
    defined, 10; emotional display and, 13;
    reading of, and choice of actors, 42;
    softball fan community and, 122; ter-
    ritories of the self and, 136
Tilly, Charles, 267n43
traces of identity, 229
traditional research. *See* research traditions
transgressions: in bars, 136, 141, 143, 149,
    154–155; by children *(see* children,
    adult social control of*)*; civil inatten-
    tion to prevent, 11, 33, 117; context
    and definition of, 136; defined, 11–12;
    face time and, 28, 31, 34–38, 40–41,
    229, 253n24; as overt public harass-
    ment, 19, 28; remedial work to repair
    (see remedial work*)*; responses to *(see*
    avoidance; confrontation; cooling-out
    response; exit; remedial work; studied
    seriousness*)*; street gangs and, 20;
    women as subject to, 28, 41, 120, 155,
    229; youth hanging out as, 104–105.
    See also conflict; trouble; violence
transient relationships. *See* fleeting per-
    sonal relationships
trouble: adult-child *(see* children, adult
    social control of*)*; defined, 184,
    261n18; softball fan community
    response to, 125–126, 132–133; in strip-
    clubs, 78–79. *See also* conflict; trans-
    gressions; violence
Turner, Ralph H., 250n40
twelve-step programs, 160, 260n9

university recreation centers: discussion
    and implications of research, 38–42;
    face time as goal in *(see* face time*)*;
    methodological notes, 42–45,
    253nn27, 29; as site, 28–29, 252nn1–2,
    253n27; social role of, generally, 26,
    41–42, 252n2

Compositor:	International Typesetting & Composition
Indexer:	Victoria Baker
Text:	11.25/13.5 Adobe Garamond
Display:	Adobe Garamond and Perpetua
Printer and binder:	Maple-Vail Manufacturing Group